Pelican Books

ASTROLOGY
Science or Superstition?

Dr H. J. Eysenck, who was born in 1916, obtained his Ph.D. degree in psychology at London University after school and university experience in Germany, France and England. Having worked as psychologist at the war-time Mill Hill Emergency Hospital, he was appointed Professor of Psychology in the University of London, and Director of the Psychological Department at the Institute of Psychiatry (Maudsley and Bethlem Royal Hospitals). Known mainly through his experimental researches in the field of personality, he has written some seven hundred articles in technical journals, as well as some three dozen books including *Dimensions of Personality*, *The Scientific Study of Personality*, *The Psychology of Politics*, *The Dynamics of Anxiety and Hysteria*, *Uses and Abuses of Psychology*, *Crime and Personality*, *The Biological Base of Personality*, (with Glenn Wilson) *Know Your Own Personality*, *Sex and Personality* and *You and Neurosis*. His more recent publications include *The Causes and Effects of Smoking*, (with M. Eysenck) *Mindwatching*, and (with J. Kamin) *Intelligence: The Battle for the Mind*. He has also edited a *Handbook of Abnormal Psychology*. He is Editor-in-Chief of the journal *Personality and Individual Differences*. He advocates the highest degree of scientific rigour in the design of psychological experiments and is very critical of much loose thinking current under the guise of 'psychology'.

Dr D. K. B. Nias obtained a Ph.D. in psychology after completing a clinical training programme at the Institute of Psychiatry, London University. His research has been in the areas of social attitudes, leisure activities, and sports psychology. His previous books are *Love's Mysteries* (with G. D. Wilson), which has been translated into a dozen languages, and *Sex, Violence and the Media* (with H. J. Eysenck). Like Professor Eysenck, he became interested in astrology upon discovering research which appeared to support astrological doctrine and so ran counter to accepted scientific principles. The present book describes and evaluates this epoch-making evidence, and represents the culmination of their quest after the truth.

H. J. Eysenck and D. K. B. Nias

ASTROLOGY

Science or Superstition?

Penguin Books

Penguin Books Ltd, Harmondsworth, Middlesex, England
Penguin Books, 40 West 23rd Street, New York, New York 10010, U.S.A.
Penguin Books Australia Ltd, Ringwood, Victoria, Australia
Penguin Books Canada Ltd, 2801 John Street, Markham, Ontario, Canada L3R 1B4
Penguin Books (N.Z.) Ltd, 182–190 Wairau Road, Auckland 10, New Zealand

First published by Maurice Temple Smith Ltd 1982
Published in Pelican Books 1984

Copyright © H. J. Eysenck and D. K. B. Nias, 1982
All rights reserved

Made and printed in Great Britain by
Richard Clay (The Chaucer Press) Ltd,
Bungay, Suffolk
Set in Film Baskerville

Contents

Acknowledgements

In our evaluation of the research on astrology, we have been greatly aided by previous reviewers, particularly by Geoffrey Dean and his colleagues, whose monumental *Recent Advances in Natal Astrology: A critical review 1900-1976* has been invaluable. We have also found the books by Michel and Françoise Gauquelin very useful, especially for surveys of the non-English literature, and are indebted to them for many personal comments and criticisms. There are four journals, *Phenomena* (which ceased publication in 1979), *Skeptical Inquirer*, *Zetetic Scholar*, and *Correlation*, which contain critical discussions of astrological research, its significance, and its value, and we have benefited from consulting them.

We are especially indebted to Geoffrey Dean for reading the whole manuscript and making helpful criticisms and suggestions in equal measure. Arthur Mather has also read the entire manuscript and made many helpful and perceptive comments. Similarly, selected chapters have been read and commented upon by Michel Gauquelin, John Addey, Simon Best, Charles Harvey, Alan Smithers, Michael Startup and Beverley Steffert. Other help has been kindly provided by David Hand, Patricia Blackie, James Bourlet, Nona Hemsley and Christopher Jeans. We have also been helped by constant referrals to astrological journals of a serious nature, such as the *Astrological Journal* and *Cosmecology Bulletin*, and by talking to astrologers and critics alike, too numerous to mention. We thank all these people for their contribution to this book, but absolve them of all responsibility for any errors that remain. These are exclusively our own responsibility.

Preface

Man's most valuable trait is a judicious sense
of what not to believe.
Euripides

The title of this book by itself will be enough to bring down on us the wrath of both scientists and astrologers. Scientists will argue that even to raise the question is absurd, and that no sensible person could truly believe there was anything whatever to be said for astrology. For them, it is an ancient superstition that survives only in the minds of suggestible people who lack any knowledge of scientific methods. Astrologers, on the other hand, will bristle at the very possibility that their craft might be considered superstition. They will object that there is so much evidence for astrology, collected over thousands of years, that to doubt its value is to take an absurdly sceptical view, determined more by prejudice than by a genuine desire for knowledge.

As we shall try to show in the first chapter, both sides beg the question. Before we assume that astrology is nonsense – or that it has a genuine contribution to make to knowledge – we must first look for direct factual evidence. It is not enough to declare, as some scientists do, that astrology is simply impossible. When it comes to declarations of impossibility, scientists have a bad track record. Johannes Müller, one of the best known and most widely respected physiologists of the nineteenth century, and the author of the authoritative handbook on the subject, declared that it would never be possible to measure the speed of the nervous impulse; three years later Helmholtz had measured it quite accurately. The philosopher G.W. Hegel declared that it was absurd to look for an eighth planet; he proved to his satisfaction that there could only be seven – just before Herschel discovered Uranus. Einstein and Rutherford, the greatest theoretical and experimental physicists of this century, both declared quite explicitly that the splitting of the atom could never have any practical application; a bare dozen years later the atomic bomb exploded over Hiroshima. Perhaps some modesty is called for in declaring something to be impossible.

It may be true, as Santayana said, that 'Faith in the supernatural is a desperate wager made by man at the lowest ebb of his fortunes,' but the universe is full of mysteries. Therefore, we must ask whether astrological assertions really are supernatural. Could they be the outcome of the long and acute observation of happenings whose causes are as yet unknown, but in principle knowable, and possibly not counter to the teachings of modern science? After all, what would physicists a century or two ago have made of tales of black holes, quarks, quasars, and the like? Electricity and magnetism were once considered magic and the work of the devil. Times change. We know much less than we think; let us keep an open mind on all questions.

It may seem odd that on what one would have imagined was a simple empirical question – can astrological assertions be verified or not? – there should be two such contradictory reactions, given by two groups so vehemently opposed to each other. The answer to this problem may be found in one of the few reliable and valid generalisations in social psychology, the 'principle of certainty' first enunciated by R.H. Thouless in 1935: 'When, in a group of persons, there are influences acting both in the direction of acceptance and rejection of a belief, the result is not to make the majority adopt a low degree of conviction but to make some hold the belief with a high degree of conviction while others reject it also with a high degree of conviction.' Thouless originally enunciated this law in connection with his research on religious belief; in 1954 one of us (H.J. Eysenck) showed that it applied to all sorts of social attitudes. It clearly applies in the case of astrology. All the more necessary, then, to take an unbiased look at the evidence.

A few years ago our own position would have been that of the 'hard scientists' who reject astrology and all its works without question. We began to have doubts when we were involved in some research with Michel and Françoise Gauquelin, the famous French psychologists who, over the past twenty years or so, have demonstrated a surprising correspondence between personality and planetary position at birth. Their work has been carefully checked and successfully repeated by highly critical scientists in other countries, and it poses very interesting and important problems which have certainly not found a ready answer yet. The remarkable demonstrations provided by the Gauquelins encouraged us to make a systematic search of the literature to discover just what was the empirical evidence for and against astrology, and this book is the outcome of our search.

The final result is not, perhaps, what either party to the dispute would have expected. We find, as the sceptics would have predicted, that much of the published research in astrology is of poor quality, badly designed and with many statistical errors in the evaluation. But we also find that there are clearly demonstrated facts which defy rational explanation by present-day theories and which would tax the ingenuity of the most determined sceptic to deny or explain away. We have done our best to point out faults in design and execution when these became apparent; we do not think we can be accused of being woolly-minded, uncritical, or credulous. Neither do we believe that we can be accused of starting with such strong prejudices that no demonstration would ever convince us of the truth of astrological beliefs. We have no doubt failed in complete impartiality; our innate scepticism may still show here and there. But this may be all to the good. As Stanislaus I of Poland said, 'To believe with certainty we must begin by doubting.'

We start the book by taking a look at traditional astrology. We ask what it is that astrologers believe and then go on to consider how true it is – and indeed how one can decide whether a particular astrological belief is true or not. This question, incidentally, is often harder to settle than you might think. We bring forward a number of instances in which what seemed like a convincing demonstration turned out to be based on a fallacy. Whatever his view of the outcome, we hope the reader will find this part of the book interesting; it gives a glimpse of the scientific method applied in an unusual field.

In this way we examine a number of particular astrological beliefs and ask what evidence there is for and against them. It is only fair to warn the astrologically minded reader that we feel forced to conclude that most of these beliefs do not stand up to rigorous examination. In this part of the book we look at and discard a great part of traditional astrology. In itself this is necessarily a negative sort of undertaking and, if that were all, this book would be of limited interest. What we ourselves find exciting, however, is that when everything that will not stand the test has been put aside, there does remain a body of extraordinary evidence that cannot readily be explained away. It lies mostly in the area of what we refer to as *cosmobiology*.

Cosmobiology studies the ways in which vegetable, animal and human life is influenced by bodies in the solar system other than our own earth. We are none of us surprised to know that the moon governs the tides or that the seasonal rhythms of many forms of life follow the yearly orbiting of the earth around the sun. Because we are so used to these facts we find them unremarkable. But what about the ability of certain marine animals to follow the phases of the moon even when they are cut off from its light and are many miles away from the wash of the tides? What about the effect of the weather on our own moods, the apparent connection (in turn) between the weather and the incidence of sunspots, and the strange and little-reported work of researchers linking sunspots with the motion of the planets? There are a number of pieces of research in this field of cosmobiology which we believe need to be taken seriously. In the end many of them will no doubt be discredited, but those that stand the test may turn out to reveal a whole web of subtle connections between life on earth (including our own life) and the motions of the planets that revolve with us around our sun.

Above all, there is the work of the Gauquelins which first set us off on this investigation. We deal at length with their findings and with the impressive evidence which seems to show that, however weird it may appear, a baby predisposed to develop a particular type of personality will tend to be born at the moment when one of the planets is at a certain critical position in the sky. There are different opinions about the interpretation of these findings, but can there be any doubt that, if they do turn out to be true, they are of revolutionary importance to psychology and the other sciences?

In writing this book we have aimed essentially at the intelligent layman interested in astrology but not necessarily very knowledgeable about it. We hope that academics scientists and astrologers will also read it, even though some of the things we have to say may already be familiar to them. We have based ourselves on scientifically documented facts, but have looked critically at the way these facts were derived, the degree to which they were confirmed by other experimenters, and the statistical analysis which justified (or did not justify) the claims made for them. We have tried to explain, where relevant, the logical basis of the statistical tests used, and the weaknesses encountered in published articles, but we have not gone into detail about the mathematics involved as this would clearly have gone beyond the limits we set ourselves. If the general reader will accept our judgement on the fairly low-level statistics involved, he should have no difficulty at all in following our argument. He will find that it takes him into some unexpected and fascinating regions of discovery.

1 Closed and Open Minds

There is no bar to knowledge greater than contempt
prior to examination.
Herbert Spencer

There is no doubt about the popularity of astrology. According
to various opinion polls roughly a third of the population of
Western countries believes in it and another third is interested
enough to read astrological predictions, at least occasionally.
The last third remains unconcerned or sceptical. As the *New
York Times* said (13 August 1977): 'In the cyclical way of the
world, we have been passing through a period of resurgent
mysticism. Educated people ask each other what signs they
were born under; witchcraft is discussed seriously on college
campuses, occult bookshops flourish, and cults of all kinds
contend with pornography for the side-walks of our cities.'

In reaction to this surge of credulity, other people hurry in to
denounce everything to do with astrology as an absurd fraud,
and among these opponents a number of scientists have been
prominent. The American *Humanist* (a magazine devoted to
discussions of social problems and irrationality), in its
September 1975 issue, carried the following statement, entitled
'Objections to Astrology'. It was endorsed by 186 leading
scientists, including 18 Nobel Prizewinners.

Scientists in a variety of fields have become concerned about the
increased acceptance of astrology in many parts of the world. We, the
undersigned – astronomers, astrophysicists, and scientists in other
fields – wish to caution the public against the unquestioning
acceptance of the predictions and advice given privately and publicly
by astrologers. Those who wish to believe in astrology should realize
that there is no scientific foundation for its tenets.

In ancient times people believed in the predictions and advice of
astrologers because astrology was part and parcel of their magical
world view. They looked upon celestial objects as abodes or omens of
the Gods and, thus, intimately connected with events here on earth;
they had no concept of the vast distances from the earth to the planets
and stars. Now that these distances can and have been calculated, we

1

can see how infinitesimally small are the gravitational and other effects produced by the distant planets and the far more distant stars. It is simply a mistake to imagine that the forces exerted by stars and planets at the moment of birth can in any way shape our futures. Neither is it true that the positions of distant heavenly bodies make certain days or periods more favorable to particular kinds of action, or that the sign under which one was born determines one's compatibility or incompatibility with other people.

Why do we believe in astrology? In these uncertain times many long for the comfort of having guidance in making decisions. They would like to believe in a destiny predetermined by astral forces beyond their control. However, we must all face the world, and we must realize that our futures lie in ourselves, and not in the stars.

One would imagine, in this day of widespread enlightenment and education, that it would be unnecessary to debunk beliefs based on magic and superstition. Yet, acceptance of astrology pervades modern society. We are especially disturbed by the continued uncritical dissemination of astrological charts, forecasts, and horoscopes by the media and by otherwise reputable newspapers, magazines, and book publishers. This can only contribute to the growth of irrationalism and obscurantism. We believe that the time has come to challenge directly, and forcefully, the pretentious claims of astrological charlatans.

It should be apparent that those individuals who continue to have faith in astrology do so in spite of the fact that there is no verified scientific basis for their beliefs, and indeed that there is strong evidence to the contrary.

In the editorial it was explained that both the American Ethical Union and the American Humanist Association – the co-publishers of *The Humanist* – had long been opposed to cults of unreason and irrationalism (under which they also classify religion, of course). The editor went on to ask: 'What better way to demonstrate this in this anniversary issue than by a major critique of astrology?' Professor Bart J. Bok, a former president of the American Astronomical Society, was invited to draft a brief statement listing some scientific objections to astrology. This was subsequently revised and expanded to the statement quoted above, and then sent to a selected list of distinguished members of the American Astronomical Society and the National Academy of Sciences for endorsement.

The signed statement was subsequently sent to thousands of newspaper editors in the United States and abroad, with the suggestion that they print it, especially if they carried a daily or weekly horoscope column. The intention, of course, was to counter the ever-increasing trend for astrology to be foisted on an unsuspecting public which is rarely exposed to scientific criticisms of it. This was an honourable intention, but as we shall show it is questionable whether the statement is true. It is also unscientific in its approach. This point was well made by Carl Sagan, a scientist who declined to sign, in the following letter to *The Humanist*:

I find myself unable to endorse the 'Objections to Astrology' statement (September/October, 1975) – not because I feel that astrology has any validity whatever, but because I felt and still feel that the tone of the statement is authoritarian. The fundamental point is not that the origins of astrology are shrouded in superstition. This is true as well for chemistry, medicine, and astronomy, to mention only three. To discuss the psychological motivations of those who believe in astrology seems to be quite peripheral to the issue of its validity. That we can think of no mechanism for astrology is relevant but unconvincing. No mechanism was known, for example, for continental drift when it was proposed by Wegener. Nevertheless, we see that Wegener was right, and those who objected on the grounds of unavailable mechanism were wrong.

Statements contradicting borderline, folk, or pseudoscience that appear to have an authoritarian tone can do more damage than good. They never convince those who are flirting with pseudoscience but merely seem to confirm their impression that scientists are rigid and closed-minded. . . .

What I would have signed is a statement describing and refuting the principal tenets of astrological belief. My belief is that such a statement would have been far more persuasive and would have produced vastly less controversy than the one that was actually circulated.

Authority or evidence?

The scientists who signed the *Humanist* statement agreed that astrology was folklore and superstition and that there was no scientific basis for it. Unfortunately, they do not seem to have

3

investigated any evidence that would have supported or disproved their claim, and so their response seems to have been largely emotional. Rather than appealing to their authority, it would have been better if they had simply presented evidence. This point was well made by Einstein in response to criticisms of his work. In 1920, a racist German group tried to refute the theory of relativity by holding an emotional meeting in the Berlin Philharmonic Hall, and then by persuading a hundred professors to condemn Einstein's theory in a book. Einstein commented: 'Were I wrong, one professor would have been quite enough.'

In addition to the 'appeal to authority', other weaknesses occur in the statement. Feyerabend (1978) points out that the 186 scientists made the mistake of criticising the basic assumptions of astrology rather than the way in which it is practised. He observed that 'it is interesting to see how closely both parties approach each other in ignorance, conceit and the wish for easy power over minds.' He also notes that, following the statement, many of the scientists declined interviews because they had not studied astrology. It appears they had signed merely on the basis of a 'religiously' felt conviction.

Feyerabend claims that this conviction led the astronomers to overlook even evidence they were familiar with. For example, in an article accompanying the statement, Bok (1975) had stated that because of their distance from us, the planets could not influence human affairs; he similarly assumed that the walls of the delivery room would shield the newborn child from radiation emitted by the planets. He made these statements even though, as an astronomer, he should have known that the planets might influence solar activity which in turn has various effects on us; it is also known that certain types of radiation can penetrate very thick walls to which a delivery room would not be an exception.

The scientists' statement prompted a contrary statement published in 1976 by the astrological journal *Aquarian Agent*. This statement claimed that astrology is at least a valid area of research, and that it is important to distinguish 'sun sign frauds' from genuine astrologers, who take far more factors into account than the sign of the zodiac under which one is born.

Signatures for this statement were obtained from 187 (!) people with academic degrees. This, while also appealing to authority, does seem to take a less prejudiced view. Of course, simply to state that you are in favour of further research is to say little more than being against sin and for motherhood, but even this is an advance on the simple, prejudiced refusal to examine the evidence.

It is of course possible that there is no truth in any part of astrology. The point is that the 186 scientists have not *demonstrated* this. To do so would involve systematically examining all the available evidence in favour of astrology and then showing how it is invalid.

The attitude of more moderate scientists is illustrated by J. Allen Hynek, Chairman of the Department of Astronomy at Northwestern University. As a member of another of Professor Bok's committees, the Harvard Committee on Astrology, he cast twenty thousand horoscopes from entries in the *American Men of Science* directory and found no association with sun signs or with aspects of the planet Mercury, which is claimed to be the 'planet of the mind'. The director of the observatory where he did this work refused permission to publish even this negative result lest it be thought that his staff spent any time on matters of this sort! Similarly, Hynek wrote in his foreword to a book of Gauquelin's published in 1978: 'It is with considerable hesitancy . . . that I write this foreword, because for an astronomer to have anything to do with anything remotely related to astrology seems enough to rule him out of the scientific fraternity.'

It is against this background of undisguised hostility, rather than of receptiveness to new ideas and experiments, that open-minded scientists have had to fight in their attempts to establish whether or not there is any truth in astrology. They have even had to defend their right to do research in this field. As a result, established scientists have often found it best to say nothing, rather than incur derision; only a few have had the courage to admit that 'there might be something in it'.

Sceptics and believers

Scepticism is of course not a new attitude towards astrology. Views among the ancients, and in medieval times, differed as much as they do now. Pythagoras, for instance, born in Samos around 580 BC and one of the great mathematicians of all time, was one of the leading advocates of astrology; whereas Hippocrates, born 460 BC and called the father of modern medicine, is said to have specifically dissociated himself from it. Plato and Aristotle, who lived during the fifth and fourth centuries BC, accepted the astrologers' belief in the influence of the stars. Plato believed in planet gods and thought that our souls originated from the stars and, once life had ended, returned to them. Aristotle taught that 'This world is inescapably linked to the motions of the world above.' But Lucretius and Cicero disagreed. The latter, in his book *On Divinations*, lists and discusses eight arguments on the futility of horoscope belief and superstition. Finally, after drawing attention to the vast space separating the heavens from the earth, he writes: 'The usual methods of divination are neither reasonable nor scientific.'

During the Renaissance, almost all the great scholars are said to have studied astrology; it was not until after the Renaissance that the scientifically-minded ones became more and more hostile. Not only did many early scholars believe that the planets determined personality and fate in life generally, but they also related astrological factors to specific diseases. Galen, born in AD 130, who was to become the father of experimental physiology, wrote a book on the prognostication of disease by astrology; he believed that the position of the stars played an important role in the dosage of medicine to be prescribed. Linking each sign to a part of the body dates back at least to the *Astronomicon* written in AD 10 by the Roman poet, Manilius. This system was extended by Paracelsus (born in 1493) who argued that the principal organs of the body are ruled by the planets. Paracelsus was unusual in that he insisted that observation should come before theory, had no respect for authorities, and spent his life trying to find things out for himself. He promoted the idea that the heavens correspond to earthly events rather than influence them; this idea is currently in vogue among modern astrologers but in his time it was directly contrary to the prevailing views. He rejected the beliefs of popular astrology and wrote 'The stars determine nothing, imply nothing, suggest nothing; we are as free from them as they are from us,' and 'it is absurd to believe that the stars can make a man' (Hartmann, 1973).

The brilliant mathematician and inventor, Girolamo Cardan (born in 1501) was also an astrologer; according to legend, he committed suicide on the day he predicted for his own death. So too was the Danish astronomer Tycho Brahe (born in 1546), who is renowned for his precise planetary tables which allowed Kepler to work out the laws of planetary motion. In pointing out that a conjunction of Jupiter and Saturn in 1593 near stars traditionally said to be pestilential was in fact followed by a plague which swept Europe, he asked whether this did not 'confirm the influence of the stars by a very certain fact'. In spite of his belief in astrology, however, he was responsible for undermining the astrological belief, dating from Aristotle, that the fixed stars were eternal, unchanging and godlike. He did this when he proved that a nova which flared in 1572 was a fixed star.

Psychologists look at astrology

We have noted what modern physical scientists feel about astrology; how about psychologists? In view of the immaturity of their science, they might be thought to be more open-minded, but this does not seem to be so. Indeed, only a few have taken any notice of astrology. C.G. Jung, the well-known psychoanalyst, wrote a book entitled *The Structure and Dynamics of the Psyche*, in which he said: 'Had the astrologers (with but few exceptions) concerned themselves more with statistics and questioned the justice of their interpretations in a scientific spirit, they would have discovered long ago that their statements rested on a precarious foundation.' (It is interesting to note, as we shall discuss in Chapter 5, that Jung himself carried out a statistical survey, one of his few scientific endeavours, on astrology and married couples.)

Gordon Allport is another well-known psychologist who took

an interest in astrology; in 1940 he prepared a statement entitled 'Psychologists State their Views on Astrology', which was endorsed by the executive council of the Society for the Psychological Study of Social Issues, and which read in part:

Psychologists find no evidence that astrology is of any value whatsoever as an indicator of past, present, or future trends in one's personal life or in one's destiny. Nor is there the slightest ground for believing that social events can be foretold by divinations of the stars. The Society for the Psychological Study of Social Issues therefore deplores the faith of a considerable section of the American public in a magical practice that has no shred of justification in scientific fact.

One cannot help wondering how pyschologists, who in their clinical practice often use unreliable, invalid, and theoretically unsupported tests like the Rorschach, can so definitely accuse astrologers and others of being 'unscientific'. But it seems clear that they, like other scientists, can be prejudiced against astrology. There is in fact some experimental evidence to show this.

Goodstein and Brazis (1970) describe how they sent a questionnaire about an astrological study to 1,000 members of the Americal Psychological Association, chosen at random. The psychologists were asked to rate the quality and scientific merit of the study, which was concerned with the question of whether planets at birth are related to subsequent vocation. The study was in fact a fictitious one, and two versions were prepared, each of which was sent to half of the psychologists being questioned. In one version, results were inserted to show that there was indeed evidence of a connection between the planets and the choice of work. The other version was identical except that the results showed no connection.

It was hoped that the psychologists would be objective in their judgements, but the test showed that they were not. Many returned the questionnaire unanswered with rude comments. Only 282 provided usable returns, and those who had been sent the study with a negative outcome rated it as significantly better designed, as having more validity, and as reaching more adequate conclusions, although it was of course the same study. This evidence of bias, coupled with the emotional comments added by some of the psychologists, prompted Goodstein and Brazis to write: 'It is unfortunate that psychologists who should be more aware of the bad effects of bias and emotion upon critical thinking seem no more objective or unbiased than any of their scientific colleagues.'

Objections to astrology

We have already mentioned in passing some of the objections made to astrology, and we shall discuss others in more detail as they arise in dealing with specific experiments. Here we will merely note some objections which are frequently voiced, but which in our view have little value. One of the commonest is illustrated by the words of Bok (1975), whom we have already encountered as one of the authors of the *Humanist* statement. This is what he has to say: 'At one time I thought seriously of becoming personally involved in statistical tests of astrological predictions, but I abandoned this plan as a waste of time unless someone could first show me that there was some kind of physical foundation for astrology.' But this is putting the cart before the horse. Newton postulated a gravitational force, and arrived at detailed formulae describing how it worked, even though nothing was known about the nature of the force. In fact, although Newton used the concept of action at a distance, he was very dissatisfied with his own theory; and modern views of gravitation, whether we taken Einstein's field theory or the quantum theory of particle exchange (gravitons), are still in debate. But even though Newton's theory of action at a distance was almost certainly false, it was spectacularly successful in advancing our knowledge of gravitation. If scientists had to wait until a physical foundation had been established for events, then sociology, psychology, and much of medicine would be beyond the pale. Even the 'hard scientists', had they taken this advice, would never have been able to begin their studies of the material universe!

Jerome (1977), in a book entitled *Astrology Disproved*, puts forward the basic position that *astrology is false because it is based on magic*. He points out that the ancient 'principle of correspondence or analogies' is still used; for example, as Mars has a reddish colour it is associated with blood and war. Because of this obviously irrational foundation in magic and superstition, Jerome thinks that the case is closed. To quote him: 'If the basic assumptions of a hypothesis are not valid, there is no need to collect data to verify it.' He concludes: 'For modern man, astrology is, and should remain, a historical curiosity.'

Jerome may well be right but he has failed to demonstrate it. It is not enough to say that astrology originated as a system of magic and as a result cannot be valid. Such an origin, if it is true – and some historians have doubted even this – may cast considerable doubt on astrology as a whole, but it does not automatically condemn all aspects of astrology. The primary assumptions of a theory do not automatically prove or disprove its results. We have already given the example of Newton's theory of gravitation. Another is provided by Dalton's theory of the atom as a single and indestructible entity. This theory was found to be erroneous since the atom can be split and analysed in terms of different components. Nevertheless, by drawing attention to the possibility of qualitative differences between elements, Dalton's theory laid the foundations for modern chemistry. Many other examples could be given from the history of science and medicine. Why should astrology be an exception?

Jerome's criticisms, while incorrect, at least resemble in essence the rational discussion that goes on in scientific circles, and among philosophers of science, concerning the admissibility or otherwise of certain theories. But much that passes for scientific criticism in the books and articles we have read is in fact little better than defamation and prejudice. As Rockwell and others (1978) have documented there are constant *argumenta ad hominem* (personal abuse, to put it succinctly), assertions of guilt by association (some astrologers have believed in other unlikely things), prophecies of consequences (a list of the dangers into which belief in astrology could lead us), and above all, appeal to authority. None of these, clearly, are scientifically relevant.

Feyerabend (1978) gives a devastating critique of the manner in which scientists and philosophers have dealt with astrology; he compares the *Humanist* statement with the *Malleus Maleficarum* or 'Hammer of Witches', a book on witchcraft published by the Catholic Church in 1484 that was for two centuries the standard inquisitor's manual for tracking down witches. His conclusions are much to the disadvantage of the statement! Clearly, he says, the authors of the *Malleus* knew what they were talking about; they had examined the contrary arguments; they did not descend to *argumenta ad hominem*; they used logical discussion to establish their point of view. Feyerabend quotes the opening words of the *Malleus*, which come from a bull by Pope Innocent VIII, and points out that 'the words are almost the same as the words in the beginning of the "Statement", and so are the sentiments expressed. Both the Pope and the "186 leading scientists" deplore the increasing popularity of what they think are disreputable views. But what a difference in literacy and scholarship!'

Plan of the book

By now it should have become apparent what our approach is going to be. Here we set out some of the main principles which have guided us.

First, the issue must not be pre-judged. Astrology may be entirely false or it may contain elements of truth. Only a fair trial can hope to decide. We must argue rationally with an open mind.

Second, only a scientific approach can hope to lead us to the truth. To argue that astrology is false because of its origins, or because of the shortcomings of the scientists who have investigated it, is not enough. In spite of its magical or dubious beginnings, astrology may still be partly valid. It is only facts that can settle the issue.

Third, in evaluating research it is necessary to be critical. Many studies have failed to take into account statistical and psychological factors which ought to be considered. No single book except the often highly technical account by Dean and others (1977) gives a proper scientific review of the evidence. Gauquelin (1970, etc.), West and Toonder (1970), Gallant (1974), Culver and Ianna (1979) and Playfair and Hill (1979), amongst others, have all attempted a scientific review but have been surprisingly lax at times in applying the appropriate standards of evaluation.

Fourth, as well as being critical it also helps to be constructive. Often accidental discoveries are made while pursuing something else. There is the outstanding example of Johannes Kepler (born in 1571). He was interested in relating planetary orbits to perfect geometric solids and to musical scales or harmonies, and he devoted the best part of his life trying to prove Pythagoras' theory of the Harmony of the Spheres. (The seven planets were believed to emit the seven notes of the musical scale while orbiting at different speeds.) Much of this is now known to be nonsense, but whilst searching he arrived at results of great scientific value – the first true geometric description of the orbits of the planets. This led him to write: 'No one should regard it as impossible that, from the follies and blasphemies of astrologers, may emerge a sound and useful body of knowledge.'

Bearing all this in mind, then, what do we hope to establish in this book? We must begin by making some distinctions.

First, we must distinguish serious astrology from the columns in newspapers and magazines that pretend to make predictions applying to everyone whose birth falls under a particular sun sign – what your future holds if you are an Aquarian or a Sagittarian, or whatever. The best that can be said for this sort of thing is that it provides harmless amusement – harmless so long as you do not take it seriously. No real astrologer believes in it. As Truzzi (1979) put it: 'A manifesto denouncing newspaper astrology columns could as easily be signed by the leading astrologers as by a group of respected scientists.'

Next comes what we refer to as traditional astrology. This deals with the connections believed to exist between the positions of the planets at the moment of someone's birth and that person's character, development, profession, marriage and general life history. This type of astrology can be descriptive (trying to help someone to understand himself) or predictive (trying to forecast what will happen to him) or postdictive (trying to interpret and make sense of his past life). Predictive astrology can also concern itself with broader issues, such as the fate of nations, treaties and battles, arguing from the position of the planets at the time the treaties were signed, the battles were joined, kings or presidents inaugurated, and so forth. If there is truth in any of this, then its significance for science, let alone life, is obviously enormous.

Lastly there is astrology in the sense of 'cosmobiology', as we call it (although the term is sometimes used in a different sense by astrologers). This looks at the association between living organisms, especially man, and extraterrestrial phenomena of all kinds, including the positions of the planets, solar activity, seasonal fluctuations, and so forth. These factors may have a fairly direct and obvious influence, as do the changes of the seasons, or they may be more recondite and at present debatable, as with the influence of sunspots. If any of the claims being made in these areas turn out to be justified, then they are directly relevant not only to astrology but also to such subjects as astronomy, meteorology and psychology.

The purpose of our book, then, is to decide if astrology, in any of the senses we have described, is just mystifying nonsense, or constitutes the beginning of a science. We do not claim to be experts in astrology, and we could not interpret a birth chart with any degree of confidence; but that is not important. Training in psychology and statistics enables us to evaluate evidence for the kinds of statement made by astrologers. What is important is the ability to look at the design of the various studies with a critical eye, and the statistical knowledge to examine the results obtained.

Why statistics?

Many people complain that 'There are lies, damned lies, and statistics,' or that 'You can prove anything with statistics.' This is not a reasonable complaint. Ordinary lies are difficult to check, but statistical mistakes are much easier to discover. Fortunately the statistics involved in our subject are not very obscure or difficult, and we do not believe that anyone trained in statistics would disagree with our conclusions; but for the general reader it may be useful to mention the main underlying purpose which is served by statistical treatment of the kinds of data discussed in this book.

If it is true, as astrologers claim, that 'the stars incline, they do not compel', then statistics provide by far the best means of disentangling the different influences at work. Let us assume that we are interested in a particular astrological claim, say the hypothesis that extraverted people tend to be born under the odd-numbered signs of the zodiac, and introverted people under the even-numbered signs. Now clearly the position of the earth in its orbit round the sun (which is what all talk of the signs of the zodiac really boils down to) is not going to be the only thing that determines someone's extraversion or introversion; quite apart from the other astrological factors which are said to be just as relevant, conventional factors like heredity, upbringing and culture are all known to be important. So, even if there is some truth in this assertion, the 'signal-to-noise ratio' would be rather low. If we carry out an experiment in which we give personality tests to a number of people born under the various signs of the zodiac, we will undoubtedly find that the average extraversion-introversion scores differ between the signs; but we must then decide whether these differences are the product of chance, or are evidence of genuine cause and effect.

This is where statistics come in. They cannot give us any finally conclusive answer, but what they can tell us is *the probability that the results we have obtained might have arisen by chance*. If that probability is less than one in twenty, then by common consent the result is regarded as 'statistically significant'. If it is less than one in a hundred, we regard our results as 'very significant'.

These are fairly arbitrary criteria, and there is nothing sacred about them, but in practice they have proved to work well. Of course they can never *guarantee* that chance has been ruled out. For example, suppose that twenty people have independently carried out an astrological experiment where no actual effect exists. By chance one out of the twenty would be likely to obtain apparently 'significant' results, while the others would not. But now that one person, convinced that he had found evidence for an astrological claim, might rush into print, while the other nineteen might simply throw their data away as proving nothing; we would then find a 'statistically significant' result in the literature when in reality there was nothing significant in the total data collected by all the twenty investigators taken together. This sort of thing happens much more frequently than you might suppose; editors of journals are rather hostile to negative results, and often refuse to publish them. Positive results get into print far more easily.

There are other complexities. The number of astrological influences that have been postulated at one time or another is enormous, and what is often done in an investigation is to take a single measure, such as a test of personality, or the incidence of some disease, or some life event, and relate it not to one, but to a very large number of astrological factors. Now here again, if we test twenty factors, none of which is really related to the event in question, then by chance one out of these twenty will appear to be significant on the basis of our statistical test. If we test a hundred factors, then five will appear significant and one of these will appear very significant. So, even when there is nothing but chance at work, results may give the impression of being statistically significant, and it needs some care to be sure that this has not happened.

This is fairly easy when the investigator states precisely the number of statistical tests he has carried out, and lists all the factors he has tested. But many people do not do this; what they do instead is to try out hundreds or even thousands of such factors, and only mention in their reports those that come out with a positive result. This may make the results appear very highly significant statistically, when in actual fact we are dealing with pure chance data. An analogy is drawing a particular card from a pack and then saying that the odds of drawing it were one in fifty-two. This would be so only if we had predicted beforehand which card would appear.

The only way out of this difficulty is what is known as 'replication': the study must be repeated, and only if this replication produces similar results can they be accepted as true. Even then, of course, there is still the possibility that we might be dealing with chance effects, but this possibility is greatly reduced and could be eliminated almost completely by having further replications. Replication is the life blood of science, and it is disturbing to find that in astrology very few of the apparently significant findings have been replicated. We will come back to this point again and again in the course of this book.

It is even more important to take a critical look at the methods used in an experiment or study, because only this will allow us to judge what kind of conclusions can be based on it. This is not the place to run through the scientific 'rules of evidence', but one particularly important rule must be mentioned because it is so often disregarded, not only in astrological research but also by psychologists and particularly by sociologists. The fact that two things tend to go together (that there is, in scientific terms, a correlation between them) does not prove that one is causing the other. Over the past twenty years the population of Copenhagen has decreased, and so has the number of storks reported in the town. Do we conclude that fewer storks have brought fewer babies? The correlation is very high but it has no causal significance whatever. To put the rule briefly: correlation must not be interpreted as causation.

Let us take a less obvious example. Psychologists have found that children who are severely beaten by their parents tend to be less law abiding and more violent as adolescents and adults. Many people have concluded that these youngsters are violent *because* they have been beaten as children. This may be true, but there are also other possibilities. For instance, it is known that the behaviour in question is to a large extent genetically determined; perhaps the same genes that caused the parents to beat the child also cause the child when grown up to behave in an aggressive and violent manner? Or perhaps a child that is hostile and unmanageable provokes the parents into beating it? By itself the correlation does not allow us to say anything about the causal sequence; that requires much more specialised and complex experimental designs. So, even when chance has been more or less effectively ruled out, we still have the job of deciding just what causes what.

The demarcation dispute

When is a science not a science? If we are going to decide whether astrology can be regarded in any way as a science, we must obviously take some position on this demarcation dispute, which has been frequently discussed by philosophers of science for most of this century. The best introduction to the topic is perhaps a recent book on *The Structure of Scientific Theories* edited by Frederick Suppe (1974). It clearly shows that what seems at first sight to be a simple question may not be all that easy to answer.

There have in fact been three major positions, which may be simplified as follows. Sir Francis Bacon originally advocated the collection of facts, and then the basing of theories on these facts (the method of 'induction'). The Vienna School of Logical Positivism, at the time of the First World War, suggested that science essentially begins with the statement of theories, followed by their verification or otherwise by research. Sir Karl Popper, more recently, has argued that no theory can ever be finally verified: however often we produce results verifying the theory, we can never be absolutely certain that one more experiment might not produce a disproof. Popper therefore believes that a theory is scientific if it is open, not to being proved true (which it never can) but to being proved wrong. In other words, falsification not verification is the distinctively scientific approach.

Our own belief is that it would be incorrect to call any of these views right or wrong, and it would be equally incorrect to assume that any of them applies to all the different states of science in its growth from early beginnings to later mastery. Science begins by making observations, and then by making inductions from these observations (Bacon). At this stage these inductions may be little more than primitive hunches and there is probably no very obvious distinction between science, on the one hand, and folklore, magic and ordinary work practices on the other. Gradually, as more facts become available, hypotheses are stated, and verification or otherwise of these begins (Vienna School). When we have a number of reasonably well verified hypotheses, more far-reaching theories are constructed, and these give rise to so many possible deductions

17

that verification of them all becomes impossible. Falsification now becomes a more crucial issue (Popper). Finally, when a theory has been subjected to many tests without being falsified, we establish laws, such as Newton's law of gravitation. These can only be overthrown when anomalies accumulate, scientific revolutions are staged and alternative theories presented, such as Einstein's theory of relativity.

Rules of demarcation which are suitable for one stage of development are not necessarily suitable for other stages, and indeed we may obtain quite erroneous results by applying the wrong rule. Thus Popper gave as examples of pseudo-scientific theories those associated with Freud, Marx and astrology; he declared that these did not give rise to falsifiable theories, and were therefore not scientific. But this is quite untrue, at least as far as astrology is concerned, because many testable hypotheses and theories are found in the textbooks. To give one example, we have already mentioned the assertion that extraverted people tend to be born under the odd-numbered signs of the zodiac, introverted people under the even-numbered signs. This is a testable hypothesis and accordingly we would have to call astrology 'scientific' by Popper's criterion.

In practical terms, we would suggest that the study of astrology has not advanced far enough to make general theory statements and falsification very useful in a decision about its scientific status; we should return to an earlier stage and concentrate on attempts at verification. Only if a number of astrological claims could be verified would it be useful to go on to later stages in our progression.

As a warning example consider the well-known story of Charles II, who set the newly-formed Royal Society the following problem: 'Why is it that when we take a glass brim-full of water and put a frog into it the water does not overflow?' The sages and scientists of the Royal Society pondered this problem for several days, until someone actually produced a glass of water and put a frog into it. The water promptly overflowed! We will have to wait for the elaboration of theories until we have some reasonably well established facts.

It is from this point of view, then, that we have in this book examined some of the assertions made by astrologers, some of their hypotheses and theories, and in particular some attempts to verify them by empirical studies. We have looked particularly and critically at the statistics and methods used in these studies, and have tried to see how far the data justify the conclusions.

In concluding this chapter one last word must be said about our choice of material. Dean and others (1977), in their *magnum opus*, surveyed practically all the numerous studies that had been done in the field of astrology, but had to dismiss most of them for various inadequacies. We have not tried to be anything like so inclusive. We have eliminated a very large number of studies which, by virtue of their design, their statistical treatment, the small size of the sample, or for other reasons, clearly did not produce worthwhile results. Our judgement may be subjective, but we are glad to see that in practically every case we agree with Dean and his fellow authors, and with the Gauquelins and other well-informed critics in this field. It would be boring to cite these worthless studies merely in order to shoot them down. Instead, we have concentrated on studies which not only have a positive outcome but also are regarded by many as giving strong support to the claims of astrology. We have described these at some length, and have tried to show the reader why, in many cases, we do not believe that the results and conclusions claimed are the correct ones. In other cases we have found nothing to criticise, though we have often pointed out the need for replication, or the dangers of drawing conclusions beyond what the data will support. We have acted in the belief that, if there is a core of sense and fact beneath the exaggerated claims and fraudulent pretence that too often go under the flag of astrology, then it is only by careful examination of positive studies that such a core can be revealed. It is simply a case of finding out whether or not the best available positive evidence stands up to scientific scrutiny.

We have tried to answer those astrologers who denigrate the scientific approach, and claim that the scientific method cannot deal with such complex and subtle theories as theirs. As we shall see, there are ways and means which enable the scientist to grapple with even very complex hypotheses, and studies

19

using these methods will be cited in detail. Anyone who denies the possibility of studying certain theories scientifically shows an ignorance of the methods available; and he may also reveal a certain fear of the outcome.

Throughout this book, we have tried to work with as little prejudice as is humanly possible, but we are under no illusions. Should our survey favour astrology, scientists will denounce us. Should we find astrology wanting, astrologers will vilify us. That is the way of the world and we shall not complain.

2   What is Astrology?

Curiosity is one of the permanent and certain characteristics
of a vigorous intellect.
Samuel Johnson

The origins of astrology

Accounts of how astrology began have filled entire books, and
we can give only a brief outline here. To begin with we must distinguish between astrology and astronomy, which originated
together in Babylonia. Astrologers usually claim that astrology
is very ancient and that it was the mother of astronomy, but the
actual beginnings of either discipline are not known. From
evidence dating back to the invention of cuneiform writing
around 3000 BC, it seems likely that the precursors of
astronomy were the observations of the sky made in response to
the need for a calendar to regulate hunting and sowing
activities, and that the precursors of astrology were simply
omen predictions.

A common calendar was important because Babylonia was a
large centralised empire in which local variations in a calendar
would have caused problems. According to an excellent historical account by Toulmin and Goodfield (1965), omen
predictions were the natural consequence of the Babylonian
belief that the celestial bodies were gods who could influence
everything from the weather to the fortunes of men and states.
Because these gods moved in patterns which could be seen and
recorded, reading omens was seen not as a delusion but as an
intellectual challenge to understand the patterns of fate.
Moreover, religious beliefs and political affairs in Babylonia
were interwoven to a degree that would be inconceivable today.
Hence although we have distinguished here between astrology
and astronomy there was probably no essential difference
between them to start with. As soon as observers linked the
sun's height in the sky with the seasons and the moon's phases
with the tides and with the female cycle, such correspondences
between heaven and earth were probably assumed to extend
without limit.

In their survey of the origins of astrology, Culver and Ianna (1979) point out that the Babylonians could hardly have been more superstitious. They saw portents in every kind of phenomena from simple everyday happenings to the state of the entrails of specially sacrificed animals. Hence the heavens were only a small part of their inventory of omen material. Typical of the earliest surviving Babylonian omen predictions is this one from circa 2470 BC: 'If the moon can be seen the first night of the month, the country will be peaceful . . . If the moon is surrounded by a halo, the king will reign supreme.' Such omens were little different from those based on other phenomena. On this basis there seems to be little doubt that superstition was the ultimate mother of astrology.

There are many prehistoric stone monuments around the world, such as the pyramids and Stonehenge, which may have served as observation points for studying the sky. Stone towers up to 300 feet high were commonplace from about 2000 BC in Babylon (the Tower of Babel was probably one of them). From these towers, it is believed, systematic nightly observations were made of the heavenly paths of the moon and planets. The few instruments that the Babylonians used, such as direction finders based on the same principle as the sundial, were not accurate. But this was not important. The precision of Babylonian astronomy (which remained unsurpassed for centuries until matched by the Greeks around AD 100) came not from the accuracy of individual observations but from the antiquity and continuity of their carefully-kept records, and the existence of a reliable calendar by which to interpret them. When centuries of daily records are available for analysis, inaccuracies in the individual observations are of little consequence.

Biblical references to early astrology date from about 760 BC, with the Old Testament providing several examples. To quote from Isaiah: 'Let now the astrologers, the star gazers, the monthly prognosticators, stand up and save thee from those things which have come upon thee.' But astrology as we know it was not possible until the Babylonians had invented the 360 degree zodiac around 700 BC for astronomical purposes. By 600 BC, they had divided this zodiac into 12 equal parts, each

22

named after the constellation occupying most of that part. As we shall explain later, due to precession (of which the Babylonians were not then aware) these constellations today have all moved on by nearly one sign. By 300 BC, they had developed the mathematical astronomy necessary to calculate the motions of the moon and planets. Thus the claim often made by astrologers that astrology began in antiquity as empirical observation is not supported, because up to this time the required astronomical knowledge did not exist.

The earliest known horoscope based on the moment of birth comes from this period and is for 29 April 410 BC; it consists largely of a simple list of the sign positions of the moon and five planets. Later horoscopes are similar but more sophisticated and sometimes there is a brief interpretation concerning future prospects such as wealth and longevity.

No Babylonian horoscope mentions the ascendant or any factor other than planets in signs. Hence it seems that most of today's astrology was invented by the Greeks after they acquired Babylonian ideas (by 400 BC they were using Babylonian sign names for the months of a solar calendar) and especially after they conquered Babylon in 331 BC. It was the Greeks who first attached special significance to the ascending sign, which is the one rising on the horizon at the moment of birth. Thus the word horoscope comes from the Greek 'horoscopos' which means literally 'I watch that which is rising'.

The earliest surviving astrological treatise is actually the *Astronomicon* by Manilius of Rome, composed during the reign of Augustus, and followed 130 years later, in AD 140, by the classic *Tetrabiblos* of Ptolemy, whose comprehensive and detailed account is taken as gospel truth by many modern astrologers and contains most of the technical essentials of astrology as practised today. Both Manilius and Ptolemy constantly referred to earlier works, so that their books represented a compilation of previously known lore. Some minor changes resulted when astrology was introduced to the Romans by the Greeks; for example, the planets were renamed after the Roman gods.

Greek astrology passed to India (especially after the Greek

23

invasion of 327 BC) where it became embroidered with Hindu ideas. Because subsequent Indian astronomy and astrology was tied to the fixed stars, whereas subsequent Greek astronomy and astrology were not, there began a fundamental difference between Eastern and Western astrology which still exists today.

By the Middle Ages astrology had spread throughout the world. It was only with the emergence of astronomy following the invention of the telescope in 1610 that astrology became lost on the rising tide of scientific reason. In 1666 it was banished from the universities in France, and elsewhere in Europe soon after. Little happened until it was revived and slightly modernised over 200 years later, largely by the Theosophist Alan Leo (1860-1917). It spread to America at the start of this century, and since then it has experienced a marked resurgence of interest, especially in the last decade or two. Today the number of people studying serious astrology in Western countries has been estimated by Dean and others (1977) to be roughly 1 in 10,000 of the general population, or about the same abundance as psychologists.

The principles of astrology

How does astrology relate the heavens to earthly matters? The rules of interpretation differ somewhat depending on whether the issue being considered is a person's character, the events in their life, a business, a nation, the best time for an event, the answer to a question, a relationship, and so on. But there are certain principles which are fundamental to most of them, and it is these that we will now describe. Readers wanting a more detailed description should refer to a suitable textbook such as that by Parker and Parker (1975).

The first step in the process is to calculate the birth chart, which is simply a stylised map of the heavens at the moment of birth. The birth in question can be that of a person, a company, an event, a nation, a question, or anything which has a distinct moment of beginning. The heavens are usually drawn as seen from the earth. Most birth charts today consist of a pre-printed form (of which there are many designs) on to which the astrologer enters the twelve signs of the zodiac, the planets (taken from a book of planetary positions called an ephemeris), and the houses (explained later and taken from a table of houses). Note that in astrology the term 'planets' includes the sun and moon; this is technically incorrect but is used for convenience. A typical birth chart is shown in the figure.

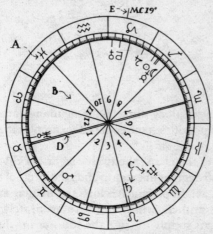

A *signs of the zodiac*
B *Houses*
C *Planets in the houses and the signs which they occupied at the time of birth*
D *The ascendant: the degree of the zodiac which was rising at the time of birth*
E *The Midheaven: the degree of the zodiac which was culminating at the time of birth*

Ludwig van Beethoven was born in Bonn on 16 December 1770 at 13:30 hours. This birth chart represents a map of the heavens at the time of his birth. In practice the chart would include the exact planetary positions, a list of aspects, and other information, all of which have been omitted here for clarity. A key to the symbols is given below. (Based on Geddes, 1976.)

A typical interpretation of this chart would begin as follows: Musical gifts are indicated by the ascendant in Taurus (a sign much associated with music by astrologers) and by Uranus near the ascendant (a position said to indicate genius). Beethoven was a difficult and quarrelsome person, as shown by Mercury (mentality) exactly opposite Mars (energy), and had a disordered personal life, as shown by Uranus (change) opposite the descendant (friends). Astrologers have made a

SIGN		PLANET	
Aries	♈	Sun	☉
Taurus	♉	Mercury	☿
Gemini	♊	Venus	♀
Cancer	♋	Moon	☽
Leo	♌	Mars	♂
Virgo	♍	Jupiter	♃
Libra	♎	Saturn	♄
Scorpio	♏	Uranus	♅
Sagittarius	♐	Neptune	♆
Capricorn	♑	Pluto	♇
Aquarius	♒		
Pisces	♓		

detailed analysis along these lines of many famous people. Mann (1979) provides some colourful examples in his book *The Round Art*.

To return to the chart, the twelve signs are divisions of the zodiac each 30 degrees in extent. Thus the circle of signs is both the celestial backdrop against which the planets are seen, and the reference grid by which they are accurately positioned. Your sun sign is simply the sign the sun was in when you were born. It is the only astrological factor which can be readily determined without an ephemeris, hence it necessarily forms the basis for all popular astrology. However, because the earth's orbit is not circular but slightly elliptical, the sun does not spend the same time in each sign. It spends its longest time in Cancer (31½ days) and its shortest (29½ days) in Capricorn. These fractions, plus the effect of leap years, mean that the sun does not always change sign on the same day each year, so that the dates given in the newspapers are only approximate. The table shows a typical division.

We now come to the other important astrological series – the 'houses'. Imagine the space around you divided into twelve sections, like twelve slices of melon with their inner edges running north-south. Six of these divisions will be above the horizon and six below, and in the course of twenty-four hours every celestial object will appear to swing round through all twelve of them, taking on average two hours to pass through each one. These divisions are the houses.

	Zodiac sign	Approximate dates
1	Aries the ram	March 21 to April 19
2	Taurus the bull	April 20 to May 20
3	Gemini the twins	May 21 to June 21
4	Cancer the crab	June 22 to July 22
5	Leo the lion	July 23 to August 22
6	Virgo the virgin	August 23 to September 22
7	Libra the scales	September 23 to October 23
8	Scorpio the scorpion	October 24 to November 22
9	Sagittarius the archer	November 23 to December 21
10	Capricorn the goat	December 22 to January 20
11	Aquarius the water-bearer	January 21 to February 18
12	Pisces the fish	February 19 to March 20

Sun signs and corresponding birth dates. To this astronomical base, astrologers have added their own interpretations. (Based on Parker and Parker, 1975.)

There are 12 houses and they start downwards at the ascendant, which is that part of the zodiac on the eastern horizon. The areas of sky just above the east or west horizons are therefore the 12th or 7th houses respectively. The sign of the zodiac in which the ascendant falls is called the ascending or rising sign. To calculate this for someone's birth we therefore need to know the exact time and place of birth as well as the date.

Another important measurement in astrology concerns the apparent angles between pairs of planets or other significant points. These angles are known as 'aspects', and the five principal planetary aspects are *conjunction* (two planets superimposed); *sextile* (two planets 60 degrees apart); *square* (90 degrees); *trine* (120 degrees), and *opposition* (180 degrees). The astrologer notes any of these aspects that appear in a birth chart. The degree of inexactness allowed is called the *orb* of the aspect; for example, if the orb is 5 degrees, then anything from 85 to 95 degrees would be called 'square'.

Aspects of 60 degrees and 120 degrees are called easy or soft, and aspects of 90 degrees and 180 degrees are called difficult or hard. Conjunctions are in between the soft and the hard. Victorian astrologers often used the terms good versus bad in this connection, but this usage has now largely disappeared.

As well as signs, planets and houses there is also a seemingly

27

inexhaustible supply of additional factors such as stars, asteroids, eclipses, nodes, midpoints, parallels of declination, retrogradation, distance, and harmonic aspects which can be used, but their use is not widespread and is beyond the scope of this brief survey.

Drawing up the birth chart may take anything from fifteen minutes to over an hour, depending on the astrologer and the type of chart involved. Alternatively it can all be done by computer. Once the birth data are entered it will produce a complete chart in seconds or minutes, depending on the computer. As we show later in this book, computers can be an enormous help in any large-scale investigation of astrology. In fact the recent advent of home computers is currently bringing to astrologers their own computer revolution, the results of which will probably facilitate the confrontation of science and astrology like nothing else.

We have seen how the basic birth chart shows the signs, planets and houses as they were at the moment of birth. From this chart the astrologer traditionally identifies the ascending sign, the signs and houses that each planet is in, and the planetary aspects, and from the individual meanings of each factor he will carefully build up his overall interpretation, as shown in the next section. So far everything seems surprisingly logical and straightforward. Nevertheless, on closer examination, we can see how complex the underlying chart is. There are ten planets including the sun and moon, twelve signs and twelve houses, and in addition to that, five main aspects for the planets taken two at a time, giving a total of hundreds of variables, each of which can have a theoretical influence on the personality and fate of the newborn baby! As each of these factors may add, subtract, cancel out, or interact in many other ways with any other factor, the possibilities for prediction are almost infinite.

Add the other factors previously mentioned (totalling thousands of variables) plus the fact that for most factors their exact use is disputed (thus astrologers disagree on where the zodiac starts, how the houses should be divided, what orbs to use, and so on), and we can begin to understand the comment of Dobyns and Roof (1973) that 'astrology is almost as confused as the early chaos it is supposed to clarify'. In other words it is almost impossible not to find some congruence between astrological factors, on the one hand, and the known facts on the other. We need to bear this in mind when we come to discuss the significance of astrological findings.

Interpreting the birth chart

Interpretation is the real contribution of the astrologer, since the construction of the chart, which simply means calculating the celestial configurations at the time of birth, is a matter of astronomy.

Planets		Signs		Houses	
Sun	Self-expression	Aries	Assertively	1	Personality
Moon	Response	Taurus	Possessively	2	Possessions
Mercury	Mentality	Gemini	Versatilely	3	Mental interests
Venus	Harmony	Cancer	Sensitively	4	Home
Mars	Energy	Leo	Creatively	5	Pleasures
Jupiter	Expansion	Virgo	Critically	6	Work
Saturn	Limitation	Libra	Harmoniously	7	Friends
Uranus	Change	Scorpio	Intensely	8	Legacies
Neptune	Nebulousness	Sagittarius	Freely	9	Exploration
Pluto	Elimination	Capricorn	Aspiringly	10	Career
		Aquarius	Independently	11	Objectives
		Pisces	Nebulously	12	Self-sacrifice

Some basic keywords which appear in more elaborate form in most astrology textbooks for the planets, signs and houses. (Based on Parker and Parker, 1975.)

Examples of interpretation will appear throughout this book, so all we need here are a few principles. Each of the planets, signs and houses has a basic meaning, as set out in the table. How these meanings were originally settled on is not clear. Some astrologers claim, without providing historical documentation, that they are based on centuries of observation. Others consider their derivation to be purely symbolic. For instance, the planets are sometimes associated with qualities suggested by their appearance. The red of Mars suggests blood and war, and so a martial, energetic temperament. The brightness of Jupiter suggests gaiety and a jovial, outgoing personality. The pale glow of Saturn suggests a saturnine, cautious type. In the zodiac, too, each sign is associated with a different personality trait which tends to correspond with the qualities suggested by the animal or object named in the sign or by the time of the year. The sun sign Leo which appears under the burning August sun is thus associated with the fiery and royal power of the king of the jungle.

To take another example, the sign of Capricorn, the goat, suggests climbing, and so an aspiring temperament. As Capricorn is the tenth sign, the tenth house is seen, by analogy, as the one concerned with aspiration and careers. Whatever their original derivation, these meanings have been handed down by tradition and are repeated more or less unchanged in countless textbooks.

To interpret an individual chart these meanings are combined in an ingenious manner: the planet is the basic quality, the sign is how it is expressed, and the house is where it is expressed. The following example illustrates how this works:

Moon in Libra in tenth house

Moon (basic quality) = response

Libra (how it is expressed) = harmoniously

Tenth house (where it is expressed) = career

Interpretation: charming harmonious manner which could be the basis for a successful career.

The interpretation is modified by various complexities which need not concern us in detail. For example, it is modified by any attributes which the signs occupied by planets share in common (polarity, quality and element) or which they share with the occupying planet (rulership and exaltation). Each planet may also be in aspect to another planet, which simply combines the meanings as shown in the following example:

Sun (self-expression) in aspect to Mars (energy)

Easy aspect = forceful, energetic

Difficult aspect = pugnacious, bad tempered

These interpretations of aspects would also be modified by sign and house positions. For example, if in the difficult aspect the sun was in the second house (possessions) and Mars was in the fifth house (pleasures), as well as pugnacity and bad temper a wasteful squandering of possessions in pursuit of pleasures would be indicated.

When he has interpreted each factor individually, the astrologer then brings them all together and carefully synthesises the overall interpretation of the chart. This is where the problems start, because the factors are both numerous and often contradictory, and it is all too easy for astrologers to see in a chart what they want to see. For example, Beethoven's chart can easily be made to fit the exact opposite; thus absence of musical gifts could be related to Saturn (limitation) opposite the MC, a pleasant non-quarrelsome person is shown by the ruler of the chart, which is Venus (harmony), and an ordered personal life is shown by Saturn (order, limitation) in the fourth house (home) and by Venus (love, harmony) in Capricorn (ruled by Saturn).

Clearly everything depends on the process of chart synthesis, and one would therefore expect unambiguous rules to say just how one factor should be weighed against another. But astrologers have been unable to agree on such rules (in fact many claim that rules are irrelevant to what they feel should be a purely intuitive process), and the only generally accepted rule is that no factor shall be judged in isolation. Thus from this point on anything goes – including any hope of quick results by investigators of astrology!

It is obviously pertinent to ask how such a subtle and subjective process can form the basis of a scientific investigation. But this objection misses the point. If the most basic tenets of astrology are true, they should be detectable in their own right, regardless of other subtleties. To take an analogy, suppose we were investigating the belief that there is a connection between diet and body weight. Of course many other factors come in, such as genetic make-up, age, exercise, health and so on. Nevertheless, if we took a large enough sample, we should certainly expect to see indications that fat people tended to be well fed and starving people tended to be thin. If astrology is true, it must pass that kind of test. Let us look and see.

3   Could Astrology be True?

What has not been examined impartially, has not been well examined. Scepticism is therefore the first step toward truth.
Denis Diderot

Can we believe in astrology, or is the whole thing simply too implausible? The question needs to be confronted, and we shall try to do so in this chapter in a general way before we go on to look at specific astrological beliefs and the evidence for and against them.

Symbolism

A great deal of astrological prediction (if not all of it) is based on symbolism, whereby one thing is used to represent another. For example, Venus symbolises love as well as a host of related ideas. For an astrologer, symbolism is central to his work: for his critics, it is all just nonsense, far-fetched and meaningless. They point out, for example, that the stars in the constellations do not really fall into groups at all. They are spread out one behind the other in space, unimaginable distances apart, and it is only by chance that, seen from our earth, they appear to cluster together. Even then, the patterns they form bear no relation to the objects they are meant to represent. They do not even look like them—a point conceded even by astrologers. (In a small-scale experiment we showed the actual configurations of stars making up the twelve signs to a number of people and asked them to say which looked like a lion, a scorpion, a pair of twins and so on. Nobody scored better than chance.)

Again, the moon and the planets appear to be inside the constellations only because of the misleading effects of perspective. The founders of astrology thought they all lay close together, a few miles at most away from the earth.

The question of distance is important, for, whatever influence the planets may exert on human affairs, it is much easier to conceive of it as coming from bodies that circle close above our heads. In fact, the planets are millions of miles away, and they

32

in turn are many, many times further than that from the constellations with which they are supposed to interact.

In other ways, too, the basis of symbolism can sometimes be shown to be factually inaccurate. Ptolemy in his *Tetrabiblos* provides many symbolic interpretations which suggest a physical basis for the astrological rules and much of this was mistaken. For instance, Mars was believed (incorrectly) to be near the sun and to be hot and arid, having a drying influence. The moon, being nearest to the earth, was believed to soak up moisture and so to have a dampening influence. We now know that Mars has considerable water (albeit frozen) and that the moon is bone dry!

Too often, astrologers seem to close their eyes to inconsistencies. For example, perhaps the most serious arises from what is known as the 'precession of the equinoxes'. The earth, as we know, spins on its axis, but as with a spinning top this axis does not point in a constant direction. Instead it describes a circle, taking about 25,800 years for a full circuit. As a result, the constellation in which the sun appears to lie on a particular day slowly changes. In the time of Ptolemy, the sun was in the constellation Aries on the day of the spring equinox (21 March); two thousand years earlier, it had been in Taurus; today it is in Pisces. (Coming up next is Aquarius, so giving rise to the 'dawning of the Age of Aquarius'.)

Because of precession there are in effect two zodiacs, the zodiac discussed previously (the 'tropical' zodiac) which is tied to the vernal point, and the 'sidereal' zodiac which is tied to the stars. The first is favoured by astrologers in the West, the latter by astrologers in the East (who outnumber those in the West). In Ptolemy's time the two zodiacs coincided, but due to precession they are now nearly one sign out of step. However the meanings have not changed, and signs of the same name still have the same meaning in both zodiacs. This means that almost opposite meanings can be given to the same piece of sky. Eastern astrologers also use other methods which are in conflict with Western methods; for example, most of them ignore the three modern planets now judged to be so essential in the West.

These are particularly telling objections because they mean essentially that if Western astrologers are right in making any particular interpretation, Eastern astrologers are wrong, and vice versa. Yet both sides claim to be extremely successful! Typically the response of astrologers has not been to resolve these impasses by experiment, but to ignore them.

Another example of the way in which astrologers can turn their backs on inconvenient facts can be seen in Ptolemy. He recognized that, in fixing the moment at which a human life begins, it might be better to take the moment of conception rather than birth. The problem is, of course, that it is not usually known, so Ptolemy neatly side-stepped this by claiming that birth will be under the same constellation as reigned at the time of conception, although there is in fact no reason at all to suppose that it is.

Confronted with this sort of objection, astrologers sometimes answer that 'there is more in our total experience of reality than lends itself to mathematical equations'; or that the only approach to reality may be in 'the language of images, metaphors and similes'. But this simply evades the issue of whether predictions based on this symbolic substructure turn out in practice to be true. That is something that can be checked empirically, and it is a large part of the purpose of this book to do just that.

Many other general objections to astrology have been raised. Why is it that the birth chart – supposedly the source of all kinds of subtle insights – cannot predict something as basic as sex, intelligence or race? How are we to explain, too, those occasions when a whole community is wiped out in some sudden disaster like a volcanic eruption or an atomic explosion? In such a large sample, perhaps containing thousands of people, birth dates and times will be spread throughout the year, with all the various signs and influences represented. Should not such a dramatic end be signalled in their birth charts? If it were, then the births of people dying together in that way should cluster together at significant times. There is no reason to suppose they do.

Again, what are we to make of the fact that children born north of the arctic circle cannot have a normal horoscope? In those latitudes most of the planets stay, like the sun, above or below the horizon for months at a time, and some signs cannot rise or set at all. If it is not astrology that rules the fate of people born in Siberia, Lapland and Alaska, then what does?

Empirical research

The objections to astrology, like the claims of the astrologers themselves, can only be judged by means of factual, empirical research. Unfortunately not many researchers in this field have a good knowledge both of astrology and of research methods. Very few astrologers understand the requirements of science, and conversely many of the scientists who have become interested in this field have little understanding of astrology.

One great exception is Michel Gauquelin. He has systematically looked at many astrological experiments, and invariably he claims that alternative explanations can be found for the results obtained. Culver and Ianna (1979) have come to a similar conclusion. They argue that claims for the validity of traditional astrology can always be refuted, and the results explained in other ways. To quote from Gauquelin (1979): 'No law of classical astrology has been demonstrated statistically by astrologers or scientists.'

Since he reached this conclusion, further evidence has become available and we shall be looking at it in later chapters, but Gauquelin's own conclusion was clear. In all his researches on what is clearly recognized as traditional astrology, he found nothing that was statistically significant.

In one typical study he charted the horoscopes for 623 murderers on file in the Paris Courthouse. They were notorious for the horror of their crimes, and had mostly met a violent end under the guillotine. Astrology should have something to say about the fate of these characters. Traditionally, Mars is associated with violence, blood and crime, so Gauquelin noted the position of Mars in the charts of these arch-criminals. The pattern was random. Even in the astrological house sometimes associated with death, Mars made only chance appearances.

In investigating mistaken claims by researchers in traditional astrology, we can see three types of error in particular. The first of them is quite straightforward. Interesting results are thrown up by one study, but when it is repeated they disappear. Paul Choisnard, for example, found in a French study based on two hundred cases that Mars or Saturn tended to be in conjunction with the natal sun at the time of death; that is, at the time of death one of these planets tended to coincide with the position of the sun at birth. The trend was three times more likely than would have been expected by chance and, if confirmed, it would have had important practical applications. We would have been able to predict the time of death for people 'at death's door' and it would have been obviously useful in planning the timing of risky operations and in nursing the sick generally. Unfortunately, when Gauquelin (1979) repeated the study on a much larger number of cases (7428) the effect disappeared. The times of death followed chance expectations and Choisnard's result appeared simply as a stroke of luck.

Choisnard and a Swiss-born astrologer named Karl Ernst Krafft were the first astrologers to apply statistics, and their findings have been widely quoted. Gauquelin carried out a complete analysis of other research by these two pioneers, but although they had often presented their results as supporting or at least being consistent with astrology, Gauquelin found, using conventional statistical analyses, that the laws of chance could explain all of them. It was only in the study on death that an original result stood up to statistical scrutiny (though not to replication).

The second type of error occurs when effects turn out to be the result of ordinary astronomical laws rather than astrology. For example, when Choisnard charted the horoscopes of people famed for their exceptional intelligence he found an excess of ascendants in Gemini, Libra and Aquarius. That is, these zodiac signs tended to be on the horizon at the time of the births of famous intellectuals, a rule Choisnard subsequently formulated in his 'law of ascendants for superior minds'. What Choisnard failed to take into account was that, because the earth's axis is inclined to its orbital plane, the twelve signs do not all spend the same amount of time on the horizon. The only sure way to guard against astronomical problems of this kind is to have a control group. Choisnard should have picked a group of people with only average intelligence and achievement but matched in other ways with his group of 'superior minds'. Since the same astronomical laws would apply to both groups, any astrological connections with mental excellence should show up in differences between them. When other researchers tried to replicate Choisnard's study with different groups their results did not support his theory. We are obliged to relegate his 'law of ascendants for superior minds' to the dustbin of astrological history.

What is true of ascendants is also true of aspects. Not all planetary aspects occur equally often. (Some, indeed, cannot occur at all. For example, Mercury can never be more than twenty-eight degrees from the sun, as viewed from the earth, and Venus never more than forty-eight degrees. These two planets, therefore, cannot realise most of the recognised astrological aspects.) If certain planetary aspects occur more often than others in connection with certain human events, it may merely be because they occur more often altogether.

The third type of error is rather similar, and comes from distortions caused by demography. Krafft noted the birth sign for 2817 musicians and found that Taurus was the most common. This looked like evidence for astrology since Taurus is governed by Venus which is traditionally associated with an artistic tendency. But matters are not as simple as this. In Europe, there tend to be more births in the spring than at other times of the year, and Taurus is a spring sign. As with the last example, a control group would have revealed the fallacy: quite apart from musicians, everyone in Europe has a slightly increased chance of being born under Taurus.

The sort of investigation on which we are embarked is always complicated by the fact that most events have a number of causes, some obvious and some subtle. Let us take as an example death from aeroplane crashes. Astrologers often use the birth chart to explain why a crash occurs at one time rather than another. But there is no shortage of other explanations, and there is even evidence that aeroplane crashes, along with fatal motor vehicle accidents and suicides generally, increase after newspaper publicity about suicide or murder.

In one such study, Phillips (1978) investigated the effect of eighteen well-publicised murders in the USA. There was a significant tendency for (private) aircraft crashes to occur after the newspaper accounts of these murders, with a peak occurring three days after the first report. Further, there was a significant correlation between the amount of publicity given to a murder story and the number of crashes afterwards.

Various control procedures were introduced in this study. Could the finding that crashes tended to occur three days after a murder be a day-of-the-week effect? For instance, if murders tend to occur, say, on a Friday night and aircraft crashes on a Monday morning, then this would explain the apparent connection: it would be what statisticians call an 'artefact'. Phillips investigated this possibility by looking to see if, in addition to the three-day peak, there was another peak a week later. There was no sign of this, and so he was able to conclude that newspaper publicity probably really did trigger off a number of suicides disguised as accidental aircraft crashes.

While on this morbid subject, it may be pointed out that a number of psychological factors have been identified as contributing to the exact time of death, including the strength of people's motives for staying alive. For example, there is a decrease in a country's death rate in the days leading up to an important event such as the Olympic Games. Dean and others (1977) mention several such studies, and make the point that time of death obviously depends on many factors quite apart from the position of certain planets. It is against this background of contributing factors that the effect of astrology has to be detected.

There are various ways in which the claims of astrology can come to look more convincing than they really are. There is, first and obviously, the possibility of genuine errors in research. Many studies are poorly designed, carelessly analysed, and inaccurately reported. Fortunately science is self-correcting; such errors can be detected and put right in future research.

Then there is the problem of biased selection of data: 'If ye search hard enough, ye shall find.' We mentioned in Chapter 1 the simple statistical fact that, in the nature of things, we will expect a result that is 'significant at the five per cent level' to crop up on average once in every twenty times when we are examining chance occurrences. That is what we mean by that level of significance: it is something that will occur by chance in five out of every hundred trials. So if we carry out a hundred experiments on coin tossing, say, we will expect to get five results significant at the five per cent level and one at the one per cent level (that is, with a probability of a hundred to one against its occurring by chance).

When we come to assess experiments in any field, including astrology, we must therefore look not only at those that produced apparently significant results but at all those that did not. Since these are very unlikely to have been reported in the literature, we are thrown back once again onto controlled replication of the experiment. That alone, not the occurrence of a single striking result, can count as real evidence.

Then there is the question of bias. There is probably a whole range of bias, stretching from simple carelessness to intentional cheating. Subconscious biases probably go a long way toward explaining the 'experimenter effect', the evidence for which was reviewed by Rosenthal (1964). He demonstrated that even when research information was collected by assistants who did not know the hypothesis or expected outcome of the study, bias still operated if they had been in communication with the designer of the study. It seems that, despite intentions, the expected outcome somehow got through to the assistants. Even when studies are designed as 'double blind' – that is, with both the experimenter and the subject kept in ignorance of the way the results of an experiment are going – it can often be shown, if the researchers take the trouble to check, that the control failed. More recently Rosenthal (1978) has shown that the detectable error rate in twenty-one research studies (themselves designed to assess error rates!) was about one per cent, and tended to favour the hypothesis of the researcher.

Hudson in *The Cult of the Fact* (1972) argues that researchers tend to obtain results consistent with their own theories. According to this, astrologers would tend to obtain results that supported astrology and scientists would not. As we shall see, to some extent this has happened.

Checking the results

Whether or not astrology can predict the patterns of people's lives, it does have reasonably fixed rules, so that different astrologers should give the same responses to the same birth data. Naturally the reading must be in context: that for a bank clerk would hardly be relevant to a Kalahari bushman. Nevertheless if they really believe in astrology they should be governed by its rules rather than by other pieces of information. But are they?

Sechrest and Bryan (1968) responded to advertisements from eighteen mail-order astrologers offering marital advice. They asked for advice on a fictitious forthcoming marriage, and they sent the same birth details to each astrologer. An accompanying letter also provided other information which was either favourable, neutral or negative about the marriage. The test was to see if the astrologers were influenced by this extra information, or whether they based their advice entirely on the horoscopes for the couple involved.

In only one case did the reply appear to be based on astrology, this astrologer making an explicit analysis of the birth chart. In the rest, the advice offered clearly depended on information other than birth data. (One of the astrologers actually wrote: 'Marriage is a personal thing and cannot be foretold from the stars.')

In general, all the replies were friendly, reassuring and remarkably inexpensive considering the amount of time that must have gone into composing them. The astrologers appeared to be giving a genuine and possibly useful social service. The only element of fraud was that they advertised themselves as astrologers.

Other mail-order astrologers are more obviously in business simply to make money. Gauquelin (1979) responded to a computer firm which promised 'to reveal your character and destiny in return for your birth data and a cheque'. He sent the firm the birth data of a group of people with a clear character and a known destiny, namely criminals convicted of murder! The hour of birth was obtained from the birth certificates of ten such villains. The computer firm sent back a horoscope chart complete with interpretations for each of the ten murderers.

The planetary positions as given by the computer were accurate. The ten interpretations varied, although it was noted that some standard paragraphs were duplicated and, presumably due to an error of programming, some contradictory statements appeared in the same interpretation. In none of the ten interpretations was there any indication of a criminal or even a non-conforming disposition, nor did any of the portraits bear any resemblance to the general character of the murderers.

In response to another computer advertisement with the same address as the original, Gauquelin sent in birth details of one of the murderers. The resulting interpretation was quite different; and it still did not match the character of the murder.

In both cases it was claimed that the computer programming was supervised by a famous astrologer, the author of twenty-six books and 'a leader of modern astrology'. Only one man among French astrologers (André Barbault) has written this number of books, and in them he asserts that 'The Ascending sign has as much – if not more – influence than the Sun sign.' Yet interpretation of the Ascendant does not appear in any of the murderers' horoscopes.

The computer firm qualified its profiles by saying that the hour of birth, accurate to the nearest few minutes, is needed for an accurate horoscope. It is of course rare to know the exact time of birth. But the point is that the firm made this qualification about time of birth only after the client had paid his money.

France is not the only country with computer astrology. A New York electronic horoscope service asks for 'Time of birth' and then goes on to state: 'If unknown, we will use 12 noon of birth date.' Apparently they do not wish to lose clients who do not know their time of birth. Worse than this, they are not even consistent: another advertisement states: 'If no time is given we will use 6 a.m.' On the basis of all this evidence, we are inclined to agree with Gauquelin who concludes that the only goal of computer astrology is sales.

Another way to gauge the value of astrology is to look at the success of predictions about public events. Culver and Ianna investigated the claims of astrology in their book *The Gemini Syndrome* (1979), keeping track over a number of years of specific astrological predictions which were made in the printed media.

Predictions were rated as unsuccessful if the event did not occur within the time limit given by the astrologers themselves. Altogether 3,011 predictions were recorded, and of those only 338 (11 per cent) came true. The predictions in question came from various American astrological magazines, from noted astrologers, and from other sources; the proportion of 'hits' was pretty much the same for all these sources, never exceeding 15 per cent.

As the authors point out: 'In each case, any predictions which could have been attributed to shrewd guesses (the SALT talks will continue to be stalled for another year), vague wording (there will be a tragedy in the Eastern United States during the spring months), or "inside" information regarding the person(s) involved (starlet A will be married to director B before Christmas) were all counted in the astrologer's "successful" columns.' These results paint a dismal picture indeed for the traditional astrological claim that 'astrology works'. Certainly one correct guess in ten is not impressive, particularly when we include among the 'successes' those which could be due to shrewd guesses, vague wordings, or inside information.

Unfortunately, Culver and Ianna do not give predictions by a control group of intelligent people claiming no astrological knowledge. They might well have scored better than eleven per cent. One of us has for many years made predictions, mainly of a political and social kind, based simply on general knowledge, information gained from newspapers and political magazines, and other similar sources: his success rate is over fifty per cent. When one thinks that the public tends to remember correct predictions and forget failures, it is easy to see how a belief in astrology could be reinforced.

Why people believe

The willingness to believe is clearly a crucial factor, and a number of investigations show how it can be brought into play.

In one well-known study by Louise Omwake, students were asked to rate their 'sense of humour'. Over ninety per cent claimed to be 'above average'. In one of our own studies, to be dealt with in Chapter 4, people were asked to select from sixty-nine words the ones that best described themselves. The words most often chosen included 'sensitive', 'emotional', 'likes freedom', 'active', 'practical' and 'pleasant'. Trait words that were hardly selected by anyone included 'bold', 'restless', and 'sympathetic'. Clearly, there are some traits that nearly everybody is likely to see as applying to them. If we now make up a personality description consisting almost entirely of these traits, then most people are going to accept it as a description of themselves.

This tendency for people to identify themselves with personality descriptions of a general and vague nature is called the Barnum effect and has been demonstrated in a large number of studies. One of the first was by Forer (1949). Thirty-nine students were given a personality test and a week later were given what they thought were their results. In fact, all the students were given the same personality profile consisting of thirteen statements taken from a sun sign book. They were asked to indicate for each statement whether they considered it a true description of themselves. The table shows the number of times each statement was rated as true by the thirty-nine students. Most of the students saw the whole profile as applying to themselves.

Forer refers to statements of this sort as having 'universal validity', and notes that astrological interpretations tend to include a lot of them. Even psychology students who ought to be immune to such deception, are susceptible. Gauquelin (1979) describes a study by Meili in which twenty-five judgements of character were given out *at random* to a class of pyschology students. Most thought that the descriptions matched their own personality.

Even more striking was a test by Sundberg (1955). He presented each of forty-four students with two descriptions of themselves. One contained the results of a genuine personality test that the student had completed; the other was a set of fake results based on the idea of universal validity. When the students were asked to select the description that best fitted them, only eighteen of the forty-four selected their own. The fake results proved slightly more acceptable than the true ones.

	Statement	Rated as true
1	You have a great need for other people to like and admire you.	28
2	You have a tendency to be critical of yourself.	38
3	You have a great deal of unused capacity which you have not turned to your advantage.	23
4	While you have some personality weaknesses, you are generally able to compensate for them.	31
5	Your sexual adjustment has presented problems for you.	18
6	Disciplined and self-controlled outside, you tend to be worrisome and insecure inside.	35
7	At times you have serious doubts as to whether you have made the right decision or done the right thing.	38
8	You prefer a certain amount of change and variety and become dissatisfied when hemmed in by restrictions and limitations.	37
9	You pride yourself as an independent thinker and do not accept others' statements without satisfactory proof.	34
10	You have found it unwise to be too frank in revealing yourself to others.	35
11	At times you are extraverted, affable, sociable, while at other times you are introverted, wary, reserved.	34
12	Some of your aspirations tend to be pretty unrealistic.	12
13	Security is one of your major goals in life.	28

Personal qualities regarded as typical (Based on Forer, 1949)

As well as seeing 'universal' characteristics as applying particularly to themselves, people tend to read into their own personalities the traits that astrology predicts.

Dean and others (1977) cite a study by R. Ebertin in which readers of a serious astrological journal were asked to indicate, from sixty traits listed under their own sun sign, those that were true of them. The highest-scoring traits averaged 80 to 90 per cent and tended to be in agreement with tradition. For example, 84 per cent of Arians ticked 'self-confident', 92 per cent of Geminis ticked 'versatile', and 77 per cent of Pisceans ticked 'imaginative'. Do these results support astrology? Unfortunately there was no control group, so it is impossible to evaluate the results. All that can be said is that they conform to what we have already seen, that when people are given a general list of traits they will rate a large proportion as applying to themselves. Moreover, since most of the subjects had an advanced knowledge of astrology, they might be expected to see themselves in the appropriate terms.

Support for this explanation is provided by Silverman (1971). Students with little or no knowledge of astrology were asked to select, from the twelve standard sun-sign personality descriptions, the four that best fitted themselves. When the descriptions were labelled only with numbers, so that the students did not know which one applied to their own birth date, the number of students who chose their own sun-sign description was almost exactly what chance would predict. But when another group was given the descriptions labelled with the sun signs and the dates of birth covered by them, they did tend to choose their own. (The figures for the two groups were 18 out of 60 and 26 out of 51, compared with chance expectations of 20 and 17.)

It seems, then, that people do tend to accept, as a description of themselves, the one that they believe is predicted by astrology. Gauquelin (1979) put this to the test in a practical situation. He placed an advertisement in *Ici-Paris* offering a personal horoscope absolutely free. Applications came in from all over France. Everyone was sent the same horoscope, obtained from the computer firm mentioned earlier, and based on the birth data of Dr Petiot, one of France's most notorious mass murderers. (He had pretended that he could help people escape from the Nazi occupation of France. When they arrived at his house with their money and possessions he murdered them, and dissolved their bodies in a tub of quicklime. He was executed in 1946 for murdering twenty-seven people; in the death cell he claimed sixty-three victims.)

The applicants were asked to reply saying whether they recognized themselves in the horoscope. Their responses were predominantly positive, and some people were so impressed that they offered money for more detailed analyses. Of the first 150 replies, 94 per cent claimed that the fake horoscope accurately described their character, and 90 per cent found the accuracy to be confirmed by their family and friends.

It is not difficult to see why so many people accepted this particular horoscope since it included traits such as 'warm, adaptable, organised, worthy and right-minded'. What is not so easy to see is how the computer managed to come up with this astrological description, when the one person to whom it should truly have applied was a peculiarly repulsive murderer.

It might be argued that so many people claimed to be happy with their free horoscope because to have said otherwise would have been ungracious. There is probably some truth in this, but Gauquelin got round the objection in a subsequent study. Instead of simply asking people whether they agreed with a description of themselves, he presented each person in his new sample with two descriptions, one genuinely based on the subject's own horoscope and the other not. When the subjects were asked which of the two descriptions best fitted them, they were just as likely to pick the false as the true one.

Another study, by Snyder (1974), showed that people's acceptance of a description is influenced by whether they think it is based on their own astrological data. Snyder took a sample of students and gave all of them the same personality description, taken from Linda Goodman's *Sun Signs* book; but those in one group were told that it was 'generally true of people', those in a second group that it was based on their own month of birth, and in a third that it was based on their day of birth. It was those in the third group who most often accepted the description as applying to themselves.

There is evidence, however, that a psychologist with a personality questionnaire has more prestige than an astrologer. Rosen (1975) got a group of students to complete a personality test and also to reveal their birth-dates. They then were all given the same set of results – supposedly a profile of their individual personalities. Half were told that the results were an assessment from a psychologist and the others that they were from an astrologer. When the students were asked to rate the accuracy of the profile, their ratings showed that they thought the psychologist had done a better job in describing their personality. Even so the students in the 'astrology' group also tended to accept the profile as an accurate description of themselves.

A similar study was conducted by Snyder and others (1976). Students were all given the same personality profile but were told that it was based either on psychology (the inkblot test) or graphology (the study of handwriting) or astrology. Students in all three groups tended to accept the profile as applying to themselves. Acceptance was highest, but not significantly so, for the psychological method, followed by graphology with astrology last.

We can see from these few examples (which could be multiplied many times) how astrologers are able to satisfy their clients. People are ready to accept almost anything as gospel as long as they are the subject of it. As a result, astrologers can truthfully boast of enthusiastic testimonials; and if most of their clients are going to be satisfied with the product offered, the astrologers themselves can hardly fail to believe in astrology! In this way a circle of reinforcement is established whereby the astrologer and his clients become more and more persuaded that astrology works.

At this point it would be easy to conclude that in reality it works only because of universal validity and gullibility. But many believers in astrology are discriminating, highly intelligent, and anything but gullible. Abell (1976), who taught introductory astronomy to arts students, found that 'about a third of them profess to believe in astrology'. Salter and Routledge (1974) equally found that university students disconcertingly often believed in astrology and witchcraft. Salter and Routledge also looked at the association between intelligence and belief in astrology, and found that at the start of university education there was only a small tendency for the more intelligent to disbelieve in astrology. Furthermore, after a year at university this tendency seemed to diminish! Gallup polls do indicate that believers in astrology tend to have lower-status jobs and less education than non-believers, but even here the relationship is by no means close.

There must be a further factor, and Hyman (1977) has supplied a likely answer. He points out that our normal process of comprehension involves using our own experiences and expectations to make sense of what is usually a disorderly array of 'inputs'. For example, an abstract work of art becomes meaningful only when interpreted in terms of our own personal values. This process of trying to find patterns and meanings in the world about us is vitally important, so much so that in order to exist we do it automatically all the time, even in situations where no actual message is being conveyed. When this happens we are likely to find meaning where none exists, and indeed this is the basis of certain psychological tests such as the Rorschach ink-blot test.

On this basis it is easy to see why astrological descriptions work: they work partly because of universal validity and gullibility, and partly because they involve the fundamental human process of comprehension. Of course this does not mean that there is no truth in astrology; it merely makes it harder to discover. It is ironical that the same process which makes us able to see meaning and order in life, and to make new discoveries, also makes us very vulnerable to mistaken beliefs – especially as the vulnerability increases with the ability to comprehend and so with intelligence!

4 Sun Signs and Personality

The great tragedy of science –
the slaying of a beautiful hypothesis by an ugly fact.
T.H. Huxley

What do Tolstoy, Goethe and H.G. Wells have in common? Answer: they are all Virgos.

If the claims of astrology are true, we ought to be able to find links between people's personalities and the occupations they choose and the astrological influences to which they are subject. In particular we should be able to detect the influence of the twelve sun signs, the most basic and the best known of all the many astrological variables. For the purposes of research, the sun signs are particularly useful in that they are clearly defined and easy to determine. Without knowing the exact time of someone's birth, we cannot be sure of the house positions, aspects and other factors in his birth chart; but so long as we know his birthday his sun sign is in little doubt. Exceptions occur only for people born on the day that the sun changes sign.

It is true, as astrologers point out, that the sun sign is only one among a number of other factors which, in any particular case, may mask or even negate its effect. But if we take a large enough sample of people its influence should show up. If it does not – if on average it has no detectable effect – then clearly there is no point in taking account of it.

In one of the largest-scale studies in this field (by Mayo, White and Eysenck, 1978) the hypothesis that there is a link between personality and sun sign was put to the test.

According to ancient astrological belief, the signs are alternately positive and negative, starting with Aries, the positive or odd-numbered signs denoting masculine, outgoing, spontaneous qualities, and the negative or even-numbered signs being associated with the feminine, the self-repressive and the passive.

The signs are also linked in turn with fire, earth, air and water, again starting from Aries. The earth signs (Taurus, Virgo and Capricorn) are said to be practical and stable, while

49

the water signs (Cancer, Scorpio and Pisces) are emotional and intuitive.

In other words, astrology claims to predict the two major dimensions of personality, extraversion/introversion and emotionality/stability. In the study with Mayo a questionnaire which allows the researcher to estimate these two dimensions was completed by 2324 people. The results were striking. For extraversion/introversion they were exactly in accord with astrological prediction, while for emotionality/stability they parted from it only in giving too high a score for Aries. Is this the first clear piece of evidence for astrology that we are looking for?

Naive and knowledgeable subjects

Hailed by the astrological journal *Phenomena* as 'possibly the most important development for astrology in this century', the study has been subjected to several attempts at replication. In general, the finding has been moderately supported as we shall see, but a limitation of all this research is that it has included subjects with a knowledge of astrology. We noticed in Chapter 3 that people tend to read into their own personalities the qualities astrology tells them to expect. It is possible that this could affect the actual development of their characters, and at the very least it could affect the way they answer a questionnaire. For example, someone born under Aries may be more likely to answer 'Yes' to the question 'Are you bold and energetic?' if he recognizes that these are the two main characteristics of his own sun sign. The point is an important one and we must examine it in some detail before we go further.

Delaney and Woodyard (1974) ran an interesting experiment which demonstrates this effect. They took a sample of fifty-five high school students and asked each one to read an astrological personality description supposedly corresponding to his or her birth sign. In fact, only two descriptions had been specially prepared and represented either high or low levels of the traits of 'dominance' and 'change'. After reading his own description, each subject was asked to complete a personality questionnaire from which his level of 'dominance' and 'change'

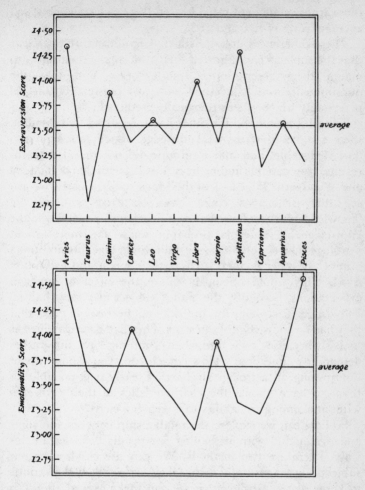

The two graphs show the scores for emotionality/stability and extraversion/introversion, plotted against sun signs. Although the differences in score between the signs are quite small, the large size of the sample makes them statistically significant. The circled points indicate the signs which, according to astrology, should have high scores. (Based on Mayo and others, 1978.)

could be estimated. The subjects who had read the statement rating their sun signs as high on these traits obtained average scores of 17·1 on dominance and 23·7 on change. In contrast, those whose statement rated low on these two traits obtained average scores of 13·0 and 21·3.

These differences are statistically significant. It was clear that the subjects had adjusted their concepts of themselves to match their descriptions, despite being told that the questionnaire was 'concerned with *your* personality and *not* personality which was astrologically predicted'.

The Mayo team, on the other hand, reported that dividing their sample in terms of knowledge about astrology into 'knowledgeable' and 'naive' groups did not reveal different results. How can this finding be reconciled with that of Delaney and Woodyard? If we look at the Mayo results closely, we can see that distortions could have occurred both in the 'knowledgeable' and in the 'naive' groups. First of all, the knowledgeable subjects probably knew far more about astrology than simple sun signs, and would take into account a number of other factors, such as their moon and ascendant signs. This would obviously dilute the effect of sun-sign expectations. Secondly, the 'naive' subject may have had no knowledge of astrology but this does not necessarily mean that they had no knowledge of sun signs. They had been classified as 'naive' because they answered 'nothing' to the rather demanding question: 'How much do you know about interpreting an astrological chart?' Clearly it is possible for them to have known the characteristics of their own sign without claiming any ability to interpret a chart.

So how can we explore the relationship between sun signs and personality without having our results distorted in this way? There are two methods. We can use children as our subjects, on the assumption that they are less likely than adults to know about astrology; or we can make special efforts to identify 'knowledgeable' subjects by giving an objective test.

We started by studying a sample of 1160 children. We knew their birth dates from school records and we had profiles of their personalities because they had already been obtained for another purpose. As in the original study, we related their sun signs to their scores for extraversion and emotionality, and the results are shown in the two graphs. They do not even begin to match those of the Mayo study.

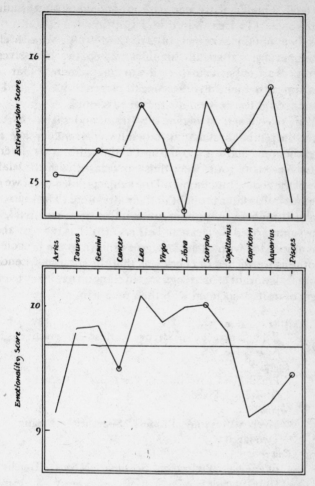

The upper graph shows the extraversion scores of the sample of 1160 children aged eleven to seventeen. The lower graph shows their scores on emotionality. Neither of them matches astrological prediction.

If we take the extraversion scores for children with odd and even numbered signs, the averages come to 15·27 and 15·24 respectively. If we compare the emotionality scores of children born under the 'water' signs of Cancer, Scorpio and Pisces with children born under all the other signs, we get averages of 9·64

53

and 9·69. Finally, if we compare emotionality for the three 'earth' signs (Taurus, Virgo and Capricorn) with all other signs, we obtain averages of 9·63 and 9·69. None of the differences are statistically significant, and two of the three differences are opposite in direction to that predicted. Thus sun signs appear to make no difference to personality.

Our second test was conducted on 122 adults. We gave each of them twelve sets of personality traits and asked them to choose the set that best matched their own personality. We also asked them to choose a second-best and third-best set. In fact, the twelve sets of traits were those associated with the twelve signs of the zodiac but almost all the subjects failed to recognize this until it was later brought to their attention. (The sets were presented to them in random order.) The traits we used were those summarized by Dean and others (1977) as the ones most often associated with each sun sign as shown in the table. The hypothesis we wished to check was that the subjects who were genuinely ignorant of astrology would show no tendency to pick the set of traits associated with their own sign.

1   *Aries*
    Bold   Energetic   Assertive   Selfish   Insensitive
    Aggressive

2   *Taurus*
    Practical   Conservative   Possessive   Obstinate
    Grasping   Fixed ways

3   *Gemini*
    Lively   Versatile   Restless   Superficial   Erratic
    Two-faced

4   *Cancer*
    Emotional   Protective   Sensitive   Moody   Touchy
    Unreasonable

5   *Leo*
    Proud   Magnanimous   Generous   Domineering
    Conceited   Shows off

6   *Virgo*
    Analytical   Logical   Industrious   Fussy   Interfering
    Unemotional

7   *Libra*
    Pleasant   Harmonious   Tactful   Indecisive   Untidy
    Stubborn

8   *Scorpio*
     Intense Passionate Secretive Resentful Vindictive
     Obstinate
9   *Sagittarius*
     Active Adventurous Likes freedom Extravagant
     Careless Tactless
10   *Capricorn*
     Cautious Practical Persevering Selfish Exacting
     Narrow mind
11   *Aquarius*
     Detached Original Humanitarian Perverse
     Eccentric Low integrity
12   *Pisces*
     Sympathetic Spiritual Impressionable Confused
     Impractical Temperamental

The personality traits associated with the twelve signs. The traits are representative of those given by four leading writers on astrology and were selected to best distinguish one sign from another. For each sign there are three positive and three negative traits. (Based on Dean and others, 1977.)

First, we had to assess the subjects for their knowledge of astrology. After they had chosen the sets of traits they thought described them best, they were told that the twelves sets represented the twelve signs of the zodiac and asked to select the one that corresponded to their own sign. Again we gave them a first, second and third choice, and it was stressed that this time they were not meant to be assessing their own personalities but merely trying to say which were the characteristics of their own sun sign, based on what they might have been told or might have read in magazines and newspapers. However vague they were on the subject they were encouraged to have a guess.

Those whose first choice was right were classified as 'knowledgeable', and 46 of the 122 subjects fell into this category. Those who got all three guesses wrong were classified as 'ignorant' (50 subjects). Those who guessed wrong first time but guessed right at the second or third attempt were classified as 'borderline' (26 subjects).

The results for these three groups are presented in the table. Even if we make allowance for possible distortions, such as apparently knowledgeable subjects choosing right by chance,

	First Assessment	Chance	Three Assessments
Ignorant Group (50 subjects)	3	4·2	9
Borderline group (26 subjects)	2	2·2	10
Knowledgeable group (46 subjects)	17	3·8	29

This table shows the number of subjects in each group whose assessment of their own personality matched the characteristics of their sun sign. The first column shows the number who selected their sun-sign characteristics as their first choice for a self-description. The right-hand column shows the number who included it as either a first, second or third choice. The centre column shows the number who would have been expected to pick it as a first choice by chance (one in twelve of the sample, since there are twelve sets to choose from).

or some people choosing the 'astrological' set of traits to match the set they had chosen as a self-assessment, we are still left with an unmistakeable message. The ignorant group show no tendency whatever for their personality to match the predictions of astrology. Indeed the number of subjects in this group whose first self-assessment corresponded to the sun-sign traits is actually below what we would expect by chance, although not significantly so. For the borderline group the result is the same: they scored slightly below the chance level. The knowledgeable group, on the other hand, showed a marked tendency to assess themselves in accordance with astrological predictions. (The probability of their producing this result by chance is less than one in ten thousand.)

If we look at the results of all three self-assessments together, it is impossible to calculate the *exact* probability of guessing right by chance; but it is clear enough that the results show the same general tendency as those for the first self-assessment alone.

We built various other tests into this piece of research, and one of them is worth mentioning here. At the start we asked the subjects to select six of the traits which best applied to them out of those listed in the sun-sign table. We presented all the traits in alphabetical order (there are sixty-nine in all of which three are repeated in the table) and once again the subjects tended to select words in accordance with their sun sign only if they were knowledgeable. We cannot avoid concluding that there is a tendency for people to be influenced in their own self-assessment by their knowledge of astrology.

A particularly interesting point is that this can happen even when their knowledge is very slight. Among our 46 'knowledgeable' subjects only 4 knew their own ascending sign, and only one of these knew his moon sign as well. (As a matter of fact, our sample could not have been expected to include many astrologically sophisticated people. It consisted mainly of students at adult evening classes in economics and art, and trainees in the Salvation Army.) In the Mayo study, on the other hand, many of the subjects were particularly interested in astrology and a number were actually students of it. It seems clear that the tendency revealed by our study is quite enough to account for the original Mayo result. It is a fact of psychology, not of astrology, that the original study really demonstrates.

A similar conclusion has been reached in Germany by Pawlik and Buse (1979), on the basis of a well-controlled study of 799 adult subjects, 68 per cent of whom were female. The subjects filled in a German version of the extraversion and emotionality questionnaire used in the Mayo study, and another questionnaire designed to establish their familiarity with astrology. The results showed that the subjects could be divided into roughly equal groups of 'non-believers', 'believers' and 'strong believers'. The personality scores for the believers and strong believers were in accordance with their sun signs as in the Mayo study, and the differences in scores were similar to those observed by Mayo. The differences were independent of age but were slightly larger for females. The results for non-believers showed no discernible astrological effect.

It is conceivable that astrology is true only for a few people who, on finding that their lives followed the astrologically predicted pattern, *became* believers. Such an effect could account for the results obtained in both this and our own study. But it would still not explain why astrology showed no indications of being true for the sample of children we studied.

It is important to realise that even people who claim no

knowledge of astrology can have picked up more than they realise. Given the pervasive influence of astrology in newspapers and magazines – for example, horoscope columns appear in over 70 per cent of the USA's 1700 daily newspapers and in every one of over a dozen glossy women's magazines in Australia – no one can be assumed to be uncontaminated. Even apparently naive subjects can be expected to know a little astrology, at least that part which applies to them, and this can be enough to influence them on a self-assessment test.

In our own study, 46 of the subjects were able to identify the set of traits belonging to their own birth sign, but earlier, when these same people were asked whether they would be able to do so, most of them said they would not. Only when they were encouraged to guess did their knowledge become apparent. It only needs quite a small 'contamination' of this kind to distort the outcome of an experiment. For example, it can be shown on theoretical grounds that a mere one person in twenty identifying with their sun sign is probably sufficient to explain the Mayo findings.

Unless a study takes account of this factor and establishes the astrological knowledge of its subjects by an objective test, it is likely to come up with findings like those of the Mayo study. This is exactly what has happened. A number of replications have been made and they have all given results which, while not as dramatic as Mayo's, have tended in the same direction. But, except for Pawlik and Buse, they have all failed to take into account the vital factor of astrological knowledge, and in our view that vitiates their results.

Mayo has attempted an exact replication of the original experiment, which allows an investigation of this effect. The results, so far unpublished, are very interesting. We divided his sample into three groups: those with a great deal of knowledge, those with a little knowledge and those who had – or at least claimed – no knowledge at all. As the stylised graph shows, those who had a great deal of knowledge showed essentially insignificant results, those who claimed no knowledge did slightly better, and the most significant result came from those with a little knowledge. How are we to interpret this?

As we remarked in considering the original Mayo study, it

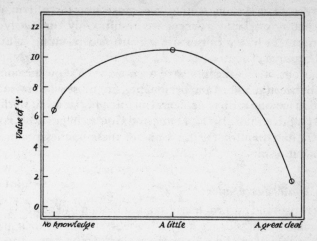

The results of Mayo's replication of his earlier study show how knowledge of astrology might have affected the subjects' answers. The figures given for 't' are a measure of the statistical significance of the relationship observed between personality and sun sign for a sample of 2274 people.

could well be that the knowledgeable group were considering many factors other than sun signs, while for those with only a little knowledge sun signs would loom much larger. If we then remember that the 'ignorant' group almost certainly knew something of the lore of the zodiac – the members of the whole sample were largely collected from people who were interested in astrology and read astrological magazines – a clear pattern emerges. Prior knowledge does influence the subject into seeing his own personality in conformity with what astrology tells him to expect; and this effect increases with increasing knowledge, up to the point when too much knowledge complicates the issue and reduces the relative importance of the factor being studied (the sun signs). It is interesting that Pawlik and Buse also got results that confirm this finding. The effect for their 'believers' was more pronounced than for the 'strong believers'.

All this should teach us to be cautious. Looking simply at the overall result of Mayo's second experiment, we see a highly significant correlation, apparently showing that sun-sign astrology does indeed succeed in predicting personality. It is only when we break the sample down that the real meaning emerges. The lesson is that we must test for alternative explanations before we accept any result. Only after we have ruled out ordinary causes are we justified in citing it as a confirmation of astrology.

Various other attempts have been made to show a connection between sun signs and personality. For those who are interested in looking further we should mention Forlano and Ehrlich (1941), Silverman (1971), Hume and Goldstein (1977), Tyson (1977) and Jourard (1978). None of these studies produced clear-cut results.

Sun signs and occupations

One way round the problem of 'contamination by knowledge' is to look, not at people's subjective assessments of their own personalities, but at the occupations they choose. Here, surely, is an objective indication of the sort of people they are. It is particularly useful if we take those who are successful, for while anyone can drift into a job that is not suited to his own personality, he will probably not succeed in it so well as someone who really fits. The timid soldier, the easy-going, uncompetitive sportsman, the introverted salesman are not likely to be found among the leaders of their professions. It is said that in the past some cultures recruited Scorpios as warriors because the sign denotes an intense, passionate and vindictive nature. If astrology is true, it was a sensible move.

The most comprehensive attempt to relate sun signs to occupations has been that of Van Deusen (1976). He systematically collected sun signs for thousands of people who had achieved enough success to be listed in biographical directories such as *Who's Who in America*, and the more specialised ones such as *Who's Who in the Theatre* and *The Baseball Encyclopedia*. A summary of some of the results obtained is given in the table.

Van Deusen claims that his results tend to be consistent with astrological lore. For example, dealing with the finding that journalists are most often born in Scorpio and least often in Capricorn, he writes: 'The natural inquisitiveness of the Scorpios is shown by their above average rating. They are willing to dig for the facts because knowledge is its own reward.

Occupation	Most frequent sign	Least frequent sign
1,552 Actors	Taurus +14%	Cancer −17%
7,118 Advertisers	Gemini +8·6%	Capricorn −8·8%
5,036 Architects	Capricorn +8·2%	Pisces −11%
2,982 Artists	Cancer +16%	Pisces −15%
4,006 Athletes	Leo +11%	Aries −6·8%
2,931 Authors	Virgo +14%	Gemini −9·5%
2,696 Bankers	Virgo +27%	Taurus −30%
5,047 Businessmen	Cancer +7·5%	Sagittarius −14%
8,762 Clergymen	Gemini +5·7%	Capricorn −9·9%
4,698 Composers	Capricorn +18%	Virgo −21%
2,842 Engineers	Cancer +11%	Libra −7·4%
2,088 Journalists	Scorpio +21%	Capricorn −19%
5,477 Lawyers	Gemini +17%	Pisces −10%
5,111 Librarians	Libra +22%	Capricorn −34%
2,616 Musicians	Pisces +23%	Cancer −14%
5,000 Physicians	Leo +12%	Aries −8·8%
5,022 Politicians	Libra +9·4%	Aries −8·0%
5,011 Psychiatrists	Scorpio +9·2%	Leo −16%
1,055 Singers	Aquarius +16%	Virgo −31%

Van Deusen's study of professions and sun signs. The two columns show which signs occurred most frequently and least frequently for each profession. The percentages are the amount by which the frequency of the sign concerned exceeded (+) or fell short of (−) its frequency in a control group taken from the general population of California.

Capricorns, on the other hand, would find the lack of recognition a serious threat to their ego and security – particularly in a profession that is characterised by unstable working conditions and modest salaries.'

We will take two other examples. In noting that Gemini is the most frequent sun sign among lawyers, Van Deusen says this 'should come as no surprise to astrologers. Lawyers must be prepared to argue either side of a case, so the two-sided (but not schizophrenic) Gemini Twins are in their element.' Similarly, of bankers he writes that 'Virgos are accountants by nature; life is a ledger in which every event must be neatly entered – and all accounts kept in perfect balance.'

One wonders whether bankers really have much in common with authors like Goethe, Tolstoy and H.G. Wells who, as we mentioned at the opening of this chapter, were all Virgos. The results also contain various other oddities. It is surprising, for instance, to find Aries least represented among athletes and politicians, while journalism is traditionally associated with Gemini, not Scorpio, and law with Sagittarius, not Gemini. More generally, it is obvious that these interpretations are being made up after the event. They may sound plausible, but are they what astrologers would have agreed on if they had been asked to predict the results *before* they were known? The only way to have established that for certain would have been to ask them to do so and for that reason alone Van Deusen's study must be seen as inconclusive.

Although Van Deusen did not do so, it is possible to devise an objective procedure. We selected ten of the occupational groups that gave clear-cut results: Actors, Athletes, Authors, Bankers, Businessmen, Composers, Journalists, Lawyers, Librarians and Psychiatrists. We then gave ten psychology graduates (who were completely unfamiliar with Van Deusen's study) a personality description for each sun sign, taken from a standard text (*The Compleat Astrologer* by Parker and Parker, 1975), referred to by Van Deusen as accurately representing 'current trends in astrological thought'. The judges were asked to read each of the twelve descriptions and then to decide which occupations seemed to give the best and worst fits for each sun sign.

Occupation	Best fit	Worst fit
Actors	Pisces 9	Virgo 7
Athletes	Aries 4	Cancer, Scorpio, Sagittarius, Capricorn 4
Authors	Aquarius 9	Libra 6
Bankers	Cancer 7	Gemini 7
Businessmen	Leo 7	Pisces 8
Composers	Aquarius 8	Leo 7
Journalists	*Scorpio* 7	Cancer, Leo, Libra 2
Lawyers	*Gemini* 7	Aquarius, *Pisces* 5
Librarians	Virgo 7	Scorpio 6
Psychiatrists	Taurus, *Scorpio* Capricorn 6	Aries, Gemini 3

Ten judges were asked to link success in ten occupations with sun-sign personality descriptions, by saying which occupation provided the best and which the worst fit for each sign. The table shows, for each occupation, the signs with which it was most often linked. (Where there was a draw, two or more signs are listed.) The numbers indicate how many judges picked each occupation as best or worst fit for the sign concerned. Where the sign was the same as the sign found by Van Deusen as occurring most or least frequently for that occupation, it is printed in italics.

Did the judges tend to link sun signs to occupations in a way that matched the results obtained by Van Deusen? The table shows the results.

It can be seen that four signs were linked with the same occupations as in Van Deusen's study: for the best fit, Scorpio with journalists and with psychiatrists, and Gemini with lawyers; and for the worst fit, Pisces with lawyers. There are 29 predictions in the table and we would expect about 1 in 12 to be correct by chance – giving 2·4 correct guesses. The score of 4 is therefore slightly better than chance, but it is difficult to apply an exact test of significance because certain statistical assumptions (such as each sun sign being equally represented) are not met. All the same, out of a possible 20 correct predictions (10 occupations each assessed twice, for best and worst fits) a score of 4 is hardly impressive. It would not be of much practical use to anyone trying to decide on a job!

We looked at these results in a number of different ways, but in the upshot the agreement with Van Deusen's results was small and did little to support his claim. One particular test we applied was to separate out the judges who had succeeded most often in matching his results, to see whether success on their part had been masked by a heavy rate of failure among the unsuccessful judges. Even this produced nothing striking, and the best judge scored only 8 correct out of a total of 53 predictions that he made – a single result well within the range of chance.

From the various analyses it emerged that the ten judges did tend to agree with one another in their predictions and that they were slightly more often right than wrong, but the degree of success was too small to be of much significance without confirmation from a replicated experiment, which we have not in fact carried out. Would the psychologists have done better if they had been given more detailed descriptions? Would experienced astrologers have done better than psychologists?

All one can say for sure is that the results as they stand are not impressive.

One way to check Van Deusen's results would be to compare them with those of other researchers. Unfortunately he makes little attempt to do so, only mentioning some earlier work on famous musicians by Krafft. The results, he claims, are similar, high on Pisces and low on Virgos; but in fact the similarity may merely be due to Van Deusen and Krafft having drawn their samples from the same international list.

This is a recurring problem, as Dean and others (1977) point out. They tried to synthesize the results from all available studies in this field, and found that the correlation between different studies ranged all the way from strongly positive, through the chance level, to the negative. But where there was a positive correlation, it tended to be high only where there was an overlap between the samples. Naturally if one studies the same people one is going to get the same results.

Bearing all this in mind, it is worth looking at some of the more interesting results to come out of other research on occupations and sun signs.

Army officers are a group that has been studied in several countries. Gauquelin (1978) looked at the birthdays of 1995 French generals to see if they tended to fall under Aries, the sign that signifies a predisposition to adventure, accidents, struggle, fights and rivalry. Was astrology correct? No. The generals' birthdays were dispersed almost uniformly through all twelve signs and Aries had only an average share of the total.

On the other hand, a survey by Cooper and Smithers (1973) found that the birthdates of 16,000 Army officers in Britain showed peaks in the summer and autumn. This contrasts with the annual pattern for the population as a whole, in which (according to information obtained from the Registrar General) most births occur in the late spring and fewest in the late autumn. Against this baseline, the Army officers' pattern represents an excess of around 10 per cent in the period from Leo to Scorpio, as shown in the figure. Since these signs are traditionally associated with a war-like disposition – Napoleon, De Gaulle, Mussolini, Montgomery and Rommel may be cited as modern examples – does this finding support astrology?

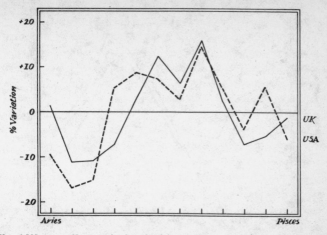

UK and US Army officers tend to have birthdays in the summer/autumn period covered by the signs Leo to Scorpio. These results are drawn relative to the average monthly birth rate for the UK. (Based on Cooper and Smithers, 1973 and 1975.)

Cooper and Smithers also conducted a similar study among 12,000 US Army officers and these results are also shown in the figure. The birth-date distribution of this sample was similar to the British one, with peaks again occurring in the summer and autumn, but this time there is at least a partial explanation (Gauquelin, personal communication). According to the US Department of Health (Rosenberg, 1966), the birth pattern in the States is very different from that in Britain. As the second figure shows, in the USA there is a peak in the autumn (August and September) and a trough in the spring (April and May), the difference being around 5 per cent either way. Although the pattern varies with area, race and year, it is basically similar for the whole country, and it is also similar to the pattern obtained for the Army officers.

We are left with the finding that Army officers in the USA and in Britain tend to be born in the summer and autumn, and that this pattern is noticeably different from the general population for the British sample. Is it possible that for some reason the mothers of future Army officers in Britain tend to conceive at the same time (winter) as mothers generally in the USA? One reason might be that Army parents, who are presumably

65

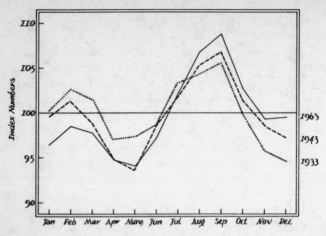

In Britain and most other countries, there is a spring peak in the birth rate. But in the USA, as shown in this graph, there is a peak instead in the autumn, evidence for which exists from at least 1933. (Based on Rosenberg, 1966.)

more likely than other familes to have Army offspring, are also more likely to get together at Christmas than at other times of the year and to have children as a result of these reunions. We could only take this finding as a demonstration of astrology when alternative explanations of that sort had been eliminated.

Many other researchers have looked for a relationship between sun signs and occupations, but the outcome has usually been negative. For the few studies with apparently positive outcomes, such as the one above, there is usually an alternative explanation, and of course chance is always a candidate. It has been calculated that, in a distribution of 2000 cases, the total for each sign will deviate from the mean by an average of 7·5 per cent by chance alone. Further, among twelve signs, the chances are that at least one sign will deviate by nearly twice that amount. This statistical principle partly explains why Van Deusen's results show such high and low peaks (up to 30 per cent and more) and it also illustrates that very little importance can be attached to isolated findings based on small groups. In spite of all the research in this area, there is little or no agreement among researchers who have studied the same occupations. With the possible exception of Army officers, we cannot be sure of a single result.

The last word on this whole issue belongs to Dean and Mather. In a letter to the *Astrological Journal* (spring 1979) they offered a prize of £500 to an eminent and outspoken astrologer if he could provide objective support for his claim that sun signs are indicative of personality. All he had to do was to demonstrate that the signs as traditionally conceived contain an element of truth – for example, to show that people born under Aries tend to be assertive, that Taurians tend to be practical, and so on. In the words of Dean and Mather: 'If signs are valid then they can be shown to be valid . . . opinions or beliefs will not do; we want facts.' The prize could not be claimed. The astrologer who, for years, had been insisting that sun signs were valid was unable to furnish any evidence to support what he believed to be true. The prize was subsequently offered to any astrologer, anywhere, who could demonstrate the validity of signs. To date it has not been seriously claimed.

5 Personal Destinies

The whole of science is nothing more
than a refinement of everyday thinking.
Albert Einstein

It is not only personality that is influenced by the stars, if traditional astrology is true. Astrologers believe that our relations
with other people, our general good and bad fortune, indeed the
whole pattern of our life can be foretold by a skilled astrologer.
All it needs is an accurate enough knowledge of the cosmic influences which mould our destiny and character.

In this chapter we are going to investigate various aspects of
human life to see how far this claim appears to hold true. As a
particularly strong example of personal relations we shall take
marriage. For the general pattern of life we shall study health
and sickness, both mental and physical; and as an extreme and
decisive moment of personal destiny we shall look at suicide.
We shall then discuss the results of some more general tests,
and finally take a glance at the life courses, supposedly so
closely linked, of twins and 'cosmic twins'.

Marriage

One of the classical assertions of astrology is that it can disclose
the affinity – or lack of it – between a man and a woman. It has
a lot to say about compatible and incompatible signs, aspects
and so on, with the seventh house (the one concerned with
marriage) being particularly relevant.

Ptolemy postulated three degrees of harmony: 'The first is
when the sun in the man's horoscope, and the sun or moon in
the woman's, or the moon in both are in their respective places
in a trine or sextile aspect. The second degree is when the moon
in a man's horoscope and the sun in a woman's are constellated
in the same way. The third degree is when the one is receptive to
the other.' Girolamo Cardan summarised this by quoting
Ptolemy as also saying: 'Generally speaking, their life together
will be long and constant when in the horoscopes of both

partners the luminaries (sun and moon) are harmoniously constellated.'

If there is truth in any of this, then it has obvious practical applications for marriage guidance; and it should be easy to test from marriage and divorce records, which provide an objective criterion of compatibility, even if a fairly rough one. The question is, do marriage partners tend to have compatible, and divorced couples incompatible contacts between their two charts?

The first scientific study was done by C.G. Jung. He examined the birth charts of 180 married couples for mutual conjunctions versus mutual oppositions and found that they revealed aspects between the ascendant, sun, moon or Venus in one chart and those in the other which tended to be in accord with traditional astrology; that is, they formed conjunctions rather than oppositions. Jung assembled a control group by pairing each person with someone other than his or her partner, and found that the three classical moon aspects occurred much more often for the married than for the control group; these were for the female's moon to be in conjunction with the male's sun, moon or ascendant.

The clearest result was for the female's moon to be in conjunction with the male's sun. This occurred for 10 per cent of the married couples compared with only 4·7 per cent of the controls. That is certainly a significant result in itself, but we have to remember that Jung claimed to have analysed 50 aspects. With such a number of possibilities it is not surprising that a few apparently significant results emerge. Admitting that he did not understand statistics, Jung took advice from a statistician who told him that, while the comparison of 10 per cent with 4·7 per cent, taken by itself, was highly significant, the overall results were not. Jung realised that the only way to check whether his result was genuine or merely due to chance was to repeat the study.

A replication with 220 new couples yielded different results. This time the most common aspect was for the two moons to be in conjunction; it applied to 10·9 per cent of the couples. This too is highly significant, but with 50 possibilities could again be due to chance. In comparing the two studies, Jung noted that the clearest results were always for moon aspects, although different ones each time. He decided to add an extra 83 couples, giving a grand total of 483 pairs.

In this third sample of 83 couples, the clearest result was for the moon to be in conjunction with the ascendant; this aspect applied to 9·6 per cent of the married couples. The table presents the results for the most prominent moon and sun aspects from the three studies, together with a summation for all three groups taken together. The clearest result is for the moon to be in conjunction in the charts of married couples – 8·4 per cent of the couples compared with 4·6 per cent of the controls.

| | Conjunction | | Opposition |
	moon-sun	moon-moon	moon-sun
180 married couples	10·0	7·2	7·2
220 married couples	4·5	10·9	6·8
83 married couples	7·2	4·8	4·8
Total group	7·2	8·4	6·6

Jung's study (1960) of conjunctions and oppositions between married couples. The figures show the percentage of the sample for which each one occurred. (The female luminary is given first, so that moon-sun means female moon with male sun.)

There are statistical methods for determining whether this result is significant over the three studies, bearing in mind that 50 tests were made, but Jung did not carry out any calculations of that sort. Apparently he consulted the statistician only for the first study.

Jung noted that these results became less clear as the total size of the sample was increased, and he realised that this was due to increased reliability. Because a different conjunction emerged as most significant each time, he suggested that any agreement with traditional astrology was due to chance, but this may not be fair (an overall result *can* be significant) and he may have been biased by his attitude to astrology. He did not believe in it, often pointed out the falsity of its predictions, and in noting that some of them did seem to succeed, suggested that this was due to clairvoyance and telepathy, the stars being used just as a pretext for premonitions. A more likely explanation of his own results is the fact that he had taken as his sample married couples who had been interested enough in astrology to have had their birth charts cast professionally. This meant that he was able to use these data in his analysis, rather than having to look up the planetary positions himself. Anyway the fact that his subjects had an interest in astrology, and presumably some knowledge of it, may just possibly have influenced them in their choice of marriage partners – another case of 'contamination by knowledge'.

Typically, other researchers have not attempted to replicate Jung's study but have looked instead at other variables. An exception is a study by Müller, who replicated Jung's work by selecting a random sample from registry offices and charting the horoscopes of 300 existing marriages and 300 divorced couples. The results were not significant and did not appear to support Jung's results.

Occasionally, significant results have been noted. Furze-Morrish (1959) sent questionnaires to married couples randomly selected from street directories. He got a response rate of about 35 per cent, and we can assume that his subjects were reasonably naive. At least most of them were not likely to be 'astrologically sophisticated'. He categorised the couples as compatible or conflicting on the basis of their questionnaire answers. In one sample of 74 couples, 47 rated their marriage as compatible and 27 as conflicting. In another sample of 49 couples, 33 were compatible and 16 conflicting. Armed with their birth data, Furze-Morrish was then able to test whether the compatible couples tended to have mutual trines and sextiles ('easy' aspects) and whether conflicting couples tended to have mutual squares and oppositions ('difficult' aspects). Relative to a control group of 35 unrelated pairs, both samples gave significant results which did tend to confirm this prediction. Furthermore (also consistent with astrological tradition) Venus and Jupiter were often prominent in the mutual aspects of the happy couples and Mars in those of the unhappy couples.

In a later replication of his study Furze-Morrish (1971)

adopted a similar procedure. He took 20 compatible, 20 conflicting and 20 unrelated pairs, and the results were reported to be similar and again highly significant. Briefly, trines and sextiles involving Venus, Jupiter or the sun were more common in the charts of compatible couples than for unrelated pairs. Moreover, squares and oppositions involving Mars, Saturn or Uranus were more common in the charts of conflicting couples than for the controls. Unfortunately, Furze-Morrish did not give his results in a form that can be properly evaluated, the most serious criticism being that he did not state the degree of inexactitude (orb) used in defining harmonious and inharmonious aspects. This makes it difficult to evaluate the results relative to chance, or, indeed, to repeat the study exactly.

Smit (1977) describes how Kuypers in Holland studied 438 marriages and analysed them for sun and moon aspects. Conjunctions, squares and oppositions were found to be significant; but a replication with 736 marriages confirmed only one of these results, and a replication by Smit himself on a larger scale did not confirm the Dutch results at all.

A more satisfactory test than any of those we have mentioned so far made use of the fact that the Gauquelins have published the birth data collected for their own research in a series of documents. Their hope is that scientists will check their analyses, and perhaps also conduct further studies on the basis of their enormous collection of raw data. Shanks (1978) is one of the few who have done so. He randomly selected 960 couples from the Gauquelins' records of family birth data collected from registry offices in France (and used originally for testing the effects of planetary heredity – as described in Chapter 10). A control group was formed by randomly matching opposite-sexed pairs. On the basis of traditional astrology, Shanks made 12 predictions about the aspects that married couples would be expected to have in common. He then tested these 12 hypotheses along with 20 other relationships. Only one of the tests reached an acceptable level of significance: the male's moon tended to be in conjunction with the female's ascendant for the married couples. Since one in 20 tests would be expected to attain significance by chance alone, it is hardly surprising that one in 32 did so in this test, although it is fair to add that the significant relationship was one of the 12 predicted by astrology. Moreover, taking the 12 'astrological' relationships as a whole and comparing them with the 20 others, there is no apparent tendency for the predicted relationships to be closer to significance. The pattern is just what would be expected if there were no astrological effects.

This carefully controlled study is important in that it involved random selection of subjects rather than relying on volunteers who might have a particular interest in astrology. Also, the birth charts were calculated by computer (as were the comparisons and analysis) thus avoiding error in what would otherwise be a very tedious task. The study has been criticised on the grounds that much of the data are from the last century when partnerships were formed for social rather than romantic reasons, but even so it might be expected that some support for astrology would still be apparent. Since it is not, any of the previous claims to have found evidence in favour of astrology must be viewed with extreme scepticism.

Other researchers, rather than covering the whole field of possible aspects, have looked specifically at sun signs, and in particular at aspects between sun signs. According to most astrologers, sun-sign relationships involving trines and sextiles are favourable to marriage whereas squares and oppositions are not. Tobey (1937) describes how J.A. Hadaller, a Californian attorney, studied the birth charts of his clients – some thousand couples undergoing divorce. He obtained clear evidence of a tendency for them to have mutual sun aspects at 45, 90, 135 and 180 degrees. Traditionally, these are all malefic aspects, which prompted Dean and others (1977) to observe: 'If true, these results must rank among the most remarkable in astrology.' Unfortunately for astrology, other studies have not yielded similar results and so doubt is cast on Hadaller's findings. As with so many other 'positive-outcome' studies reviewed in this book, replication by other researchers has usually failed to provide the necessary support.

In two studies, Daneel (1970 and 1972) investigated hundreds of birth charts of divorced couples in Bonn. The occurrence of the supposedly malefic sun-sign squares and oppositions was exactly chance, but he did obtain one interesting result. Scorpio women (but not men) tended to divorce much more frequently than those born under any other sign. According to some books on astrology, Scorpios are aggressive, passionate and rebellious – 'they are prone to jealousy, bear grudges and are difficult to live with.' Other books, however, claim that they are intensely loyal and self-sacrificing, so that Daneel's result is consistent only with one school of astrology.

Other studies, in any case, have not confirmed this result, and in one by Kop and Heuts (1974) Scorpio women were *less* likely to divorce! They analysed a random sample of 3392 marriages in Amsterdam, of which 408 had ended in early divorce. Overall, the results were not significant, but because there were 144 possible combinations (12 sun signs for each partner), many interesting patterns emerged of which some were consistent with traditional astrology. For example, Capricorn or Aquarius men tended to be married to Libra or Scorpio women; and Aquarius men who were married to Taurus women tended to divorce. Since the results overall were not significant it makes little sense to dwell on isolated successes, although astrologers have claimed them as support for their views.

Silverman (1971) looked at records of 2978 marriages and 478 divorces in Michigan. Two astrologers' books were used to designate the sun-sign combinations thought to be particularly compatible and incompatible, and their two sets of predictions were tested separately. The marriage and divorce figures supported neither of them. The proportion of marriages and divorces for the various sun-sign combinations was almost exactly what would be expected by chance.

In general, significant results have not been reproduced by different research teams, and we are forced to conclude that the isolated findings which support astrology were due to chance or error. We must, however, add that many astrologers would consider the hypotheses tested to be over-simplistic; furthermore, any comparison between married and divorced couples is ambiguous because divorced couples were once married and so presumably were once well above average in compatibility. It is not impossible that more refined techniques, or the use of more highly-differentiated couples, might give positive results. We can only wait and see.

Psychiatry

Astrologers have been comparatively little interested in psychiatric disorders, except in connection with the moon (which will be dealt with in a later chapter). Nevertheless, an important aspect of astrology is counselling, and increasingly this is being applied as a method of treatment. (The attraction of having your birth chart read is not unlike that of undergoing psychoanalysis, which until recently and in spite of not having empirical backing has been the most popular of psychiatric therapies.) Dobyns (1970) claims: 'It is my firm conviction that the psychotherapy or counselling of the future will use the horoscope as routinely as we now use the interview and background data on the subject.'

If we look for evidence on links between astrology and mental illness, we find that one area which has been researched is that of drug addiction. Newmeyer and Anderson (1973) examined the relationship between heroin abuse and sun signs, looking up the birth dates of 1386 heroin addicts at a clinic in the Haight-Ashbury district of San Francisco. Astrologers had predicted that the sun signs Pisces and Scorpio should denote personalities particularly susceptible to drug abuse, but Newmeyer and Anderson found that they were more often born under the sun sign Aquarius, and less often under Scorpio, than a control population from the USA generally. They were also born more often under the moon signs Virgo and Gemini, and less often under Capricorn.

As a whole the findings of the survey ran contrary to prediction, and even the apparently significant results noted above may in fact be due to chance. The statistics had not been corrected for the fact that there are 12 possibilities for the sun signs to come up in an apparently significant manner, and a further 12 for the moon signs, so that the authors may have capitalised on chance. Only a replication might tell us whether this was so or not.

Using more stringent measures, Shaffer and others (1977) carried out such a replication. They took both their sample and their control population from Maryland, studying 349 male narcotic abusers known to the Baltimore police. The results did not confirm the Newmeyer and Anderson study. There were no significant results of any kind, and for Aquarius an opposite trend was noted to that previously found.

Apart from being contradictory, the findings of these two studies taken together are insignificant. Even had the results been significant, and in the predicted direction, we would still not necessarily be justified in regarding astrology as having been proved right; there is always the chance of prophesies like these being self-fulfilling. It is possible that some people, knowing their sun signs and knowing the astrological predictions, would feel destined to become drug addicts and would put up less resistance than they might otherwise have done. San Francisco of course has a population in the Haight-Ashbury region where belief in astrology is particularly widespread, so the possibility is not as unlikely as it might seem at first sight. Maryland is probably less prone to astrological beliefs, and this may account for the less positive results of Shaffer and his colleagues. However this might be, there is no doubt that the results are not compatible with traditional astrological beliefs.

Schizophrenia is another area of psychiatry in which astrologers have shown some interest. Unfortunately most of these studies are not reported in sufficient detail to make any conclusion possible, or else they contain obvious errors.

One interesting unpublished study has been communicated to us by G.A. Dean and D.J. Spencer. In the first part of the study they compared the birth charts of 10 reliably diagnosed schizophrenics and 10 non-schizophrenics, finding 5 criteria which in terms of astrological symbolism seem quite appropriate and which strongly differentiated the two groups. This looked promising, but when these criteria were later tested in a double-blind trial against a further 10 pairs the results were no better than chance, thus illustrating the ease with which astrology can be made to explain anything after the event, and also the perils of investigating small samples without replication. We must conclude that the published and unpublished material contains no evidence that astrology can predict drug addiction or schizophrenia.

Medicine

If astrology shows little promise in dealing with mental problems, what are its prospects in the field of physical illness? Some of the possibilities and difficulties are clearly indicated in a study by Emerson and others (1975), who were interested in haemophilia. Using a computer, they compared 75 cases of haemophilia and a similar number of non-haemophilic subjects, using nearly 500 astrological factors. They then picked out the factors which, for those groups, seemed to discriminate best between the haemophiliacs and the others, and tested them against further groups of 23 haemophiliacs and 25 non-haemophiliacs. This application of the index derived from the first sample to the second sample did discriminate significantly: 18 of the 23 haemophiliacs were correctly diagnosed, although 12 non-haemophiliacs were incorrectly diagnosed as haemophiliacs. The numbers involved are too small to place much confidence in the results, and another replication with much larger numbers would be needed to estabish the validity of the findings. Nevertheless, it must be said that the methodology is correct, and many studies we have omitted in our account would have benefited if they had used a similar way of designing the experiment and treating the data.

Some of the difficulties that arise even with a sophisticated design like this can be seen in a study by Larry Michelson and others (1977). They were concerned with the prediction of infant mortality in the first three hours of birth due to what is known as 'respiratory distress syndrome' (RDS). Babies with this condition often die only a few hours after birth, and medically the condition is completely unpredictable. By the time doctors notice something is wrong, it is often too late to save the baby.

Michelson and his colleagues carried out both a pilot study and a replication to compare the birth charts of RDS and normal babies, using the records of 122 RDS babies screened out of 24,000 births in the north-eastern USA and compared with a random sample of 145 normal babies used as a control group. Unfortunately they have published the details only of the replication, but generally what they did was as follows. They used a computer to study several thousand astrological variables to see which ones correlated with RDS. They found no significant differences between the RDS babies and the controls for such factors as month, day or time of birth. But they did find a relationship with sun signs: RDS babies were more likely to be born in Aquarius than in Leo. Altogether, taking both the original study and the replication, they found 18 astrological variables that seemed to be significant for predicting RDS. Consistent with astrology, it was the signs and planets and not the time of birth as such that seemed to matter.

The researchers then performed a sophisticated analysis of the 11 most significant astrological variables, which 'weighted' each variable according to how well it appeared to predict RDS. The weighted factors were then put together to form a 'prediction profile' to indicate the probability of RDS. The 11 variables which tended to be present in the birth charts of RDS babies are given in the table. For any given baby, the weights for each variable present in the birth chart would be added together, and the higher the score, the higher would be the chance of RDS occurring.

Variable	Weighting
Moon aspecting midpoint of Venus and midheaven	2·78
Mercury aspecting midpoint of moon's node and midheaven	2·41
Ruler of 6th house in 3rd house (Placidus)	1·62
Midheaven aspecting midpoint of sun and moon's node	1·48
Sun in Aquarius	1·30
Sun trine the asteroid Juno	1·29
Jupiter sextile Neptune	0·99
Mars in 1st, 4th, 7th or 10th house	0·83
Ruler of 2nd house in 10th house	0·54
Ascendant in Sagittarius	-0·70
Sun square or quincunx Neptune	-1·08

The variables which most effectively distinguished RDS babies from normal babies. The two variables with a negative weighting were less, rather than more, likely to be associated with RDS. (Based on Michelson and others, 1977.)

When this index was tested against the 145 normal babies, 64 per cent were correctly classified as normal and 36 per cent were incorrectly classified as RDS. When it was tested against the 122 RDS babies, 74 per cent were correctly classified as RDS and 26 per cent were incorrectly classified as normal. Hence overall, around 69 per cent were classified correctly and 31 per cent incorrectly.

If these figures could be believed, then they would be of very considerable importance in medical practice, and needless deaths could be prevented. The proportion of normal babies misclassified as liable to RDS is of course disturbing, but might surely be a price worth paying for the sake of detecting such a high proportion of RDS babies.

Larry Michelson and his colleagues appear to have arrived at a remarkable finding. Unfortunately, there are a number of shortcomings in their reporting of the research which makes it impossible to set a firm value on their results. In particular, it is not clear from their account how they derived the index for predicting RDS. The context suggests that it was derived by analysing the same cases that they subsequently tested it against, which if so would render the whole analysis worthless. The choice of the control group is also doubtful. It seems to have been drawn at random from the 24,000 births, although it would have been better if it had been matched with the RDS group on such variables as socioeconomic status, season of birth, and rural versus urban residence. It is also unfortunate that the number of controls was so small; there should have been no difficulty in getting a much larger group from the 24,000 births available for choice. For the group that was chosen some of the astronomical data are very odd, and many of the observed differences may be due to this oddity rather than to any deviations from the norm for the RDS births.

Finally we encounter the problem that has cropped up so often. We are not told how many variables were tested, and once again this is crucially important. Judging by the specialised nature of the variables given as significant (for example, ruler of the 6th house in the 3rd house) there would have been about 2500, and if so, it would be expected that about 25 would appear highly significant by chance alone. This may

79

be the most appropriate interpretation of the results presented. We have tried to obtain clarification of these and other problems, as has Gauquelin; but we have not been able to get replies to detailed questions and our letters were frequently not answered at all. This is unfortunate in view of the possible practical significance of the data; we can only hope that others will replicate the findings, if possible.

The early beginnings of medical astrology together with the well-known claims of Paracelsus, linking planets with diseases, suggest this to be a promising area of research. But apart from the above mentioned studies, there has been little in the way of attempts to substantiate the claims made.

Suicides

Suicide is about as extreme an act as anything a person can do. If our characters or destinies are written in the stars, then surely a tendency to suicide is one thing that ought to show up in our birth charts. Also, suicides generally occur at a known time, they are recorded and they must be certified by law. This means that the data are completely objective, or at least as objective as bureaucracy can make them!

For these reasons, suicide forms a particularly good field for astrological research, and it has been the subject of an excellent study by Nona Press and others (1978). Press and her colleagues looked at the records of suicides in New York City from 1969 to 1973, selecting those who had been born in the city and whose birth certificates showed the times of birth. They ended up with 311 suitable candidates, and matched each suicide with a control born in the same year and borough and chosen from birth certificates sampled by random numbers. For the purpose of the analysis, the suicides were divided into three groups according to the year of suicide, and the matching controls were similarly divided into three.

A large number of astrological factors were then entered into a computer, and each factor was tested for significance between suicides and controls in each of the three groups. Altogether about 100,000 different factors were examined in each of the 622 charts. By hand this probably represents over a man-century of effort and is therefore a great deal more than any astrologer could possibly look at. This shows the advantages of the computer over personal hand scoring. It can deal with numbers that would defeat whole armies of astrologers, the number of variables that can be tested is therefore in principle unlimited, and we are not dependent on preconceived ideas or possibly erroneous old-fashioned views. This advantage has to be bought, of course, at the cost of adopting a sophisticated and complex research design. We need objective data and carefully matched control groups, and replication has to be built into the research design. But given these requirements the computer method of analysis is in many ways ideal for astrological research.

These criteria were all met in the Press study, and its upshot was clear. Of all the 100,000 factors examined, none correlated significantly with suicide in a way that was reproduced over the three groups. Out of all the possible astrological influences in the birth chart, this huge and very thorough study failed to find a single one that was significantly related to suicide.

Global tests

Astrologers often object to studies of the kind summarised so far in this chapter. They feel that looking at individual indices, or even combining them statistically, does not do justice to their particular skills or to the theories on which they base themselves. They say in effect: 'Give us a complete horoscope to interpret, and judge our predictions as a whole.'

A suitable test, therefore, must combine proper experimental design and statistical treatment with a relative freedom for the astrologer to put together different indices in a subjective way, and generally proceed in the experiment as he would when confronted with a client.

The same sort of problem confronts psychologists studying such methods as graphology, or projective tests like the Rorschach. There are many graphological indices, such as the size and slant of letters, their distance apart and so on, and they can be taken to show various intellectual or personality traits, either alone or in combination. Similarly, scores on the

Rorschach test (which essentially consists of asking people to say what they see in a series of black and white or coloured inkblots) can be used in an attempt to discover various psychological facts, either alone or in combination. As with astrology, such attempts have usually ended in failure; but graphologists and Rorschach experts often complain that the method used to test their claims does not give them a chance to demonstrate their real ability, which is to give a global interpretation of a subject's personality based on a subjective combination of all the different aspects of the handwriting, or the Rorschach report.

Psychologists have accordingly devised a method which makes it possible to test such claims for the global validity of a given combination of test and experts. It is known as 'the matching method', or sometimes as the method of 'blind trials'.

It can be illustrated by looking at two experiments done by Eysenck (1945) to try and assess the validity of graphological and Rorschach methods. Briefly, 50 very neurotic patients and 50 normal subjects gave samples of their handwriting; similarly 50 very neurotic patients and 50 normals were given the Rorschach test. The handwritings were then given to expert graphologists, and the Rorschach records given to expert Rorschach analysts, with the request to sort them out in each case into those which were taken from severe neurotics and those taken from normal subjects. Clearly the experts had complete freedom to use their ability in any way they liked, without being constrained by having to score individual indices or combine them statistically. Nevertheless, statistics could still be used to test their success by seeing whether they identified correctly a larger number of neurotics and normals than chance would make likely. The results were better than chance for graphology; for the Rorschach test they were not significant.

This method can clearly be applied in astrology also, and several studies have been made using it in one way or another. Vernon Clark (1961 and 1970) was one of the first to conduct a blind trial along these lines. He carried out three studies, and each gave positive results.

In the first study, Clark chose 10 people for whom accurate birth data were available, each with a different but well-defined job, including a musician, a vet, a prostitute and a librarian. Their birth charts were drawn up and sent to 20 experienced astrologers, along with a list of the jobs and a short case history of the person holding each job. The astrologers were asked to match the 10 charts with the 10 jobs. As a control, Clark gave the same task to 20 psychologists and social workers. While the non-astrologers guessed at chance level, the astrologers scored much better than chance.

A possible criticism of this study is that the astrologers could have taken the task more seriously than the controls and so might have picked up non-astrological clues. For example, the age range of the people was 45 to 65 and one could assume that the prostitute was towards the younger end of this range. But Clark was aware of this and tried to control for all such clues.

Encouraged by this success, Clark designed a similar study. This time the astrologers were given 10 case-histories and asked to match each with one of a pair of horoscopes. Only one of each pair of horoscopes was genuine, the other being based on the true birth-date plus or minus a year. Even though the sun sign was the same in each case, the astrologers tended to be able to distinguish between the true and false charts. Indeed the results were more significant than before, with 3 astrologers getting all 10 right. It is difficult to think of any objection to this study unless the people in the case-histories included some who had organised their life according to the dictates of astrology! Clark's third study, however, seems to control even for that possibility. Thirty astrologers were asked to discriminate between two charts, one being for a person with brain damage (cerebral palsy) and the other for a person who was fit and with a high IQ. This time no details were given as to life events, and Clark himself was unaware to which group each chart belonged. This was a 'double blind' trial with neither the astrologers nor the experimenter knowing the answers. Although they did less well on this study, the astrologers still performed better than chance.

The astrologers' average scores on these three studies were 6·4, 7·2 and 5·9 respectively out of a possible 10 each time. The controls averaged exactly chance with 5·0. These results taken in combination are extremely significant, although for the purposes of advising an individual client they are only marginally useful – correct judgements averaging only around 65 per cent, this is 15 per cent better than chance. No one has exactly repeated Clark's procedures, and the various outcomes of other investigations have not been as clear-cut as his. Some have been significant and some not. We shall describe three of these replications, and we shall also mention Gauquelin's research in this area.

Through the US magazine *Astrology Now*, Dobyns (1975 and 1976) attempted to repeat Clark's second study. Ten pairs of charts were published in the magazine with a request for readers to participate. Only 49 astrologers, and most of these still students, took up the challenge. (Since the circulation was 5000 and the readership some four times that number, a response from only 49 readers illustrates the lack of interest most astrologers show in testing their ability.)

The task for the astrologers was to discriminate between a true and a false birth-date for the 10 case histories they were supplied with. The case histories consisted of a summary of up to a dozen significant events in the lives of the 10 people, together with the dates of their occurrence.

It was found that the 49 astrologers' judgements were better than chance, and that the accuracy of their judgement was not related to their experience. Out of 490 judgements, 277 were correct, that is 56 per cent. This is 6 per cent better than chance – a difference which is statistically significant, although of course it has little practical value.

Joseph (1975) attempted to repeat Clark's third study (gifted versus palsied) using new data. Twenty-three astrologers, selected for competence, had to distinguish between 10 pairs of charts, each pair consisting of a highly gifted child (IQ typically over 150) and a severely retarded child (none could speak and all required custodial care). All the cases were selected by a pediatrician to whom they were known personally. As before, this was a double blind trial with neither the astrologers nor the experimenter knowing the answers. The astrologers' average score was 5·3 correct, slightly better than chance but not significantly so.

Vidmar (1979) has conducted another replication of the

Clark and Dobyns studies. Five graduate psychology students volunteered to provide anecdotal information about themselves, furnish autobiographical essays and take part in a psychological test. For each student, two birth charts were computed, one based on his or her true birth date, and the other on a false birth date, obtained by randomly adding or subtracting three months to or from the true one. The sun signs in each pair were therefore not the same. Twenty-eight astrologers at a conference volunteered to guess the true birth dates on the basis of the case histories. With 5 guesses each this meant a total of 140 guesses, so that they would be likely to get around 70 right by chance. In fact they got 95 right, a highly significant result. The accuracy of their judgements, which amount to 68 per cent, is intermediate between the results obtained by Clark in his second study and Dobyns, but closer to the former.

As a control condition, 18 mental health workers were given the same task, but without the horoscopes – which as we shall see was an unfortunate omission. The number of correct guesses by this group was 52 per cent, very much what would have been expected by chance. Vidmar concluded that the ability of the astrologers 'implies that there is some kind of relationship between planetary configuration at an individual's birth and subsequent behaviour'. He also stated that 'by no current interpretation of scientific law should the findings of this and prior studies have occurred.' This is debatable.

One serious limitation of the Vidmar study is that no check was made to ensure that the students who provided the case histories did not know about astrology. If they did, then they could easily have given hidden clues. For example, a Scorpio, knowing he was meant to be passionate, might have been influenced to list that as one of his traits. We produced evidence in the last chapter to show that this is a serious possibility.

Another limitation is that the experimenter had selected his 5 subjects from a group of 10 on the basis of the 'best written' case histories. The possibility arises that he might have subconsciously selected those who provided the best 'astrological' clues, or those whose birth charts corresponded best with their actual personalities. In all experiments of this kind, subjects should be selected who know nothing about astrology, and if there is further selection for a smaller pool, this should be done on a chance basis, by tossing coins or in some such way.

Evidence that hidden clues may have accounted for the success of the astrologers is provided by one of the control group findings. One of the mental health workers got all five guesses correct, and he explained this by saying that he had relied on sun-sign theory (he happened to know a bit of astrology) in making his guesses. This may be evidence for the validity of sun signs, but equally well it could indicate that the subjects had provided hidden clues, in which case it was a mistake not to give the birth charts to the control group (most of whom would presumably have been exposed to sun-sign astrology in newspapers and magazines). The astrologers could well have been less successful than the top mental health worker because they relied on astrological indicators other than sun signs; we saw in the last chapter that too much knowledge may affect some results as badly as too little.

There is one criticism which has to be made of all these studies, and as it relates to a statistical point of some subtlety, it may not be obvious at first to the non-statistical reader. What has been done every time is to take a relatively small number of subjects and have their birth-dates or charts matched against their professions or life histories by a large number of astrologers. The significance of the findings is tested by comparing the average percentage of correct answers with the chance level and by taking into account the number of astrologers who together reached that average. In other words, if chance level is 50 per cent and the success rate of the astrologers is 55 per cent, this would be considered significant if we had 40 astrologers, but not if we had 4.

However, this is probably not the crucial test to make. The success or failure of the experiment may have been inadvertently determined at a much earlier point, in the selection of the subjects themselves. Given the present kinds of descriptions used in astrology, clearly the life patterns of some subjects will agree with astrological prediction, while those of others will disagree. If we now pick 5 or 10 people to provide birth times and details about their profession or personality, then we will pick some who are astrological confirmers, and others who are astrological disconfirmers, that is, some for whom astrology would be judged right and others for whom it would be judged incorrect in terms of agreement between their birth chart and their personality or occupation. We can see how the outcome of the experiment is predetermined to a large extent by the selection made at this stage. If we take more confirmers than disconfirmers, then the outcome will be positive (provided the astrologers know their business); but if we take more disconfirmers than confirmers, then the outcome will be negative. With small numbers chance plays a large part in this selection, and may entirely determine the outcome.

Suppose there are five subjects, as in the Vidmar experiment, and suppose that in the population at large there are as many disconfirmers as confirmers. Chance would now make it equally likely that we would choose two confirmers and three disconfirmers or three confirmers and two disconfirmers. The former choice would give us a success rate of 40 per cent and the other a success rate of 60 per cent. The latter is of course the success rate actually obtained on the average in the three studies we are considering, but this may clearly hinge simply on the choice of a single subject. It is this probability that should be looked at statistically, independently of the number of astrologers used. It would have been much better had Vidmar used 28 subjects and only 5 astrologers, rather than 5 subjects and 28 astrologers. Quite generally it should be said that the number of subjects used is the crucial variable, and the number of astrologers relatively unimportant; this is exactly the opposite to the attitude taken by the investigators in all these studies. The reader may recall the psychological matching experiments mentioned earlier on, testing the ability of graphologists and Rorschach experts to predict personality on the basis of their particular art. In these experiments the number of subjects was large, and the number of experts small, precisely in order to avoid this possibility of getting 'good' subjects (that is, subjects behaving as the theory demands) in slightly higher proportion than chance would allow. Altogether the methodology of the matching type of experiment is much more complex than most people realise, and for this reason the figures reported by investigators of astrology cannot always be taken very seriously.

If we are right in thinking that the choice of subjects may have been influential in producing the apparently significant results of the three investigations so far mentioned we would expect that negative results could also be obtained in similar studies, and Gauquelin (1973) has provided brief details of such a study. He gave a test of 'opposed destinies' to 14 astrologers. The astrologers were given the birth charts of three celebrities – a television announcer, a racing cycle champion, and an entertainer – and asked to identify them. The outcome was very negative; chance choices would have provided a better match between birth charts and professions.

In another study, astrologers were asked to separate the birth charts of 20 notorious criminals who had been executed for murder, from those of 20 ordinary people who had led long and peaceful lives. The performance of the astrologers was at chance level.

As a result of his own work, and other studies with a negative outcome, Gauquelin concluded that the few positive outcomes on the ability of astrologers were due to chance or error. It should be noted that Gauquelin's experiments suffer from the same difficulty of statistical analysis as the positive studies we reviewed: the samples were too small. Consequently they cannot be taken to disconfirm astrologers' claims any more than the previous studies could be taken to confirm them. The comparison of 20 criminals and 20 ordinary people comes closest to having a large enough number of subjects, but even so it is doubtful whether it really provides proof that the people chosen contain an equal number of confirmers and disconfirmers. It does not tell us what the proportion of confirmers and disconfirmers might be in the general population, and that of course is the crucial question.

Concluding this section, which has dealt with some of the studies which are often claimed to be favourable to astrologers, we must come to a judgement of 'not proven'. Even the successful studies are not very much above chance level, certainly not far enough to be of much practical use, and there are obvious reasons for believing that the successes obtained may have been due to statistical or experimental errors, especially as the judgements involved were far removed from the level of normal chart interpretation and in general were very difficult. Nevertheless, the matching method itself is obviously a useful one, provided that its statistical and other limitations are properly understood, and we may hope that future work will give us a better understanding of the success rates that can be obtained with astrology.

Judging appearances

There is little agreement as to just how appearance is linked to sun signs and other astrological factors, but it is often claimed that some astrologers have the ability to judge a person's sun sign or ascendant from a chance meeting.

Controlled studies on this topic are rare, which is surprising since it is easy to test objectively. Can astrologers in fact judge a person's birth sign from his appearance? The *News of the World* ran a study in which a panel of 4 leading astrologers set out to judge the sun signs of 12 people, based on a 5-minute interview with each person, followed by a panel discussion. They succeeded with 8 out of the 12 people, and since the chance score is 1 this result appears highly significant.

How did they do it? Perhaps the subjects just happened to be of the relevant type – confirmers. But if so what was this type? Again, because the judgements were based on interviews as well as appearance, we cannot tell if it was appearance or character that provided the clues. It is well known from psychological experiments (reviewed by Smith, 1966) that some people are extremely sensitive to impressions and appearances of other people, and can tell a great deal about their character from just seeing them and watching them move and carry out quite ordinary actions, like lighting a cigarette. Perhaps some astrologers are of this sensitive type. Even if they are, it still requires the subject to project the relevant image, so important clues would be provided by a replication in which the subjects were divided according to familiarity with astrology. It is not yet necessary to go as far as some observers who have suggested that telepathy or extra-sensory perception may be responsible for success in this task.

One way of ruling out the direct assessment of personality is to use photographs. Harvey (1965) did an experiment of this kind in which no clear relationship between appearance and birth data was apparent in a collection of 500 photographs provided by the UK Astrological Association. In another study Addey (1968) looked to see if red hair was associated with sun signs, and in particular with Aries, but found no such relationship. The table shows that Culver and Ianna reached a similar conclusion.

Sun sign	Number of people	Sun sign	Number of people
Aries	27	Libra	34
Taurus	22	Scorpio	23
Gemini	25	Sagittarius	21
Cancer	28	Capricorn	31
Leo	30	Aquarius	20
Virgo	21	Pisces	18

The sun signs of 300 red-haired people. (Based on Culver and Ianna, 1979.)

An apparent exception to this run of negative results was provided by Metzner (1979) who studied 156 subjects and claimed to find a significant relationship between eye colour (blue, green, hazel, brown) and sun signs grouped according to the four elements; blue eyes tended to be related to fire signs, and brown eyes to air. The trouble is that Metzner did not use objective standards of colour but simply relied on the subjects' own assessments. That would obviously make for a lot of uncertainty in classifying borderline cases (eg. grey eyes), and is probably enough to invalidate his claims. Moreover, no significant relationship was found between hair colour and the four elements. A later study by Metzner and others (1980) looked for relationships between body build and other groups of sun signs (cardinal, fixed and mutable) for the same 156 subjects; overall the results were at chance level. Once again we have to conclude that without a successful replication study one cannot take 'unexpected' results too seriously.

Twins and cosmic twins

If two people are born at the same time and place, should not astrological influences give them similar characters and destinies? Astrologers rightly point out that even twins are not born at exactly the same moment and they argue that a few minutes can make a vital difference, which is why such precision is needed in drawing up a birth chart. At the same time they often quote examples of twins who had very similar careers and deaths.

This is clearly a very useful line of approach in any assessment of astrology and it is unfortunate that there has been very little work on it. The problem of establishing the exact time of birth of each twin is, of course, a serious one, and although many countries today do record these times they may not show them on birth certificates. Even when they do, the registry office may not release the information to researchers.

One interesting preliminary question is whether twins tend to be born under the sign of the twins, Gemini. Tobey (1936) reported a study in which the incidence of twin births are related to the time of year and, as the table shows, found twice as many twins born in June (the month which is roughly covered by the sign Gemini) as in January. However, before we seek an explanation for this result we must ask whether it is reproduceable. Unfortunately for astrology, the answer seems to be no. Selvin and Janerich (1972) looked at the New York State record of births over an eight-year period and found that twin births followed much the same seasonal pattern as single births. There was no sign of an excess of Gemini twins. In Japan, Kamimura (1976) found that twins tended to be born more frequently not in June but in the spring and autumn. Clearly no generalization is possible.

Month	Jan	Feb	Mar	Apr	May	Jun	Jul	Aug	Sep	Oct	Nov	Dec
Number	53	78	83	95	85	106	89	83	85	65	75	85

Tobey's study of 982 sets of twins born in South Carolina from 1856 to 1859. The month with most twin births coincides with the sign of Gemini.

To gauge how far it is astrological influences that produce similarities in the lives and personalities of twins we need to

91

compare identical twins with fraternal (unalike) twins. The interval between the births of identical twins is not appreciably different from that between fraternal twins. Hence, astrologically, twins of either type are just as similar, but in reality fraternal twins are usually as different as brothers and sisters born several years apart while identical twins are usually very alike in personality and intelligence as well as in appearance. Genetically this is easy to understand but astrology has no convincing explanation.

It is sometimes popularly held that marriages, accidents, illnesses and even deaths of identical twins often occur at the same time, even when the twins are separated and are unaware of each other's existence. However, the many studies which have been made of twins show that except for marriage (which can be entirely explained by social factors) there is little evidence that any similarity is not simply due to similarity in age and upbringing. In fact, the lives of identical twins almost never follow precisely the same course. It is very rare for both identical twins to develop the same illness at the same time and even rarer for them to die naturally or commit suicide on the same day. Even extra-sensory rapport, supposedly very marked between identical twins, has been found to be not consistently greater than between family members in general (if it has been demonstrated at all).

An even more powerful test of astrology can be made by looking at 'cosmic twins' (otherwise known as astral or time twins). These are people who are born at the same time and place but are unrelated. Surprisingly, this test has been neglected, although there are a number of anecdotes.

One of the best known and much repeated stories of cosmic twins concerns King George III and one of his subjects, an iron merchant. Their lives had many interesting parallels: they were married on the same day, the merchant took over his father's business on the same day that George ascended to the throne, and both died on the same day aged eighty years. Unfortunately we have not been able to trace the origin of this historical anecdote, and neither has Gauquelin (1979), so its authenticity must be regarded as doubtful. The fact that a story is much repeated does not of course mean that it is true. For example, it is just as frequently said that the astronomer Halley (of comet fame) once rebuked Newton for his belief in astrology, to which Newton pointedly replied, 'Sir, I have studied these things, you have not.' But according to Cowling (1977) this quotation is incorrect, there being no evidence that Newton believed in astrology, and no reference to astrology in any of his unpublished writings. Yet both this and the King George III story have been widely quoted in support of astrology.

Many other anecdotal accounts exist of how 'doubles' have been discovered and then shown to have been born at the same time, but these examples have not been systematically studied and probably just reflect chance coincidences. The same applies to a study of cosmic twins by Krafft. He made a collection of cosmic twins including his own, who happened to be another astrologer! But of course statistical analysis is needed, and all that Krafft did was to provide interesting examples of similarities. There were no controls (unrelated people not born at the same time) although these might also have provided many surprising coincidences.

A statistical study has, however, been attempted by Goodavage (1976), perhaps the leading worker in this field. He obtained many cases of twins from hospital records, but was able to obtain questionnaire results from only 18 pairs. Nevertheless, he claimed they indicated that 'some kind of parallelism was indeed at work.' He also made an earlier study (1966) of cosmic twins and many of his examples do show a provocative similarity of character and circumstances.

Eriksen (1976) decided to check Goodavage's work. When he investigated the stories of cosmic twins that supported astrology he found there were flaws in each of the case studies he checked. In one case, in which two boys crashed and died at the same time, it was found that their birth times were not exactly the same. In another case, in which two women had the same name and then chose the same names for their children, and married husbands with the same name, it was found that the details were not as Goodavage had reported them.

Goodavage (1979) subsequently acknowledged these errors and attributed them to the inaccuracies of newspaper and magazine articles from which he had gathered the information.

He continued to claim of the many dozens of cases he had collected that, even allowing for such errors, 'a dim but discernible pattern clearly existed between time of birth and major events (including death) in the lives of people born at the same time and place.' However, in spite of over fifteen years of work in this area, he has yet to do the one thing that would remove all doubt, namely publish a complete and fully documented account of his findings. Until that is done we are entitled to be suspicious of his claims.

Gauquelin (1973) also looked for examples of cosmic twins in his collection of over 50,000 horoscopes. On the basis of his own work (of which he has published only scant detail) and that of others he concluded that nobody has demonstrated similarity in the lives of people born on the same day of different parents. It is unfortunate that the negative results reported by Gauquelin, like the positive results given by others, are at fault in not supplying enough detail to judge them on any proper scientific basis. Negative results in this field are more readily accepted by scientists than positive results, but it seems unjust that the scales should be weighted in this way. If an investigation is worth reporting, it is worth reporting in sufficient detail to make a scientific judgement possible.

Conclusion

In this chapter and the previous one we have looked at the major claims of astrology to predict personality and destiny, and we are forced to conclude that these claims are at best unproved. Wherever a properly scientific test has been carried out on a large enough sample and reported in enough detail for its validity to be judged, and has then been replicated, it fails to support the beliefs of traditional astrology.

Is that the end of the matter? Before we decide that it is, we must look at some broader possibilities. Can it be that the seasons of the year or some other rhythms of the solar system do influence our lives in ways the astrologers did not foresee? It is to that fascinating possibility that we now turn.

6 Seasons of Birth

Science is built of facts the way a house is built of bricks;
but an accumulation of facts is no more science than a pile
of bricks is a house.
Henri Poincaré

Suppose that we could discover a link between the season of a man's birth and his chances of becoming, say, a genius or a madman or a cancer patient. What immense and obvious benefits for the human race would follow! Simply by planning conceptions for one time of the year rather than another we could notably increase our children's chances of becoming happy and successful people and of avoiding disease and pain.

The prospect is attractive enough to have led a number of people to investigate it and we shall look at some results in this chapter. Strictly speaking, of course, these seasonal effects are not astrological. Several sun signs occur in each season, supposedly with different characteristics, and the motions of the planets follow their own rhythms which are quite independent of the arrival of spring, summer, autumn and winter on earth. All the same, most astrologers would feel that the existence of seasonal differences of the kind we are discussing gave some sort of support to their general approach, and in practice they have often claimed that apparent seasonal differences arise from astrological causes.

One interesting example, which shows how one can distinguish between astrological and seasonal effects, is the remarkable result obtained by Pellegrini (1973) in a study using a personality questionnaire given to 288 students. He found that students born during the six months of the year that fall under the signs from Leo to Capricorn (that is, from mid-summer to mid-winter) tended to obtain high scores on Femininity, whether they were male or female. Their scores on this scale averaged 23 points whereas for those born under the six signs from Aquarius to Cancer the average was only 17. This clear-cut result was claimed to be evidence of an astrological effect, even though by tradition it is the even-numbered signs throughout the year that are classified as 'feminine'. Various astrological theories have been advanced to explain it, but of course an explanation in terms of a lasting effect from season of birth is equally tenable.

Illingworth and Syme (1977) decided to accept the result at face value and to test for a seasonal versus an astrological explanation. They used a clear and simple method. If the result was due to the season of the year, then people born in the southern hemisphere should show the opposite pattern: if it was due to astrological influences there should be no such reversal. Accordingly, Illingworth and Syme used the same questionnaire to assess students from Perth in Australia. The results they got supported neither hypothesis, the scores for Femininity showing little or no tendency to vary according to the sign of the zodiac or to season of birth; and in a similar study with 615 students carried out in South Africa by Tyson (1977) there was again no indication of a heightened Femininity score for those born in the seasons covered by Leo to Capricorn, or indeed of any sun-sign effect.

The need to check whether the result obtained originally could be reproduced had by now become obvious. Mayes and Klugh (1978) tested 120 students in Michigan and found no significant tendency for signs of the zodiac to be related to Femininity; what slight correlations there were tended in the reverse direction to those in the original study.

Earlier Standen (1975) had raised doubts about the results of the original study by pointing out an anomaly: the scores for males and females did not differ significantly on the Femininity scale. Normally, a much higher Femininity score is obtained by females and there is little to suggest that Californian students should be different in this respect; the Feminist Movement has not had that much effect! In all the other studies, the usual male-female difference was apparent, and because of this Standen suggested that the original result was due to 'some undetected gross error in the data'. More charitably it could be put down to the effect of chance or to a hoax. Anyway, the moral is that it is unnecessary to consider differing explanations of the original result if that result cannot first be replicated.

Animal rhythms

In 1938, Huntington published the results of his monumental survey *Season of Birth: Its Relation to Human Abilities*. In it he provided graphs from many countries showing seasonal variations in birth rates related to a number of traits including intelligence and insanity.

He offered theories to account for these seasonal trends, but he did not believe in astrological explanations. He wrote:

. . . . the old astrologers were quite wrong, and the modern ones are still more so, in thinking that there is value in a horoscope based on the positions of the planets at the time of birth. Nevertheless, the cold facts as to millions of births leave no doubt that on an average the people born in February and March differ decidedly from those born in June and July. In the middle latitudes of the northern hemisphere, as we shall soon see, they tend to be more numerous, more evenly divided as to sex, and longer-lived. By a curious quirk of fortune they also include a larger proportion not only of distinguished people, but also of unfortunates who become criminals or are afflicted with insanity or tuberculosis. Man is like the lower animals in having a definite seasonal rhythm of reproduction with a maximum of births in the late winter or spring.

This tendency for more births to occur in the early part of the year is backed by evidence from several countries. In the northern hemisphere the trend is for more births to occur in the first half of the year and in the southern hemisphere the pattern tends to be reversed, with more births occurring in the second half of the year.

This suggests a climatic explanation, but other factors must also be involved since there are exceptions to the general rule, notably in America where the maximum number of births occurs in August and September.

One can, in fact, suggest two different types of explanation for seasonal variations in birth rates. One is based on ordinary practical or social facts: for example, summer holidays might provide more stimulating opportunities for making love and this would be reflected in a peak of births nine months after the holiday season. The other type of explanation is the one put forward by Huntington, who suggested that the variations were due to the existence of a 'basic animal rhythm' of human

97

sexuality. Other animals have strongly marked seasonal rhythms of reproduction. Why should not man have at least the remnants of such a rhythm, which might easily have had evolutionary advantages for our ancestors? Mating in the summer would mean that offspring would be born at the start of milder weather in the spring. At that season food supplies are steadily increasing and children could build up strength to deal with the hot weather of summer and then the cold of winter. It is a plausible hypothesis, and in prehistoric times, before the days of clothing, year-round food supplies and modern housing and heating, such a rhythm could have been sufficiently marked for men to have observed it, and perhaps even incorporated it in the beginnings of astrology. Unfortunately we cannot know about that, and in our time, contrary to Huntington's theory, there is no consistent evidence of a breeding season in humans as there is with animals.

Faced with such major anomalies as the radically different birth patterns in Britain and the USA we are thrown back on 'social' explanations. The spring peak for births in Britain may simply reflect family planning for tax or social reasons, or the fact that June happens to be the peak month for marriages and honeymoons. Similarly, the September peak in the USA may be due to heightened sexual activities in the Christmas period, although why this should happen only in the USA is not clear.

The best time to be born?

If the excess of spring births in some countries occurs because there are biological advantages in being born at the start of warmer weather, we should expect children born at that time to show evidence of thriving better. On the simple criterion of birth weight this is not so. On the basis of 20 studies, birth weight has been found to be very slightly higher in late summer and autumn (Pintner and Forlano, 1943), but the evidence varied from study to study and the general finding probably reflects something like parental class differences rather than a direct effect of the seasons.

On the other hand, Huntington thought he had found evidence supporting the biological theory. It showed that in the eastern USA people born in March lived on average nearly four years longer than those born in July. Consistent with this, Taurus males in California were found in another study to live to an average age of 81 years, while Sagittarians of both sexes were the shortest lived at 61 to 62 years. This surprising result has been investigated by the British astrologer John Addey (1961). He analysed 51,000 birth-dates and the data did not confirm the theory that spring or summer sign people are longer-lived and winter sign people shorter-lived. Addey also looked at the charts of 977 nonagenarians in *Who's Who*. Capricorns are reputedly long-lived and Pisces short-lived, but he found no truth in this. Nor could he find any evidence for any of the other traditional astrological pointers to longevity. To quote from West and Toonder (1970): 'The opponent of astrology, seeking to disprove it, would have given up after the more obvious statistical avenues had been explored, while the astrologer, feeling from experience that a correlation *must* exist, will keep looking. And ultimately Addey did find at least one significant factor.' This factor was a multiple-of-$3^1/3$-degrees aspect (the 108th harmonic) between the sun and Mars, Saturn or Uranus, but it has yet to be replicated. It may simply be an example of 'significant' findings emerging by chance when enough opportunities are provided for this to happen.

Huntington noted that several researchers had found that the seasonal pattern of births is more marked in the case of illegitimate births. It would seem likely that illegitimate births are less often planned than are legitimate births and so might reflect biological rather than social causes. Perhaps 'spring fever' really does stimulate love-making among the more impulsive, or perhaps a change in hormonal secretion during warmer weather increases their fecundity at this time of year. One can easily suggest mechanisms to explain the effect: the trouble is that not all countries show an exaggerated pattern for illegitimate births at specific times. It is clearly a case of many interacting factors, with some being more important in some cultures than in others.

Crime, eminence and the seasons

A number of researchers have claimed to find evidence that personality, intelligence, high achievement and mental and physical illness are related to the season of birth. In reviewing these claims we shall have to disentangle social from biological and meteorological – let alone astrological – causes. But first we must make a statistical point that will recur many times in this book.

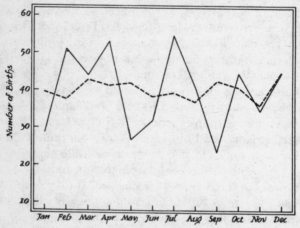

Aggressive criminals in Amsterdam tended to be born in July rather than September. The dotted line gives the birth frequency for the general population of Amsterdam. (Based on Heuts and Kop, 1974.)

Two Dutch researchers were interested in finding out whether the perpetrators of aggressive crimes tended to be born at any particular time of year (Heuts and Kop, 1974). They noted all the convictions for murder, manslaughter and ill-treatment in Amsterdam over a two-year period, which involved 481 males and 27 females. We may disregard the female data, since the number is too small to be useful. The graph shows 55 males were born in July, and only 24 in September; whereas to be in line with the general population, the number should have been around 40 for each of these two months. The authors point out that these results are statistically significant, but this applies only if the two months are evaluated in isolation. What they have not taken into account is that, with twelve months in the year, there are twelve chances of an extreme result. The correct procedure is first of all to test the whole distribution statistically; only if it varies significantly from what might occur by chance is it 'permissible' to conduct tests for individual months. In the present case, the whole distribution could well be a product of chance, so the July and September extremes could themselves be merely chance variations. This is the kind of error that occurs frequently in astrological studies. One thing to note is that if there were a genuine seasonal effect at work we should expect to see the numbers rising towards the peak month and falling away afterwards – in other words, 'spreading' to the months on either side. In this study that did not happen, as the graph makes clear.

Returning to Huntington, let us take a look at some of his most striking results, which were to do with eminent people. He noted that of the first 31 American Presidents in office since 1774, 26 were born in the winter period from October to April and only 5 in the summer period from May to September. (Since then the figures have become less marked – 27 and 12.) Washington and Lincoln were both born in February, which appears to be the peak month for famous people. Huntington also spotted a similar distribution for eminent Americans listed in the 1930 edition of the *Encyclopedia Britannica*.

Kaulins (1979) decided to check this finding using the 1974 edition, and extended the sample to include everyone for whom a birth-date was given. He plotted the birth-dates of all the people listed since 1400 (totalling over 11,000) and found a striking seasonal trend, as the figure shows. Eminent people show a strong tendency to be born in the months between the winter solstice and the spring equinox: at the peak, 36 eminent persons are born per day compared with 27 at the trough. This provides good confirmation of Huntington's result, although it is not all that good since the two samples were not completely independent (the Americans who formed Huntington's list would mostly have been included in Kaulin's).

The figure also shows the average monthly temperatures in New York City over 107 years, which is seen as generally reflecting temperature patterns in the northern hemisphere at a

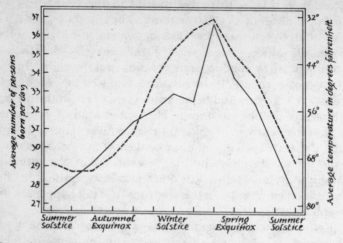

Persons listed in the Encyclopedia Britannica *tended to be born around the month of February. The dotted line gives the seasonal temperature pattern for New York City. (Based on Kaulins, 1979.)*

latitude from which a large proportion of the eminent persons originated. The annual variation in temperature is remarkably similar to the annual variation in births of eminent persons, with most being born at the coldest time of the year at temperatures of around 32 degrees Fahrenheit.

Huntington draws a parallel with animal rhythms and notes that the clear pattern for eminent people suggests that 'the births of people of unusual ability conform to the basic animal rhythm more closely than do those of people as a whole.' (This prompted him to comment that his book 'might be better if the author had been born in February instead of September'.)

Here we run into a problem. If the 'basic animal rhythm' produces a peak of births in the spring because that is the most advantageous time to be born, why do eminent people's births peak a few months earlier than average? You cannot claim a special evolutionary advantage both for eminent births in winter and for ordinary births in the spring.

It also seems that, for intelligence generally, the opposite trend applies. Pintner and Forlano (1943) analysed the intelligence test scores of 17,502 New York children and found the

102

winter-born to be duller than the summer-born, with January and February actually getting the lowest scores. Another study with 7,897 college students in New York gave a similar result. IQ scores were highest for those born in the spring and summer, and lowest for winter-born (Forlano and Ehrlich, 1941). In reviewing these and other studies, Dalén (1975) concluded that IQ tends to be very slightly higher for people born in the summer.

How can the finding of eminent people being born in winter be reconciled with the finding that intelligence tends to be slightly higher in the summer-born? The difference in IQ has typically been of the order of only one or two points, and so small a difference could easily be masked by other factors. Eminence involves more than just intelligence; personality factors are involved as well. A high energy level, wide interests and obsessiveness seem to be important factors, and a link with eccentricity has often been suggested. This is especially true of geniuses, and Huntington marshals evidence that it is only the very famous who show the winter peak. The figure shows how the peak tends to occur later when less eminent people are considered, and also how a winter peak is more noticeable for those who have more space devoted to them in the *Dictionary of American Biography*.

These results may explain why other researchers, such as Pintner and Forlano (1934) who looked at the birth dates of successful men, have not always replicated Huntington's finding of a winter peak; they have not studied truly eminent people.

Since eminence may be the result of personality as much as intelligence, Forlano and Ehrlich (1941) also gave personality tests to the students in their study. There was a very slight tendency for the winter-born to be extravert, and for the summer-born to have inferiority feelings, but later studies (admittedly using rather small samples) have not replicated these trends (Farley, 1968; Kanekar and Mukerjee, 1972). Anyway, a better test would be to classify the eminent persons in the *Encyclopedia Britannica* as to personality and then see if this is related to season of birth; Gauquelin has in fact carried out research along these lines in relation to planetary positions at birth, and as we

103

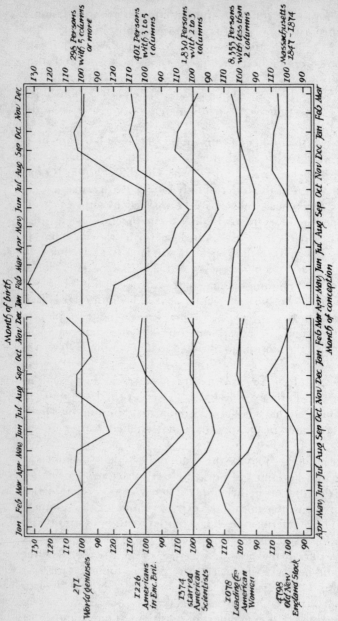

Huntington's data showing (left) 'season of birth among persons with varying degrees of eminence' and (right) 'seasonal distribution of births among eminent Americans in the Dictionary of American Biography'. In each case the bottom graph is of a control sample. (Based on Huntington, 1938.)

shall see in a later chapter, the importance of eminence was strikingly confirmed.

Subnormality and mental illness

At the opposite end of the scale it has been claimed that the mentally subnormal also show a slight tendency to be born in the winter rather than the summer. Knobloch and Pasamanick (1958) looked at the birth-dates of 5,855 mentally handicapped children admitted to Columbus State School from 1913 to 1948. Relative to the number of births per month in the whole of Ohio State, the mentally subnormal tended to be winter-born with a peak of 1,507 children in February and a trough of 1,297 children born in August.

One possible explanation for this result was offered in terms of a critical stage of foetal development occurring during the hottest time of the year. Hot weather is known to reduce the appetite of women in the early stages of pregnancy, so there might have been a vitamin or protein deficiency in the mother's diet. Moreover, the cerebral cortex of the foetus begins organizing itself at around three months and, apart from reducing appetite, hot weather might alter the mother's metabolism, again causing damage to the foetus.

In an attempt to test this, Knobloch and Pasamanick looked at the birth rates of their subjects following hot and cool summers. There was indeed increased incidence of mental retardation when births followed a hot summer.

Unfortunately for this neat and apparently convincing study, other research has not given a similar picture. As Dalén (1975) points out, the majority of more recent studies have, if anything, given a summer rather than a winter peak for the births of the mentally subnormal, but the tendency is really so slight that it is difficult to state it as a conclusion. It is certainly nowhere near as marked as the tendency for fame to be associated with winter births.

The clearest example of a seasonal trend in births is provided by schizophrenia. The story begins in a Swiss clinic with an investigation of 3,100 psychotic patients. Tramer (1929) compared their birth-dates against general population

105

statistics and found a 15 per cent excess of patients born in the period December to March. Many subsequent studies have confirmed this finding, to the point where there is no longer any reasonable doubt about it. Hare (1975) has pointed out its importance in that it established 'the first clear association between the incidence of schizophrenia and a simple, objectively definable factor in the environment.' (Unfortunately for astrology, there seems to be nothing in astrological tradition to suggest that schizophrenics should be born under Capricorn, Aquarius or Pisces.)

Barry and Barry (1961) reviewed the work of seven independent research teams involving a total of 30,000 psychotic patients. All the research teams found a tendency for northern hemisphere schizophrenics to be born in the first three or four months of the year. On average, the excess is around 10 per cent, and there is evidence that it is increasing, at least in Britain (Hare, 1978). Since the Barrys' review, a similar trend has been found for 16,238 schizophrenics in Sweden, this being the only mental illness to present a seasonal pattern which was clearly significant (Dalén, 1968). The figure shows this result. In England and Wales, a survey of 46,000 psychiatric patients revealed the same pattern for schizophrenics, manics and manic-depressives, but not for other groups such as neurotics (Hare and others, 1974).

Replications in the southern hemisphere have provided partial confirmation of this seasonal pattern. For example, Parker and Neilson (1976) examined the birth-dates of 20,358 psychiatric patients in New South Wales and found an excess of winter births for schizophrenics.

One of several explanations offered for this pattern is that schizophrenia tends to be associated with lower socio-economic status, and that such a group may suffer from dietary deficiency at a critical stage of foetal development during the summer preceding birth. Higher social class, it is argued, protects the developing foetus from this effect. (This is, of course, similar to the theory advanced by Knobloch and Pasamanick (1958) to account for their finding of an excess of mentally subnormal children born in the winter.)

Support for the hypothesis was put forward by Barry and

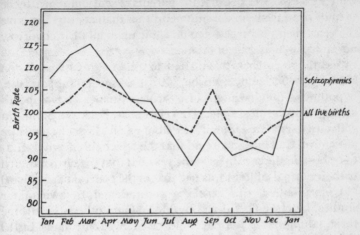

The births of schizophrenics in Sweden show a clear bias towards the first months of the year. (Based on Dalén, 1968.)

Barry (1964). They found that the births of 5,677 schizophrenics in two private mental hospitals in Connecticut followed the usual pattern of the general population, rather than the special pattern of schizophrenics. The Barrys' sample of patients was similar in social class to the general population, so coming closer to the 'ideal' scientific requirement of matching the two groups to be compared in every respect save for the one characteristic which is under investigation, in this case schizophrenia.

However, it is the social class of the parents and not the patients that should be critical, and one can easily see how schizophrenics could drop into a lower social class simply because of the handicapping effects of their disorder. Hare and others (1974) reported in their survey that there was no difference between the distribution of social class in the fathers of schizophrenic patients and that of the male population as a whole.

A more critical test is to compare the birth pattern of schizophrenics with that of their non-schizophrenic brothers and sisters. If schizophrenia is associated with damage at a critical stage of development then the healthy siblings should not show the same birth pattern. On the other hand, if the

107

winter excess arises because the parents of schizophrenics tend to mate or conceive in the summer rather than at other times of the year, then that excess should show up in all their children, normal as well as schizophrenic.

Several researchers have tried to answer this question. A study by Buck and Simpson (1978) seems to support the hypothesis that winter-born schizophrenics have been damaged at a critical stage of development. Buck and Simpson collected birthdates from 1,039 siblings of 545 schizophrenic patients in Canada, and found that the schizophrenics did tend to be born in the early part of the year but that the birth pattern of their normal siblings was like that of the general population.

Unfortunately, this result is contradicted by two other studies, by Hare (1976) and by McNeil and others (1976). In their samples, the normal children showed the same birth pattern as their schizophrenic siblings. It is fair to add that these results were based on relatively small samples (670 and 280 normal siblings respectively) and they were not clear cut, so that we cannot put too much confidence in them, but they do tend to counterbalance those of Buck and Simpson.

Alert readers will have noticed that both eminent people and psychotics (schizophrenics and manic-depressives) show a distinct tendency to be born around February. These two findings may not be unconnected. Since the days of the ancient Greeks genius and madness have often been linked, and most people will be familiar with Dryden's deplorable rhyming couplet from 'Absalom and Achitophel': 'Great wits are sure to madness near allied, and thin partitions do their bounds divide.' We mentioned earlier in this chapter that genius and eccentricity seem to go together, and there is evidence from empirical studies that originality and creativity are associated with those personality traits which make for psychosis. Studies by Eysenck & Eysenck (1976) and by Woody and Claridge (1977) have demonstrated that this relationship is quite close, and may be largely independent of intelligence. This finding may explain, not only the relationship between the birth-dates of eminent people and schizophrenics, but also the failure of intelligence to show a similar pattern. What makes a person eminent may be originality and creativity, rather than mere intelligence. This hypothesis might bear a closer look; it should be possible to divide eminent people into two groups, those who showed some kind of mental abnormality and those who did not. On this hypothesis the abnormal geniuses would be expected to show a more pronounced tendency to be born in midwinter than the 'normal' geniuses.

Unfortunately, this intriguing story has a disappointing ending as far as schizophrenia is concerned. The claim that schizophrenics tend to be born during the first months of the year may rest on nothing more substantial than a methodological artefact. It was two psychologists from the University of Texas, Lewis and Griffin (1981), who pointed out that because patients are characteristically first affected by schizophrenia in their teens and usually diagnosed as such by early adulthood, it is necessary to take age into account, in any season of birth survey that is made among relatively young age groups. An example to illustrate the problem involved here would be a disorder that is first detected in babies during the first year of life. A survey at any point in that year would find that babies born at the beginning of that year would be overrepresented simply because they have been in existence, and so 'at risk', for a longer period. Similarly, it can be reasoned that people born at the beginning of the year are very slightly more 'at risk' of being diagnosed as schizophrenic than those born later in the year. In all the surveys that have been carried out, schizophrenic birthdays have been averaged over several years so compounding this particular error, perhaps sufficiently to account for the whole effect.

In order to demonstrate the likelihood of this explanation, Lewis and Griffin re-analysed a set of data with an appropriate correction for age. Schizophrenic birthdays were now shown to be distributed more or less evenly over the whole year. As a second check, they re-analysed the same data without the correction for age but by taking June instead of January as the first month of the year. Now the season of birth effect reappeared but with the excess of birthdays in June and July! On this evidence it seems that the season of birth claim for schizophrenia is without foundation.

Physical illness

Is season of birth related to proneness to disease? In one case at least ·it certainly is. Mothers who catch rubella (German measles) during pregnancy have a significantly higher risk of giving birth to a child with congenital defects. Since rubella is most common during late winter and early spring, and since it exerts its most harmful effects on the unborn child at about three months, there is an increase in malformations in infants born in the autumn.

The mechanism here is obvious, and has nothing to do with astrology (but could have been so linked did we not know better!), but there have also been other claims that people suffering from certain illnesses tend to be born at a particular time of the year, usually winter. One of the best researched areas is cancer.

A very interesting discussion of this was put forward by John Addey, who is one of the most scientific and highly regarded of British astrologers. His book *The Discrimination of Birthtypes* was published in 1974, and our summary of it is included here to show how persuasive and appealing astrological arguments can be, even though, as we shall see, this one does not hold up in the end. It may appear invidious to single out one astrological work in this way, but it is important to include at least one detailed study of this kind, and following the scientific tradition we have chosen a particularly outstanding piece of work, rather than the kind of nonsense that can easily be dismissed in one paragraph.

Addey starts out by quoting two Dutch studies of the birthdates of lung cancer patients. One, by B.K.S. Dijkstra, covered 480 cases, and the other, using data collected in Amsterdam, covered the much larger total of 1,320 cases. In the upper figure the·data are grouped by month of birth, while the lower figure shows the same data grouped by season, and with the addition of another group of 2,042 lung cancer cases observed in Chelsea, England, by Davies (1963). Addey concludes that 'altogether, the case for some sort of seasonal rhythm in cancer birth seems to be very strong indeed.'

He goes on to discuss this and other diseases in terms of astrological theory because, as he says 'all these fluctuations are based on the harmonics of cosmic periods.' But the question he

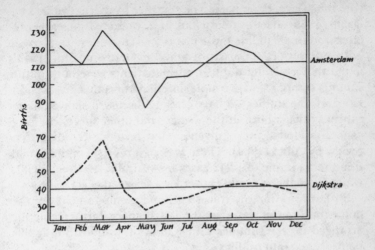

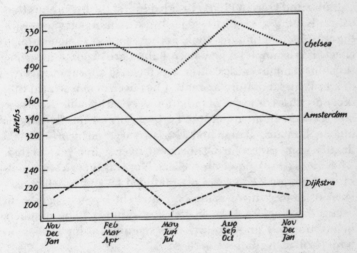

In the upper figure, cancer patients tended to have been born in March according to two sets of studies in Holland. The lower figure, in which the results are grouped by seasons rather than individual months, shows how, in England, cancer patients tended to have been born in the autumn rather than the winter. But the overall pattern matches that found in Holland. (Based on Addey, 1974.)

does not answer is the one that readers of this book will by now be all too familiar with: do the results stand up to replication with much larger numbers? The evidence has been reviewed by Dalén (1975) so let us take a look at it, working from earlier to later studies, including those mentioned by Addey.

In a survey of 2,829 cases of cancer in Germany, Stur (1953) found that a smaller number of the patients were born in the summer compared with people suffering from other diseases. In Holland, the studies we have already discussed showed more cancer patients born in the winter; and other surveys of lung cancer in Holland have given similar results, according to a review by Allan (1964). There is even a reversal of the Dutch trend in a sample of 1,242 cases in Australia (Nolting, 1968), which is what one would expect for a seasonal effect.

So far everything is consistent, and seems to hold out the hope that cancer rates might fall if more births could be arranged for the summer rather than the winter. But at this point we run into trouble.

Bailar and Gurian (1964) decided to test the hypothesis that cancer is induced very early in life by an irritant that varies with the seasons, and that this could account for any season-of-birth effect. For example, if new-born babies are exposed to strong sunshine it might cause cancer which would appear much later in life. With laboratory animals it has been demonstrated that certain viruses or forms of radiation very early in life can cause later cancer. In an attempt to find support for this hypothesis among humans, Bailar and Gurian surveyed nearly 20,000 deaths from cancer in Connecticut over a five-year period. There was no season-of-birth effect. Nor was there a season-of-birth effect for 2,278 cases of childhood leukemia, which is a form of cancer, there being only a slight but not significant excess for children born in the late summer. The numbers involved in this study are well over ten times as big as those in both the Dutch studies together.

Other negative results have been obtained in English surveys of lung cancer which are reviewed by Allan (1964), and the danger of relying on results from just one or two surveys is well illustrated by Dean and others (1977). They compared the monthly birth rates for two samples of cancer patients from two independent studies in France and America, each of which showed clear differences between different sun signs. The problem was that the two samples did not agree with each other: in the first most cases were born in Pisces – but in the second, the least. Overall, the correlation between the two sets of data was only 0·1.

In summary, then, we must conclude that the evidence for cancer cases tending to be winter-born is inconsistent, applying only to Holland, if at all. While there is in general some evidence that season of birth has a detectable effect later in life, the phenomenon has a 'now you see it, now you don't' nature. Two apparent exceptions are eminent people and schizophrenics, who both show a tendency to be born during the coldest part of the year. Both these generalisations have been taken as indicating that the seasonal effects are real. This has been especially so since the association between eminence and schizophrenia agrees with reasonably well substantiated theories linking genius and madness, through the intermediary concept of originality, creativity, or unorthodoxy. It is unfortunate that this link means that parents cannot plan for an eminent offspring without also running the risk of producing a schizophrenic, although of course the chance of either is slight. However, as in so many other astrologically related claims, the season of birth effect for schizophrenia (although not for eminence), has been shown as probably nothing more than an artefact arising out of inadequacies in the analysis of survey information.

7 Cycles and Sunspots

> Science is the great antidote to the poison
> of enthusiasms and superstition.
> *Adam Smith*

A cautionary tale: it is called 'How to discover the secret rhythms of the digestive system of the unicorn.'

The feat has been achieved by a Cornell University zoologist named LaMont C. Cole (1957). Since he was unable to obtain any actual unicorns for his experiment, he decided instead to use a series of random numbers to represent the metabolic changes in the missing animal. The purpose of the study was to see whether these numbers could be made to yield some kind of recognizable pattern.

First of all Cole constructed a graph covering five days in the unicorn's life, and on it he plotted his series of numbers to stand for the unicorn's metabolic rates over that period. There was, of course, no apparent pattern, since the numbers were truly random. To simplify the graph, Cole then averaged groups of figures, but still no pattern emerged. It is inconceivable that the unicorn should really be such a haphazard beast, so Cole continued his search. Arguing that the unicorn's cycle might well be governed by the moon, he adjusted the scale for the hour of the moon's rise and – look! – an unmistakable daily rhythm emerged. When the graph was 'smoothed' (a common and legitimate statistical practice) the pattern became clearer still, showing a peak of metabolic activity in the early morning and a trough twelve hours later. The rhythm of a unicorn's day was clear at last.

Cole had, of course, succeeded in showing what he set out to show – that if you keep on playing with any set of numbers you can eventually pull some sort of pattern out of them. As the saying goes: 'Seek long enough and ye shall find.' To safeguard against this effect one should decide in advance what mathematical treatment of the data would be justified, not simply go on trying different procedures until some pattern emerges. If one does discover a pattern in that way, then it is necessary to repeat the study on a new set of data, using exactly the same procedures. If Cole had performed the same manipulations on a new lot of random numbers it is highly improbable that the same rhythm would have shown up again.

It is easy enough, then, to fall into the trap of producing statistical artefacts and mistaking them for the rhythms of the cosmos; but this in no way proves that there are not genuine cycles that could have a bearing on human affairs. Mark Twain put what you might call the astrological hypothesis as boldly as anyone:

By the law of Periodical Repetition, everything which has happened once must happen again and again and again – and not capriciously, but at regular periods . . . the same Nature which delights in periodical repetition in the skies is the Nature which orders the affairs of the earth.

We need not even believe in traditional astrology to accept that there are certain cycles with which our lives are intimately linked. Sleeping and waking; seed-time and harvest, depend on the motions of one particular planet around a star. Could there be other cycles whose causes are less obvious but which could be shown by scientific means to exist, and perhaps eventually explained in scientific terms? Many such cycles have been suggested, ranging from the workings of individual bodies to the broadest patterns of history. Let us take a look at some of the most likely ones; and let us begin with our own bodies.

Biological rhythms

Gay Gaer Luce (1971) has reviewed the evidence on biological rhythms. Daily rhythms, such as variations in temperature, blood pressure and blood sugar level, are fairly easy to study. Body temperature, for example, follows a cycle which takes most people to a high point during the day and a low point in the middle of the night. For any given person these high and low points occur at much the same time each day, but for early morning 'larks' (usually introverts) the high point tends to occur in the morning and for 'night owls' (usually extraverts) in the afternoon or evening. Athletes can, with advantage, arrange their time of sleeping and waking so that they compete

115

when they are at their peak time of day.

It is the constancy of such cycles and their resistance to change that causes problems to the international traveller. 'Jet lag' is the tendency for the body to keep to its existing rhythms in spite of the change in sleeping times as we cross into different time zones. When people travel to the other side of the world, it takes about a week for their temperature cycle to revert, and for a while the different cycles of the body can be out of step with each other. Poor sleepers, incidentally, seem to be permanently out of step with their own sleep cycle, with their temperature cycle peaking at the wrong time.

Interestingly, people do not all naturally fall into a twenty-four-hour rhythm when they are left purely to the guidance of their own 'biological clocks'. Subjects who have been studied for long periods living in special environments such as deep caves where there are no clues as to time show a lot of individual variation, with the average 'day' nearer to twenty-five hours. (It has often been noted that, whether or not there is any causal connection, this is close to the lunar cycle.)

During the course of the day, these cycles seem, among other effects, to produce different degrees of vulnerability to drugs and other sources of stress at different times. In a study on rats, in which they were given high doses of x-rays, those who were exposed to them at night died while those who were given an identical dose during the day all survived. Another experiment using an overdose of amphetamine produced a similar result. In humans, too, it is thought that the effects of some quick-acting medicines depend on the time of day at which they are administered, and it is possible that critical surgery is safer for the patient at a certain time in his daily cycle.

There are also longer cycles lasting for weeks, months or even years, but these are naturally harder to study. Many people, for instance, are aware of a cycle of mood, feeling more lively and energetic on some days than on others. The average length of these mood cycles is about five weeks, for both men and women, but it varies a lot between different people, though the cycle for any one person tends to be fairly constant. There are even claims for a cycle of creativity in poets and musicians, which is supposed to average 7·6 months according to a study mentioned by Dewey and Mandino (1973).

Various experiments have been designed to pinpoint the part of the body that might generate these cycles, but so far without success. It is also possible that some external factors might be involved, such as changes in the sun and moon, barometric pressure, gravity, magnetism and so on. If a link of that kind is discovered, of course, it will take us straight into the field of cosmobiology.

Incidentally, one must distinguish genuine biological rhythms from what are called by their proponents 'bio-rhythms'. According to the theory of biorhythms, we all have a 23-day physical cycle, a 28-day emotional cycle and a 33-day intellectual cycle which run from the date of our birth. Critical days occur when the cycles are changing from the positive to the negative phase, and at such times the person is particularly prone to accidents. Pocket calculators can be purchased for working out one's good and bad days, and for identifying the day when all three cycles coincide, which occurs in the fifty-seventh year. Researchers have claimed evidence that supports this theory in relation to industrial accidents, baseball and academic performance, and for self-ratings of mood (Buttery and White, 1978). But in all these cases there were no checks to make sure that the subjects were not aware of their supposedly good and bad days, and if even a few of them were aware, it may have turned the whole exercise into a self-fulfilling prophecy. In properly conducted studies – they have been reviewed by Persinger and others (1978) – none of the evidence supports the theory of biorhythms.

Cycles in history

Some external cause, rather than innate biological rhythms, would presumably have to underly the long cycles – running to years or even centuries – which some people claim to have discovered. Many such cycles have been put forward, and in 1940 the Foundation for the Study of Cycles was established in the USA with the aim of identifying cycles that could be used to predict future trends. The American stock market was an obvious first target: nothing could bring quicker rewards than a

117

system that would predict its up and downs in advance. The Foundation did claim to have discovered such a system (the story is told by Dewey and Mandino, 1973) but unfortunately so many cycles of different lengths had to be superimposed on each other to give the final result that the whole thing became too complex and unwieldy to make a useable investment guide. All the same, the researchers did detect a pattern of stock prices since the time of the American Civil War and claimed that, by following that cycle, one would have made a successful investment seven times out of ten – up to the time of the Second World War, that is: after that the pattern disappeared.

Altogether the Foundation for the Study of Cycles claims to have identified thousands of cycles, and many more have been suggested by other people. Most of them need not be taken too seriously. To take one example, R. Collin noted that fashions in clothes tend to alternate between a masculine and a feminine image and claimed to detect an 84-year period in these swings (Dewey & Mandino, 1973). Obviously a great deal of subjective judgement must come into collecting data of that sort, and during the span of history for which we have anything like accurate records of fashions the number of 84-year periods is not large. This is an important point. The persuasiveness of any theory of cycles is in proportion to the number of cycles it can claim to cover. An event which occurs at regular intervals three or four times can easily be put down to coincidence: one which occurs with equal regularity a hundred times is obviously harder to ignore.

One curious and interesting cycle has been going on since the early eighteenth century, and shows a striking regularity over its 25 peaks since then. Since 1735 the Hudson Bay Company has recorded the number of lynx furs brought in by trappers. There has been an enormous variation, from less than 2,000 skins a year to over 70,000, and for nearly two and a half centuries the cycle has had an average length of 9·6 years with extraordinary accuracy, as the figure shows. It seems very unlikely that such a regular rhythm would persist for so long just by chance, but there is no general agreement about its cause. Presumably the variation reflects a periodic rise and fall in the numbers of the whole Canadian lynx population, rather than a cycle in the efforts of the trappers, and it is interesting – though unexplained – that a similar cycle seems to govern many species of wild life and also a number of other phenomena such as the incidence of heart disease. Some examples are given in the table.

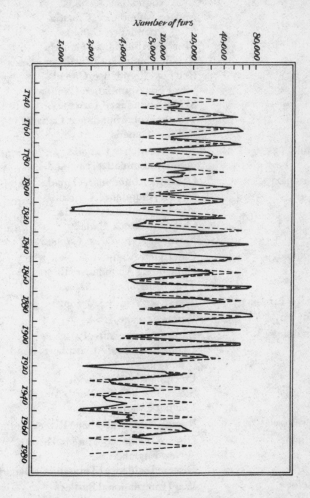

The cycle in the abundance of Canadian lynx, 1735-1969. The dotted line shows a perfectly regular cycle of 9·6 years. (The scale on the vertical axis is logarithmic.) (Based on Dewey and Mandino, 1973.)

Science	Phenomenon
Mammalogy	Colored Fox Abundance, Canada
	Coyote Abundance, Canada
	Cross Fox Abundance, Canada
	Fisher Abundance, Canada
	Lynx Abundance, Canada
	Marten Abundance, Canada
	Mink Abundance, Canada
	Muskrat Abundance, Canada
	Rabbit Abundance, North America
	Red Fox Abundance, Canada
	Silver Fox Abundance, Canada
	Skunk Abundance, Canada
	Timber Wolf Abundance, Canada
	Wildlife, Canada
Ichthyology	Salmon Catches, Canada
	Salmon Abundance, England
Ornithology	Goshawk Abundance, Canada
	Grouse Abundance, Canada
	Hawk Abundance, Canada
	Owl Abundance, Canada
	Partridge Abundance, Canada and USA
Entomology	Caterpillar Abundance, New Jersey
	Chinch Bug Abundance, Illinois
	Tick Abundance, Canada
Dendrochronology	Tree-Ring Widths, Arizona
Agronomy	Wheat Acreage, USA
Climatology	Barometric Pressure, Paris
	Ozone Content of Atmosphere, London and Paris
	Precipitation, Worldwide
	Storm Track Shifts, North America
	Magnetic Value
Hydrology	Runoff, Rihand and Sone Rivers, India
Medicine	Disease Incidence (Human Heart), New England
	Disease Incidence (Tularemia), Canada
Sociology	War (International Battles)
Economics	Cotton Prices, USA
	Financial Crises, Great Britain

Cycles alleged to be 9·6 or 9·7 years in length. (Based on Dewey and Mandino, 1973.)

One very significant point about these cycles is that at the same latitude all cycles of the same length tend to turn at the same time. Furthermore the cycles tend to peak progressively later as one passes through different latitudes towards the equator, an effect known as 'latitudinal passage'. The difference in timing between the pole and the equator is proportional to the length of the cycle concerned and averages about 0·7 cycles. Like the cycles themselves, this phenomenon remains unexplained—and is equally neglected by modern researchers. Clearly if these phenomena are genuine there is something here crying out for further investigation.

One series of cycles which could be of considerable importance to the human race relates to war, and if we accept that it is due to something more than chance we should be trying to understand it and preparing for the next peak, which this time will occur in an age of nuclear weapons. The simplest of these war cycles shows a major peak in the incidence of international battles occurring every 142 years, but three shorter cycles have also been identified and by combining all four of them and adjusting for any general up-and-down trend one can arrive at a mathematically defined curve which follows the actual pattern of battles with a fair degree of accuracy. (The figure shows these two treatments.)

One of the three shorter cycles has the same length as the Canadian lynx cycle that we have just encountered – 9·6 years. Is this significant? At present we simply do not know. There has also been a claim of a war cycle of 11·1 years, which is the average length of the cycle of sunspots – a phenomenon whose importance is well recognised.

Sunspots

It was the Russian historian A.L. Chizhevsky, a near-genius in many fields, who in the early part of this century began looking for cycles in world events and trying to relate them to the sunspot cycle. He collected data from 72 countries going back to 600 BC and covering not only wars but social upheavals such as mass migrations, revolutions and epidemics. Gauquelin (1970) describes this pioneering research. It has been sadly neglected

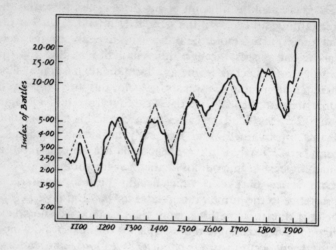

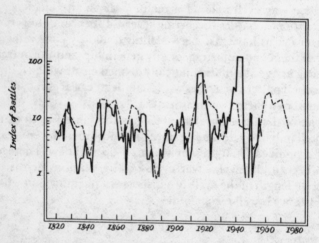

The upper graph shows a simple 142-year cycle (dotted line) and it is clear that the incidence of international battles shown by the solid line follows it quite closely. In the lower graph the solid line again shows the incidence of international battles, this time over the more recent period since 1820, while the dotted line is the result of combining the 142-year cycle with three different shorter cycles. Again, the match is quite good. (The scales on both vertical axes are logarithmic.) (Based on Dewey and Mandino, 1973.)

by modern researchers and Chizhevsky himself was poorly rewarded for his efforts. He was sent to Siberia by Stalin, apparently for suggesting that it was the sun rather than the doctrines of dialectical materialism that lay behind the great upheavals of history, and though he was released when Kruschev came to power he died soon afterwards.

Since Chizhevsky, a number of people have tried to relate sunspots to human affairs in many different fields and the whole matter is well worth examining in some detail. Before we do so we will first take a look at the nature of sunspots themselves.

It is rare for the sun to be without spots, indeed there can be several hundred on it at the same time. The largest of these curious dark patches can cover an area many times that of the earth, and they can sometimes be seen by the naked eye when the sun is low on the horizon and screened by mist or fog. They were first noted by the Chinese, whose records of them go back over two thousand years, and Galileo observed them through his telescope in 1610. Realising that it is dangerous to look directly at the sun, especially through a telescope, he devised a method that is still used today and projected the image from his telescope onto a screen.

We now know that the spots are abnormally cold areas on the sun's surface associated with a very high magnetic intensity. Although they radiate less visible light than surrounding areas of the sun they do emit large amounts of other radiation and they also send out charged particles. The radiation takes about eight minutes to reach the earth, and the charged particles a day or more. The spots also produce an increase in the strength of the 'solar wind', which is a constant outward streaming of ionised gas from the sun.

We do not know why the sun has spots, or even for sure what they really are. As the sun rotates in relation to the earth (which it does once in 27-28 days) it carries the spots into view on its eastern edge, and when one of them is right on the edge it forms what looks like a depression in the surface. One theory is that this is a vortex in the outermost gaseous layer of the sun, like a tornado on earth, but most astronomers today believe that there is not a real hollow but rather the appearance of one caused by the gases at the centre of the spot being relatively transparent.

Sunspots are continually appearing and disappearing. Their

123

life is highly variable, some lasting only a few days, while some can last for over a month, but taken all together they form a cyclical pattern which rises to a peak of activity on average every 11·1 years. The cycle is irregular and the intervals between peaks range from 7 to 17 years, but after a short interval there is usually a long one to redress the balance and over any extended period of time the average length of the cycles is surprisingly constant.

It was a Danish astronomer who first discovered the sunspot cycle and it was documented by Heinrich Schwabe in 1843. We can now trace it back into the past with a fair degree of accuracy, using a combination of direct observations and the measurement of carbon-14 in tree rings, which gives an indirect measure of solar activity. The pattern since 1610, when Galileo first observed sunspots, is shown in the figure.

Sometimes the cycle is broken and for a time the usual peaks fail to appear. This occurred, for instance, during the period 1645-1715, known as the 'Maunder minimum'. (It is named after Walter Maunder, superintendent of the Royal Greenwich Observatory in London, who in the 1890s searched through old journals and found that records of sunspots were missing for that period.) The failure of sunspots to appear during the years 1400-1510 had already been pointed out by the German astronomer Gustav Spörer, and the indirect methods of tracing sun-spots that have been developed since then confirm the existence of the Spörer and Maunder minima. They also show that similar minima have occurred roughly every 500 years for the past 5000 years (Eddy, 1976).

Sunspots and the weather

The radiation and particles sent out by sunspots have their effect on earth. Thus the beautiful and spectacular display known as the aurora borealis (the 'Northern Lights') is produced by charged particles from the sun, as are the disturbances to HF radio which we shall be considering in more detail in the next chapter.

There is also some evidence that the weather may be affected by sunspots, with such things as temperature, rainfall and

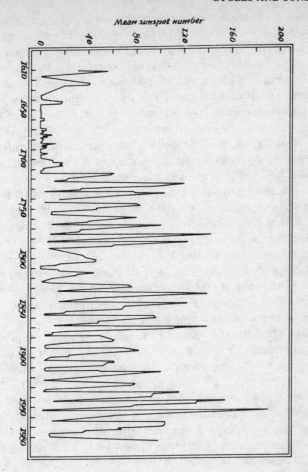

Average sunspot numbers, 1610-1980.

barometric pressure fluctuating with the sunspot cycle through the years. However, the correlation seems to be rather slight and the research in this area is largely unsatisfactory (Pittock, 1978). We will mention a few results to show the sort of work that has been done and the possibilities that are open.

Right back in 1801 Herschel, the discoverer of Uranus, suspected that there might be a link between sunspots and the average weather conditions in each year. Reasoning that good

125

and bad weather is generally reflected in low and high prices for farm crops, he tried to find a connection between wheat prices and sunspots. His results were inconclusive, and so were those of Carrington and Jevons (an astronomer and an economist) who tried to find the same link later in the nineteenth century.

These studies had covered only Britain, but an attempt to study the same effect over the much larger area of the whole USA was made by Garcia-Mata and Shaffner (1934). Oddly enough the sunspot cycle did not correlate with agricultural prices but it did with the total of American production *excluding* crops. This strange result has yet to be explained.

An ingenious study of temperature was made more recently, using the length of the 'growing season' as an index – that is, the number of days each year when the temperature rose above 5·6 degrees Centigrade. The study was made at Eskdalemuir in Scotland and the results are plotted in the figure, which certainly shows, on the face of it, a relationship between high temperatures and a high frequency of sunspots. If this holds in general then we ought to find cold weather prevailing at times where there is a dearth of sunspots. Using estimates of the average annual temperature in England, Hughes (1977) has demonstrated that this is true at least for the period of the Maunder minimum, which is also known as the 'Little Ice Age'.

There is, then, some evidence linking sunspots with temperature. What about rainfall? One way of studying this is through tree rings. Trees grow faster in warm, wet weather and this is shown in the width of the ring of new wood they put on each year. The width of these rings tends to vary over the world as a whole, for though most of us are only aware of local weather conditions there is in fact a climate of the earth. In very old trees such as the bristlecone pine, which is the oldest living thing on earth, dating back to at least 500 BC, the sunspot cycle can be seen charted in the wide rings that occur every 11 years or so. Research has shown that it is rainfall as much as warmth that is responsible, with narrow rings clearly associated with droughts (Cook and Jacoby, 1977).

Barometric pressure is something of a puzzle. One interesting cycle has been plotted for New York over the last century

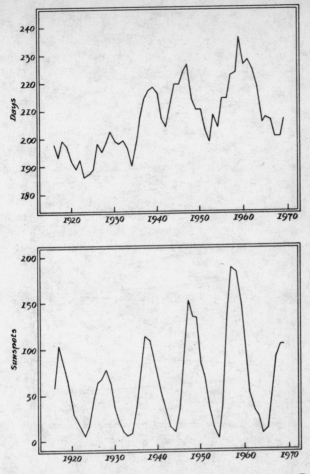

The upper half of the graph shows the number of days in the growing season at Eskdalemuir, and the lower half shows the average number of sunspots during each year. (Based on King, 1973.)

but, as the figure shows, it has a period of 7·6 years, so if it is related to the sunspot cycle there must also be other complicating influences. There are also some results from Russia and Indo-Malaya which do show barometric pressure varying with sun-spots – increasing at times of maximum sunspots in Russia and decreasing in Malaya.

127

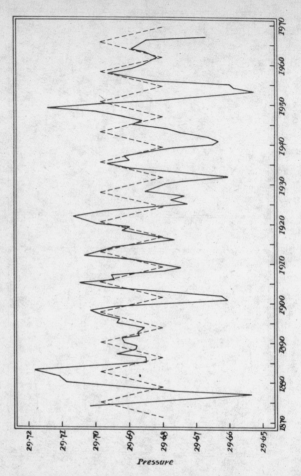

The 7·6-year cycle in New York's barometric pressure, 1874–1967. The solid line shows the pressure in inches of mercury on average for each year. The dotted line gives a regular 7·6 year cycle for comparison. (Based on Dewey and Mandino, 1973.)

Overall, we have to conclude that the relationship between sunspots and weather has not yet been clearly established. Given all the difficulties, this is not surprising. In any one place local conditions will easily override any more general effect, so that one needs to study the earth as a whole. One must also look for any pattern over a long period of time so that day-to-day

128

fluctuations in the weather will average out, and even then the relationship is likely to be slight. In addition, the sunspot cycle itself is not perfectly regular but varies, as we saw, between 7 and 17 years. One faces the problem of unravelling a small 'signal' from a great deal of 'noise'.

The weather and ourselves

It would be interesting to know more about the possible effect of sunspots on the weather, and certainly it would be interesting to know more about the influence the weather has on our own lives and emotions. A lot has been written about the latter but only a few studies have produced reliable results.

There is a certain amount of material on seasonal effects. It has been known since the early eighteenth century that the number of patients admitted to mental hospitals tends to be higher in summer, and it seems that this comes from a peak in the psychotic disorders of schizophrenia and manic-depression. (Other mental disorders do not vary seasonally in this way.) There also seems to be a peak in suicides in the spring, with a smaller peak in the autumn, and an autumn peak in depression following childbirth; but not enough work has been done to establish reasons for these results.

On the effect of weather, as distinct from the more general effects of the seasons, two interesting experiments were reported by Cunningham (1979). We are all of us used to the idea that people are more cheerful when the sun is shining but Cunningham decided to see if people's behaviour really varied if it was tested objectively. So in the first of his experiments passers-by in a Chicago street were stopped and asked to help by answering a long questionnaire of social opinions. The number of questions anyone was willing to answer was used as a measure of his willingness to help, and this was then analysed in relation to the weather. The experiment covered summer and winter months, and in both seasons the most significant variable was sunshine. The more it shone, the more helpful people were; and it was not just a matter of temperature, for people were more helpful on cooler days in summer and warmer days in winter.

129

The second experiment related the weather to the size of the tips left for waitresses in a Chicago restaurant. The results bore out those of the first experiment, with people giving higher tips when the sun was shining, although they were shielded from its more obvious effects in a fully air-conditioned restaurant.

There has also been some interesting research on the effect of certain winds. In various parts of the world there are days on which a hot dry wind blows and everywhere the effect on people is said to be much the same: it can produce lassitude, depression, irritability, insomnia and even nausea, and it can trigger off attacks of migraine and asthma, and lead to an increase in suicides and traffic accidents. In Italy this wind is known as the Sirocco, in Canada as the Chinook, in California as the Santa Ana. In the Alpine regions of Europe it is called the Föhn and in Israel the Sharav: these last two have had several studies.

The claim about accident proneness was put to the test by Moos (1964). He looked at traffic accidents in Zurich for the years 1958 to 1961, tabulated them in four-hour periods, and found that the peak times fell in the periods before and during Föhn weather; in the period after and at other times there were fewer accidents. Is there an alternative explanation? It certainly was not a matter of road visibility, since the Föhn brings dry weather with good visibility and clear skies, not the rain, snow and fog that are normally associated with accidents. Moos checked his data to make sure that Föhn weather did not happen to coincide with rush-hour times, when most accidents tend to occur in Zurich, but he found that the accidents associated with it tended to occur throughout the twenty-four hours.

It has to be admitted that the effect was only slight, but another study, on the Sharav in Israel, tends to confirm it and suggests a possible mechanism. Rim (1975 and 1977) looked at the psychological tests completed by groups of job applicants, and found that those tested on Sharav days scored significantly higher on 'extraversion' and 'neuroticism' than a control group tested on days when the Sharav was not blowing. They also scored lower on certain measures of intelligence. Interestingly, it was tasks demanding concentration and thought that were affected; 'overlearned' operations such as arithmetic and copying were not.

Now several studies have shown that accident proneness is more often found in people who are both extraverted and emotionally unstable (which is what is meant by the word 'neurotic' in this context). It seems, then, that the effect of the Sharav was, as it were, to push people's personalities in the direction of accident proneness.

Rim tried to counteract the effect of emotionality and restlessness by artificially adding negative ions to the atmosphere on the Sharav days, since it is claimed that the Sharav and the Föhn are associated with a deficiency of these ions (though we have found no good evidence for this). The results supported his theory, in that the subjects then obtained similar scores on Sharav and ordinary days, but there is a catch. The reports do not make clear whether proper controls were adopted, and if the subjects knew that the atmosphere was being treated this could well have affected their test results.

However, another study (Hawkins and Barker, 1978) did control for this. Male students were tested in a room in which the air was enhanced with either positive or negative ions and it was assumed that they did not know which group they had been assigned to. They were set a number of psychomotor tasks and their performance was found to be better with negative ions.

We do not know just what determines the ion balance, although we do know that the invigorating negative ions tend to predominate near the sea, near water-falls and after a sudden downpour, which is perhaps why rain is often said to 'clear the air'. The studies we have quoted illustrate the possibility that the weather can have real psychological effects and that the ion balance may be at least one of the links. Whether the ions are in turn affected by cosmic influences (such as radiation or charged particles reaching the earth's atmosphere) is something that must be left to the future to discover. At all events, here is a clear example of a possible cosmobiological effect, even if it is one that has no apparent connection with traditional astrology.

Sunspots and the mind

Fifty years ago two German researchers, B. and T. Düll, claimed to have found links between various phenomena such as sunspots, magnetic storms and the Northern Lights, on the one hand, and human fate, such as deaths from disease and suicide, on the other. For example, they reported an increase in suicides of about 8 per cent on days of marked sunspot activity. Could this be a case of cosmic events directly influencing human life? Unfortunately the Dülls did not collect their data in a very systematic way, nor did they analyse their results statistically, and more recent research has not confirmed their claims.

The same is true of other claims that suicides and admissions to psychiatric hospitals increase on days of high magnetic disturbance or cosmic ray activity. Pokorny and Mefferd (1966) looked at some of the most interesting of these and came to the conclusion that the results did not really hold up. In investigating one quite plausible study of this kind they took real data on homicides, suicides and psychiatric admissions, but substituted random numbers for the indices of magnetic disturbance; they found that by using the same methods as the original study they could produce results that looked just as convincing – as Cole had done with his unicorns.

One interesting area of research relates electromagnetic disturbance to accident proneness. Tromp (1963) and Lynn (1971) describe two studies done in Germany. In one of these R. Reiter analysed 362,000 industrial accidents over a two-year period and found an increase of 20 to 25 per cent on days of strong electromagnetic disturbance of the kind known as ELF (extra low frequency). The second study, also by Reiter, found that days of strong ELF disturbance correlated with a considerable increase in traffic accidents, of which 21,000 were studied over a one-year period. A similar result came out of some work by another German researcher, R. Martini, on industrial accidents attributable to clumsiness, inattention or nervousness in the worker, rather than mechanical or structural faults. (This is described by Gauquelin, 1971.)

As a result of a study of our own relating accidents to magnetic disturbance, we have reason to doubt the validity of these claims. Using data from the UK Transport and Road Research Laboratory we correlated the number of road accidents occurring each day with the daily magnetic index from the

Institute of Geological Sciences at the Hartland Magnetic Observatory in Devon. For the 365 days in 1979, road accidents in the UK correlated inversely (-0·19) with the degree of magnetic disturbance. In other words, there was a slight tendency for magnetic disturbance to be associated with fewer rather than more accidents.

If there is, in fact, a rise in accident proneness, one possible explanation lies in people's speed of reaction. During the traffic exhibition in Munich in 1953, which lasted for 71 days, 53,000 visitors were tested, and their speed of reaction tended to be slower on days of ELF disturbance. This is an intriguing result and it is unfortunate that the report does not give enough detail for us to evaluate it.

Sunspots and health

According to Tocquet (1951) in 1920 a French physician named Fauré noticed that telephone disruptions seemed to occur at the very times when his patients needed him most urgently – when they had heart attacks. After reading that a particularly severe magnetic storm had caused a major breakdown in the United States telephone service he decided to investigate. Together with another doctor, Sardou, and an astronomer, Vallot, he tried to relate deaths from heart attacks to sunspots, the presumed cause of magnetic storms. Over a 267-day period Vallot recorded 25 major sunspot days and for these days the death rate for Fauré's and Sardou's patients was twice that on other days.

Other researches have pointed the same way, but mostly the data they present are sketchy and the periods studied too short for any final conclusion to be drawn. For example, N. Romensky noted that heart attacks in Black Sea clinics increased ten-fold on an exceptional sunspot day; one day may suggest a line of research but it obviously proves nothing.

One study which did cover a longer period was made in India by Malin and Srivastava (1979). They looked at 5000 emergency heart cases admitted to two hospitals from 1967 to 1972 and related them to the daily index of geomagnetic activity published by the International Union of Geodesy and

Geophysics. (We mentioned earlier that the earth's magnetic activity increases at heavy sunspot times.) So as to eliminate any seasonal trend (in either the medical or the geomagnetic figures) they worked out the correlation separately for each month of the year and came up with a highly significant result: the correlations ranged from 0·4 to 0·8. The figure shows the overall result.

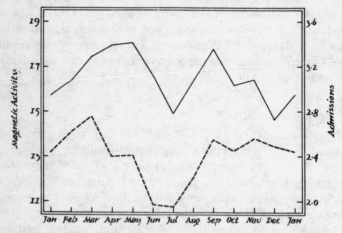

The upper line shows the magnetic activity in each month of the year averaged over the whole six-year period (1967-1972). The lower graph shows the daily admissions of cardiac emergency cases, averaged in the same way. (Based on Malin and Srivastava, 1979.)

The result might have been even clearer if it had been possible to use the times of the heart attacks themselves, but only the times of admission to hospital were known. All the same, the finding seems remarkably clear-cut, and it is puzzling that a similar study in the United States found no such connection. Lipa and others (1976) examined data on deaths from the National Center of Health, correlating heart attacks and strokes for 1962 to 1966 with magnetic indices, but found no sign of any trend. They made a detailed analysis of three metropolitan areas, but unfortunately not of rural areas, and it is just possible that a high level of artificial magnetic disturbance from cars and industry in American cities was masking the effects of the world-wide variation in magnetic activity. A study contrasting rural with urban areas in the same country might help to unravel this question.

In Britain, Knox and others (1979) ran a similar study in the West Midlands for 1969 and 1970, and again the outcome was negative. None of their correlations were significant, and again we face the puzzling question of why the data were so different from those found in India. So far no certain conclusions are possible, but further investigation is urgently needed in what might, from the medical point of view, be an important area. Investigators should also look at the suggestions described later in this chapter that there is an increased tendency for the blood to clot at times of sunspot activity, which could obviously provide a link with strokes and heart attacks.

There have been various other attempts to find a connection between sunspots and illness. For example, the Dülls investigated tuberculosis in Hamburg in 1936: their results were suggestive enough but later studies have sometimes supported and sometimes contradicted them. A more easily understood connection is with skin cancer or melanoma. Houghton and others (1978) investigated 2983 cases of melanoma from 1935 to 1974 and found that there tended to be more cases following a sunspot peak, with a lag of about two years. Other forms of cancer did not show a similar cycle. Now there is evidence that the likelihood of getting melanoma may be increased by exposure to the ultraviolet rays in sunlight. And the level of this radiation is highest at sunspot maxima. This suggests a possible link between melanoma and sunspots, but once again later investigations of that link do not yield clear-cut results.

The same is true of claims by Chizhevsky (whom we met earlier in connection with wars) to have traced a sunspot rhythm in major epidemics such as cholera, diptheria, typhus and smallpox. He claimed that plague epidemics since the sixth century took place twice as often at sunspot maxima as at minima, and he put this down to harmful cosmic radiation. He also believed that, apart from wars, other signs of human unrest, or 'mass excitement', such as revolutions and migrations, followed the sunspot cycle. Since Chizhevsky's death his work tends to have been supported by Soviet but not by Western research; but it is difficult to evaluate it since he presented his results in summary form and left out necessary details. It is also fair to say that there is an almost limitless variety of human phenomena to choose from and anyone who has an interest in demonstrating a solar influence can sooner or later do so simply by selecting the right data.

Chemical reactions

If the sun or any of the other heavenly bodies have an influence on human life, then there must be some mechanism by which they do so. Some transfer of matter or energy must take place, and on the basis of existing knowledge we assume that this energy is in the form of electromagnetic radiation. All the types of radiant energy that we know – from low-frequency radio waves, through the spectrum of visible light, to x-rays and beyond – are forms of electromagnetic radiation. If we are to believe in some new form of energy, unknown to science or to ordinary observation and with effects that are detectable only by astrologers or other students of the occult, we shall first need very good evidence that it really exists. We should never rule out the possibility that some radically new discovery of this kind may one day be made, but science progresses by trying to fit new observations into the framework of existing knowledge and changing the framework only when it is clear that there are phenomena it cannot be made to fit. If a blade of grass suddenly bends in front of our eyes on a still day it may of course have been moved by some unknown cosmic force – but we would be wise not to assume so until we are sure it was not a raindrop or an ant.

It is particularly interesting, therefore, to come across experiments which appear to show the effect of extraterrestrial radiation on chemical processes of the kind that go on inside our own bodies. One of the most striking concerns something very ordinary, the freezing point of water. Normally water freezes at zero degrees Centigrade, though there are factors that can affect this, such as changes in barometric pressure or, of course, movement which would act to prevent local freezing. However, curious aberrations have been noticed. There are times when it takes a noticeably lower temperature to freeze the water where it does not appear to have been caused by any of the known factors. At first these aberrations were put down to simple error, but about 1950 a Berlin bacteriologist, H. Bortels, thought the matter worth investigating. He studied pure water in sealed containers, with all known causes of variation controlled and only one thing changing, the temperature of the water. The freezing point of the water still varied from day to day. To test whether some outside radiation was responsible Bortels surrounded the containers with a metal screen that would block it off. The variation stopped.

Bortels suggested that an extraterrestrial force was at work and there were already some earlier experiments that pointed in the same direction. Some of these involved colloids, which are very fine particles suspended in a fluid. Colloids are interesting because they are particularly susceptible to electrical effects and also because they take part in many of the processes within any living body. One of the earliest studies of them in this context was made by Findeison (1943) who reported that even when they were kept in sealed vials under constant conditions certain non-random fluctuations in their behaviour took place.

A few years later Giorgio Piccardi, an Italian chemist and physicist at the University of Florence, encountered a similar effect. He was studying an inorganic colloid (bismuth oxychloride) and he noticed changes in the speed at which the particles precipitated out of the fluid in which they were suspended. For ten years he carried out daily tests on the rate of precipitation and compared them both with the occurrence of particular sunspot eruptions and with the eleven-year sunspot cycle as a whole. The striking results are shown in the two figures. When the solution was shielded by a copper screen the effect was inhibited, as it had been in Bortels' experiment. These important results have been replicated by many other workers in various parts of the world.

Piccardi believed that ELF waves (which we encountered in connection with accident proneness) might be responsible. He also noted that, as well as varying with sunspot activity, the reactions varied with the time of year, and he thought this was because, in its passage round the sun, the earth changes its

137

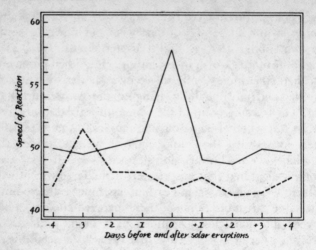

The effects of solar erruptions on chemical reactions. The two curves show the speed of precipitation of bismuth oxychloride when the experiment is performed in the open (solid line) or under a shield (dotted line). On the day of a solar eruption (marked 0) the unshielded test shows a sudden change. (Based on Piccardi, 1962.)

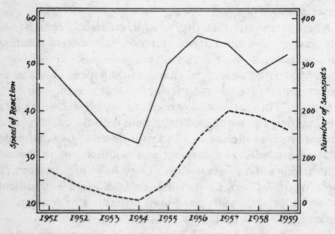

The speed of chemical reactions as a function of the eleven-year solar cycle. The solid line shows the average speed of precipitation each year, while the dotted line shows the number of sunspots. (Based on Piccardi, 1962.)

orientation towards the galactic radiation and particles that are constantly streaming through the solar system.

If the sun can have this effect on the interaction between water and a colloid it is possible that it could have a similar effect on living creatures, including ourselves. After all, the human body is about 65 per cent water and, as we mentioned, most life processes are based on organic colloids. Moreover water is especially sensitive to influences such as changes in pressure at temperatures between 35 and 40 degrees Centigrade, which is the range that encompasses most warm-blooded animals including man.

Some research does indeed suggest that the sun affects living beings in this way. Gauquelin (1970) describes an experiment in which microbes were found to reproduce more rapidly with changes in the weather. This was not an effect of temperature or barometric pressure, which were carefully controlled, and it stopped when the microbes were put inside a lead or iron screen. If the claims of Chizhevsky and others that some diseases are more prevalent during sunspot peaks turn out to be true, this could suggest a possible mechanism.

A direct effect of radiation on the human body was demonstrated by a Japanese haematologist named Maki Takata (1951) and the moral of this appears to be that if a haemophiliac is going to cut himself on a day without sunspots he had better not do so behind a metal screen! Takata had earlier developed a method of testing the level of albumen in the blood known as the 'Takata reaction index'. Albumen is an organic colloid which helps the blood to clot and its level was thought to vary in women according to the stage of their monthly cycle. What Takata found was that it also varied unaccountably in other ways, even in men, in whom it should be relatively stable.

The clue was provided by a sudden increase in sunspots early in 1938, which was when the unpredictable variations in the index was first noticed, and in a series of experiments Takata was able to show that the sun was responsible. One way to check was to see what happened when the subjects were either shielded from the sun's radiation or particularly exposed to it, so Takata carried out tests in an aircraft, at the bottom of a mineshaft and during a total solar eclipse. The index rose dramatically when the subject was taken up above the protective screen of the atmosphere, which normally isolates us from much of the sun's activity, and it decreased at the bottom of the mine and when the sun's rays were blocked by the moon during the eclipses. It was highest when sunspots were facing the earth and, by testing men in various countries simultaneously, Takata also established that the variations took place at the same times throughout the world.

X-rays and gamma rays left the index relatively unaffected. Only solar radiation had a dramatic effect, and a possible clue to the form of radiation involved was given by the fact that the index also went up just before sunrise. ELF waves are known to increase at this time as well as during heightened sunspot activity.

If the increased incidence of heart attacks and strokes at times of sunspots is eventually confirmed, Takata's finding could provide an explanation. It has also been linked to Piccardi's inorganic colloid reactions by Caroli and Pichotka (1954) who found that organic and inorganic reactions varied together. Yet another brick has been added to the building by a Soviet haematologist, Schultz (1960), who related solar activity to types of white blood cells. Tests involving 120,000 measurements were carried out on people living in a Black Sea resort, and the figure shows how the number of people with an excess of one type of white blood cell varied with sunspot activity. Other components of the blood were found to decrease; in particular, the incidence of leukopenia (which comes from a deficiency of another form of white blood cell) more than doubled – from 13 to 29 per cent – following a violent solar eruption. This took place in 1959, the year in which sunspots reached their highest average since accurate recording began in the nineteenth century.

Finally we should mention a study by Rothen (1976) who investigated why certain immunological reactions on glass slides vary with an exact 24-hour periodicity. He noted that their activity was constant and high during the night but that it decreased at sunrise and increased again at sunset. Once again, the variation was largely eliminated by the use of a metal screen, and Rothen suggested that cosmic radiation from the universe in general was acting to increase the speed of the

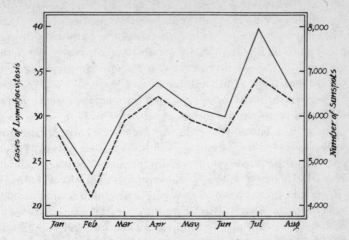

Sunspots and white blood cells. The solid line shows the number of cases of lymphocytosis, caused by an excess of one type of white blood cell. The dotted line shows the number of sunspots from January to August 1957. (Based on Schultz, 1960.)

reactions but that radiation from the sun acted in the opposite way to decrease it and during the day over-rode the general radiation.

Summing up

This chapter has covered a wide field, from the number of lynxes in Canada to accident proneness in Zurich and the behaviour of blood cells under solar radiation. What does it all amount to?

On the question of cycles in general we must keep an open mind. Some of them (like that of the lynxes) seem to be well established, but mostly they are just the sort of thing that can be produced by anyone willing to go on searching through an indefinitely large number of phenomena and then adjusting cycles and sub-cycles until something fits. We ourselves are not convinced that Mark Twain was right and that everything in our world follows a series of rhythmic patterns reflecting the motions of the cosmos. We cannot help remembering those unicorns.

Studies of the relationship of sunspots to life on earth seem to offer more plausible results, and here at least we are in a position where there is a clear and well established cycle to start with. Its influence on the weather is not yet known and may turn out to be less than many people have supposed, while the influence of the weather in turn on human emotions has been the subject of few really reliable studies.

Perhaps the most interesting area is that of the direct effect of solar and cosmic radiation on the chemistry of life. Here, as so often in this book, it is irritating to find that interesting and well-conducted investigations yielding important results have not been replicated or followed up, possibly because scientists are afraid of being labelled gullible quacks if they look at alleged effects that do not have a ready physical explanation.

Where scientists have feared to tread, astrologers have rushed in, accepting the influence of the sun and going on to assert that the sun's radiation is in turn affected by the motions of the planets. This is a startling claim, but it is not without evidence to back it. It is what we shall look at next.

8 Planetary Forces

Before the days of Kepler, the heavens
declared the glory of the Lord.
George Santayana

If sunspots influence us, and if sunspots are themselves regulated by the pull of the planets, then we have a cosmobiological connection of the most obvious and startling kind. And if the way in which the planets exert their influence is through the angles they make with each other when viewed from the sun or the earth – their 'aspects' – then traditional astrology can claim that one of its fundamental concepts has a proven physical basis and can never again be dismissed as mere symbolism or fantasy.

A man whose work is often quoted by astrologers in this matter is an American radio engineer named John Nelson. Basing his predictions on planetary aspects, he claimed to foretell radio interference caused by sunspots with an accuracy unobtainable by conventional methods. These claims were convincingly formulated and they have been widely accepted by astrologers. There is no doubt that they deserve careful consideration – more than has been given to them by astronomers and the radio industry.

To understand Nelson's work we must first look in more detail at the way sunspots behave and at the two main theories about what causes them.

The causes of sunspots

As we saw earlier, sunspots are continually appearing and disappearing on the surface of the sun. Any one spot may be large or small and may last for a longer or shorter time, up to about a month at solar maxima or several months at solar minima: as individuals they seem quite unpredictable. Taken all together, however, they show patterns of some regularity and it is in these patterns that we must look for clues to their origins.

Sunspots always occur in pairs or groups of pairs on each side

143

of the solar equator (like the earth, the sun rotates around an axis and so has poles and an equator). At the start of one of the eleven-year cycles of activity the spots first appear at about latitudes 30 degrees north and south. As the cycle progresses, they start to appear closer and closer to the equator until, at the end of one cycle and the beginning of the next, the new spots start to appear again in the 30 degree latitudes. This phenomenon is known as 'latitudinal passage' (a term which we met in the last chapter in connection with cycles of wild life on earth) and the figure shows how it works. Strictly speaking, a complete cycle lasts on average 22·2 years, because throughout each 11·1-year cycle the magnetic polarity of the leading spot in each pair in each hemisphere is the same, and opposite to that of the leading spots in the other hemisphere. At the start of a new cycle these polarities reverse.

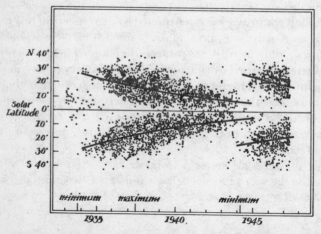

The sunspot cycle, showing how spots tend to appear closer and closer to the sun's equator until, at the time of minimum activity, they begin to appear once again around 30 degrees north and south. (Based on Abetti, 1963.)

The process by which sunspots form is still unknown, but any theory must account for the 11·1-year cycle, the lulls in it such as the Maunder minimum, the way magnetic polarity reverses from cycle to cycle, the symmetry of formation of spots on either side of the solar equator as shown in the figure and the phenomenon of latitudinal passage.

There are in fact two main theories. The first, which is held by most astronomers, is that sunspots are caused by an internal process in the sun, probably to do with some slow magnetic oscillation. The second theory holds that they are caused by forces exerted on the sun by the planets. We should note that this is not necessarily a straight either/or choice. There is no *a priori* reason why sunspots should not be generated by an interior mechanism but influenced in their timing and movement by planetary forces. To take an analogy, it would not be true to say that the way the earth spins in space sets up winds in its atmosphere. The energy that drives the winds comes from the heating of the air at the equator and its cooling at the poles. Nevertheless, the earth's rotation does influence their direction, causing cyclones to rotate clockwise in the southern hemisphere and anti-clockwise in the north, and something of this sort could in principle be true of sunspots and the planets.

The most obvious consideration in favour of the planetary theory is that there seem to be no other cyclic forces around. The planets are an obvious first choice, and in fact various planetary combinations have periods that closely match those of the sun. It is no surprise that since 1850 over a hundred scientific papers have been published claiming to establish a link.

The great objection to the theory is that the forces involved seem to be far too weak to have any effect. Presumably these forces would have to be gravitational, since planetary motion is exactly explained by gravity alone and any electromagnetic or other force must therefore be negligibly small. On the sun's surface the gravitational forces exerted by the planets are about one million millionth of the sun's own gravity, so to expect them to have any significant influence is like expecting a jumbo jet to be unbalanced by a single grain of sand.

However, as Dean and others (1977) point out, it is much too simple to view the solar system as a collection of small inert weights circling a large inert weight. The sun is fluid, it rotates faster at the equator than at the poles and the plane of its rotation differs from the plane in which the other weights revolve. In complex and unstable conditions a very small force could be enough to trigger off an event that was already on the verge of occurring.

145

There is also the question of angular momentum (the momentum that keeps a flywheel rotating). Although the sun is by far the most massive body in the solar system it only accounts for 2 per cent of the system's angular momentum, the other 98 per cent residing in the planets. Mörth and Schlamminger (1979) make the point that gravitational forces between the planets cause mutual perturbations of their orbits and this could cause a periodic transfer of angular momentum within the solar system that could affect the pattern of vortices on the sun's surface, which is of relatively low inertia and so would be the first solar material to respond.

However, if one is to back the planetary theory of sunspots one must first point to some planet or combination of planets whose periods of motion round the sun coincide with the timing of sunspots in their appearance, their latitudinal passage and their occasional lulls such as the Maunder minimum. We will not try to cover all the planetary candidates that have been put forward; as we mentioned, there have been a great many. We will explore only the findings put forward by Dean and others (1977), because they seem to fit all the main sunspot rhythms and have been ingeniously and carefully worked out.

Dean suggests that the main factor is a massive planetary resonance whose period is centred on the movement of the midpoint of a line joining Jupiter and Neptune, a movement which has remained in synchronisation with the solar cycle over the entire 320 years for which records of sunspots exist. The upper diagram (opposite) shows how the theory works and the graph below gives a measure of how closely it fits the actual rhythm of sunspots. Briefly, what Dean proposes is this. The midpoint of Jupiter and Neptune sweeps in an orbit round the sun, but the plane in which this orbit lies is not the same as the plane of the sun's equator. As a result, the midpoint passes through the equatorial plane at only two points, marked A and B, and it does so at the times of maximum activity of the 11-year solar cycle. The times when the midpoint is furthest away from the sun's equatorial plane coincide with minimum sunspot activity; this is shown by the little triangles in the graph.

A further refinement is that when the midpoint is sweeping

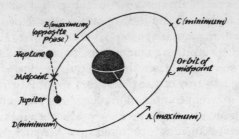

The midpoint of Jupiter and Neptune moving in orbit round the sun. The plane in which this orbit lies is tilted compared with the plane of the sun's equator so that the midpoint passes through the equatorial plane at two points only, A and B. As it passes through each of these points, the sunspot cycle reaches its maximum.

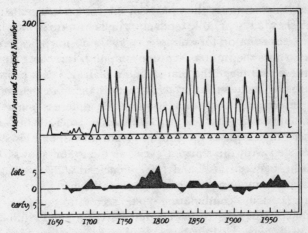

The upper line in the graph shows the average number of sunspots throughout each year and the triangles mark the times when the Jupiter-Neptune midpoint was farthest away from the plane of the sun's equator. The lower curve (filled in black) shows how many years late or early the midpoint was compared with the sunspot cycle. (Based on Dean and others, 1977.)

up through point A the sunspot cycle is in one phase (that is, the leading spots north of the solar equator have, say, positive magnetic polarity); when it is sweeping down through point B the cycle is in its opposite phase.

The most significant part of Dean's theory is that the orbital periods of various planets, or of the midpoint of two or three

147

planets, form 'harmonics' with the period of the Jupiter-Neptune midpoint. (By this we mean that the periods are in a simple arithmetic relationship with each other. For example, two complete orbits of a planet or midpoint might take the same time as one orbit of another; or three orbits of one might correspond to two of the other, and so on.) In this way the effects of different combinations of planets 'resonate' with each other, producing regular periodic peaks when the critical point on one orbit coincides with that on another, and troughs when they diverge.

The main 'resonant frequency' of the solar system coincides with the orbital period of the Jupiter-Neptune midpoint, which explains why the sunspot cycle is 22 years and not some other period. Furthermore, the phases of the component planetary cycles show a remarkable tendency to synchronise in the plane of the solar equator; for example, every time Saturn lies in this plane so does the Jupiter-Neptune midpoint. It is observations like these that make the planets more plausible as a cause of disturbance to the sun's surface. However, the coincidences are not perfect and from time to time the different planetary combinations get out of step with each other. When this happens the timing of the Jupiter-Neptune midpoint also gets out of step with the sunspot cycle, as the graph shows. The worst fit, between 1770 and 1800, coincided with an unusual number of competing planetary combinations.

One curious combination that seems to support the relevance of the solar equator is that of Neptune and Pluto. It is curious because Pluto is both small and far distant from the sun, but Dean points out that, since at least 2000 BC, every time Neptune and Pluto have been both opposite each other and in the solar equatorial plane there has been a prolonged period of solar inactivity.

Dean also mentions other planetary combinations whose rhythms appear to relate to the sunspot cycle and his whole theory seems to us to present a serious challenge to modern astronomy. Yet we know of no attempt to replicate his computations nor of any response by astronomers. But because of the fundamental importance of this issue to astronomy, it is something that will have to be faced sooner or later.

148

The work of John Nelson

The same indifference has been shown towards the work by John Nelson on planetary aspects, sunspots and radio interference that we mentioned at the start of this chapter. If Nelson's claims are justified, then his work unquestionably deserves careful scrutiny, and it would reinforce the belief that there may be a connection between planetary rhythms and the sunspot cycle. We will first describe his methods and the results he achieved and then present our own assessment.

High-frequency (HF) radio – or short-wave radio as it used to be known – works over long distances only because the waves 'bounce' off an ionised layer in the earth's atmosphere. If it were not for that they would act almost like light waves which travel in a straight line and are therefore invisible beyond the horizon. It was discovered early on that the state of the ionosphere had a marked effect on the quality of HF radio reception, and that its state is a very unstable one. It varies between night and day and also between one day and another, sometimes very markedly. When it is at its least helpful it ruins long-distance HF radio reception, sometimes to the point of imposing a total blackout.

In the early days of radio it was known that the radiation and charged particles emitted by sunspots had an effect on this ionised layer, and therefore on HF radio, and in 1946 one of the world's largest HF radio networks, the Radio Corporation of America (RCA), decided to investigate further. With about a hundred HF radio stations around the world they stood to gain immensely from a solution to the problem of radio interference, which sometimes put them out of business for days at a time. After looking for an astronomer with a knowledge of radio they decided in the end to give the job to one of their own radio engineers, who had a spare-time interest in astronomy and had even built his own six-inch reflecting telescope to observe the stars from his home. The man was John Nelson.

Nelson, who had been with the corporation since 1923, was transferred to the new department of Solar and Ionospheric Research and given the title of 'Short-wave Radio Propagation Analyst'. He began his research in 1946 and continued until his retirement in 1968, since when he has acted as a consultant to

RCA. He has described his work in several articles and in two books (Nelson, 1974 and 1978).

For the first two years of his new appointment, Nelson studied the sun and its relationship to radio disturbance. By relating the quality of radio signals to the number of spots on the sun each day, he confirmed that there was a connection, though it was by no means perfect. Sometimes there was a disturbance when no spots were apparent, although it is possible that 'undetectable' sunspots on the other side of the sun could have been responsible. Curiously, some sunspots actually seemed to improve radio signals; these tended to be large and stable spots which probably had this effect because of the stable level of ultraviolet radiation that resulted.

Nelson's interest was initially in the sunspots that caused the most trouble, which he named 'maverick spots'. These tended to be new and active spots in which the penumbra (the lighter outer area) was small compared with the darker umbra at the centre.

It also seemed that maverick spots tended to cluster in a critical part of the sun's disc, just east of the centre as seen from earth. During 405 lost radio hours in a six-month period in 1947 no less than 89 per cent of maverick spots were found to be in or around this critical area. Using this information Nelson was able to predict which sunspots were most likely to produce a radio disturbance; and because the speed of the earth's motion round the sun and the rate of rotation of the sun itself was known, he could also predict if and when a sunspot was going to reach the 'critical zone'.

One complication was that a spot could have two effects; one when it first appeared, which could even be on the far side of the sun, and again when it faced the earth from the 'critical zone'. Prediction was a complex business, but by putting together all his indicators, Nelson was able to predict radio conditions for the following twenty-four-hour period with 65 to 70 per cent accuracy. This was not considered good enough and after two years' research Nelson began to look for another solution to the problem.

He decided to investigate the theory that sunspot cycles are related to planetary motions through tidal (gravitational) forces. In answer to the usual objection that these forces are far too small, he argued that they might still be big enough to affect not the sun itself but the highly unstable electrified atmosphere that surrounds it. If the planets were even partly responsible for modulating the 11-year sunspot cycle, it seemed not unreasonable to ask whether they had any influence on the appearance of individual spots. At any rate he thought the theory worth investigating and got permission from RCA to extend his research into the field of planetary influences. He did not realise it at the time, but he had become a scientific astrologer!

Nelson started this new phase of his research in 1949 by looking up in an ephemeris the planetary positions for what was, and still is, the worst period on record in the history of radio interference. It began late on 23 March 1940 and raged on for a full month before ceasing as abruptly as it had begun. For most of this time there was a complete blackout of HF radio signals throughout the world. The figure presents the planetary positions with respect to the sun for Easter Sunday, 24 March 1940, which was the first full day of this gigantic magnetic storm. Nelson calls this diagram a 'planetary position Rosetta Stone'.

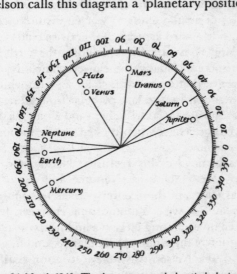

The planets on 24 March 1940. The degrees are marked anti-clockwise, following the direction in which the planets move round the sun. (Based on Nelson, 1978.)

151

Looking at it in the light of Nelson's later researches, it shows a number of critical aspects between planets. For example there are the following 'hard' aspects: Mercury in opposition with Jupiter and moving into opposition with Saturn; Venus in conjunction with Pluto and square with Saturn; Mars square with Neptune. There was also a 'soft' sextile (60-degree) angle between the earth and Venus which Nelson believed to be associated with radio disturbance only when it occurred alongside hard aspects.

The number of exact angles in this diagram persuaded Nelson he was on the right track and he immediately looked at the aspects on other notably disturbed days. The same angles tended to recur. He then looked at the correlation between planetary positions and past radio disturbances for every day of a five-year period, and this both confirmed his analysis and provided a number of extra indicators of a radio disturbance. Those that he finally adopted have been summarised by Dean and others (1977), and they can be briefly set out as follows. Nearly all radio disturbances are linked to hard aspects, the degree of disturbance being roughly proportional to the number of other aspects simultaneously present. A trine (120-degree angle) or sextile tends to worsen disturbance when it occurs alongside a hard aspect but otherwise tends to improve it. All the planets have an effect, including the earth and Pluto but not the moon. Usually the slower planets from Jupiter outwards seem to set up conditions for a storm which is then nudged into action by the fast planets (from Mars inwards) moving into critical aspects with them and with each other. The planets have more effect when they are at perihelion, that is, closest to the sun.

In the early days of his research, Nelson had not even bothered to look at Uranus, Neptune and Pluto since the gravitational effects of these outer planets is infinitesimal. It was another short-wave communications engineer, Jack Clark, who had been investigating Nelson's findings, who pointed out the contribution of these outer three planets, and by going back over his analyses, Nelson was able to confirm that they did, indeed, play an important part.

At the same time as carrying out his research, Nelson had

been making daily forecasts for RCA. He was, after all, employed by a commercial enterprise and so had a duty to provide them with any practical assistance that his research afforded. He had been making two types of forecast. The first was a daily one covering the next twenty-four hours. In this forecast he was able to make use of direct sunspot observations and any available results of ionospheric analysis as well as his planetary aspects. The second forecast was also made daily but for a month later. This long-range forecast was based mainly on planetary positions. (We are not told the exact proportion of the prediction that is attributable to the planets.)

Nelson claims that the accuracy of his short-term forecasts rose from less than 70 per cent to about 80 per cent when the inner planets were included, and to just over 90 per cent when the outer planets were also included. By 1967, he reported an accuracy of 90 per cent for a total of 1460 forecasts, this being based on prediction to within one point on a six-point scale of radio signal quality ranging from very poor to good. Accuracy is reported to have remained at this level ever since. Moreover, the long-range forecast became so accurate, attaining a level close to 90 per cent over a period of more than twelve years, that the short-term forecast was discontinued. Forecasting was now being done almost entirely on the basis of planetary positions!

Nelson was aware that he made errors in his forecasts; indeed, he would make a point of always re-analysing predictions that went wrong in an attempt to improve his methods. Sometimes a predicted disturbance was a day early or late, and sometimes it never occurred. Similarly, he sometimes completely failed to forecast a disturbance. In retrospect, he could occasionally see why a mistake had occurred; prediction was more complicated than the abbreviated account that we have given, and variables could easily be overlooked. But often there was no apparent reason for the appearance or non-appearance of a magnetic storm. (This is part of the missing 10 per cent in the forecasting accuracy of 90 per cent.)

For our purposes we do not need to have evidence of 100 per cent accuracy. If most astronomers are right and the planets have no influence on sunspots, Nelson's methods ought to have no predictive value at all. An accuracy of a good deal less than

90 per cent would be enough to make his point – providing it can be at least partly substantiated.

Assessing Nelson's claims

Astrologers have, naturally enough, embraced Nelson's work as demonstrating the effect of the planetary aspects which are such an important part of their methods. What do astronomers make of it? We have been unable to trace any detailed evaluation. However, one leading astronomer who has at least familiarised himself with Nelson's writings is Abell (1979). He points out that it is difficult to evaluate the work since the forecasts involve using other more conventional criteria besides planetary alignments; for example, Nelson takes into account ups and downs of the sunspot cycle. As a result, Abell admits to having 'found his statistical analyses unconvincing'. Unfortunately, he does not take the matter a step forward by conducting his own analyses. Rather he reports that the forecasting centre at the Space Environmental Services Center in Boulder, Colorado 'have not found his [Nelson's] methods useful'. Apparently, they had 'informally' evaluated Nelson's forecasts but found his categories of 'hits' too broad to verify the accuracy of his techniques. Similarly, Playfair and Hill (1978) write: 'We must also report that two researchers known to us have tried without success to replicate his chief findings.' However in these criticisms of Nelson's work, no details are given as to why it is unconvincing, not useful or impossible to replicate. This makes the criticisms themselves unconvincing and of little value.

What of Nelson's own justification of his methods? That too lacks many essential details. He gives various examples of outstandingly bad days on which his aspects were clearly in evidence, but although this is enough to make his theory worth examining it does not prove it true. It could merely be one more example of the fact that apparently convincing coincidences are usually there for the finding if only you look long enough.

Rather than providing illustrative examples, what Nelson should have done is to present a table summarising the planetary angles on, say, the 20 most disturbed days in radio history. Alongside such a table would be another one summarising the same information but for 20 of the least disturbed days in radio history; alternatively one could take 20 non-disturbed days chosen on some random basis, and preferably 'matched' with the disturbed days for time of year and position in the sunspot cycle. Given this control information, it would be a simple matter to conduct a probability test to see if the planetary angles on the disturbed days differed significantly from the angles on the non-disturbed days. It is only by this type of analysis that the sceptic might be convinced there is something in the theory.

Apart from checking planetary alignments for the most disturbed days in radio history, it is useful to check Nelson's forecasts. It may be, for example, that Nelson is able to forecast without being fully aware of how he does it. An independent verification of the accuracy of his forecasts would be scientifically acceptable evidence. Although they were made primarily for RCA, and so may not be readily available for checking, some were published – usually being provided months in advance in order to meet publication deadlines. For example, some three months before the event, Nelson predicted a severe magnetic storm for the period 19 to 24 September 1977. This was one of his forecasts that happened to be highly accurate, but again it is just an illustrative example and carries little weight on its own. A systematic analysis of all Nelson's published forecasts, or a random selection of them, would go a long way towards providing confirmation or otherwise of his claim to reach an accuracy of 90 per cent.

Not finding one anywhere in the literature, we ourselves have carried out such a check. We obtained details of Nelson's forecasts from 73 Magazine for the period 1 January 1979 to 30 April 1980. For each day of this period (with the exception of February 1980) Nelson had predicted some three months in advance whether it would be a good, fair or poor day for radio reception. We also obtained (from the Institute of Geological Sciences Magnetic Observatory at Hartland, Devon) information on the amount of magnetic disturbance actually occurring on each of these days.

For the 457 days in question, the correlation we obtained was close to zero (0·04). This result is of course totally inconsistent with Nelson's claims of predicting with 90 per cent accuracy, given the assumption that radio and magnetic disturbance are themselves associated. What are we to make of this discrepancy? As a first step we checked on a couple of criticisms that might be levelled at our analysis.

Since sunspots occur up to one day before the resulting magnetic disturbance on earth, it is possible that Nelson's predictions involve a lag: what applies to conditions on the sun one day may apply to radio conditions on earth on the following day. To check this possibility, we repeated the analysis using Nelson's predictions for the previous day. The correlation obtained was slightly larger, but again insignificant (0·07).

Another possibility is that Nelson was able to predict only in the case of severe magnetic disturbances, and in the period we analysed there were few severe magnetic storms. There appeared to be some truth in this suggestion since a comparison of Nelson's predictions for days on which the magnetic disturbance was relatively high with very quiet days revealed a difference that was just significant statistically. But the results were still only slightly better than chance and cast considerable doubt on the validity of Nelson's claims of a high degree of accuracy.

We wrote to John Nelson, seeking his comments on our analysis. He responded by pointing out that magnetic disturbance is not as closely related to HF signal quality as is commonly supposed, and he suggested that we repeat the analysis using data on actual radio quality rather than the magnetic indices. He provided us with copies of his predictions made for RCA, together with radio quality figures for the North Atlantic published by the Central Radio Propagation Laboratory for the period February 1964 to December 1965.

An analysis of these data for the first 516 days of the period (we did not have time to analyse the complete set of data) yielded correlation coefficients that were slightly higher than those obtained using the magnetic indices. For his RCA predictions, Nelson had made separate predictions for the twelve-hour periods of night and day, and correlating these predictions with the actual figures on quality yielded coefficients that were slightly above chance level (0·23 and 0·11 respectively).

Dean (1981) has carried out similar analyses of Nelson's RCA predictions for a period of two years and of his radio magazine predictions for a period of 11 years, a total of 4656 predictions. The correlations obtained in this exhaustive check showed not the slightest support for Nelson's claims, ranging from -0·05 to 0·07. The average was almost exactly chance (0.01).

How are we to explain this gap between Nelson's claims and the negligible success of his actual results? He himself has kindly provided details of the calculations made by RCA and this information has revealed the cause of the discrepancy.

To check the accuracy of his predictions, RCA used a method developed by the US Bureau of Standards. This method is described in a manual published by the International Union of Radio Science as follows: 'A forecast is considered to be a success when it differs from the observed figure by not more than one unit. The ratio of successes to total number of forecasts, in terms of percentage, is computed.'

Even though this method has the backing of the US Bureau of Standards it is in fact totally useless. It is liable to give very misleading results because it provides no baseline against which predictions can be evaluated. To take an extreme example, suppose that a forecaster predicts every day to be 'good' for radio conditions, then using this method an accuracy rate close to 90 per cent would be achieved since nearly 90 per cent of days are in fact 'good'. Applying a conventional correlational analysis to the same data would result in a coefficient of zero, which provides a better estimate of the true accuracy.

Why organisations such as the US Bureau of Standards should develop an invalid statistical method when satisfactory methods exist is inexplicable. Anyway, the use of this method provides the explanation for how Nelson was able to claim around 90 per cent accuracy for his predictions.

In reaching a conclusion on Nelson's work there is one other factor we must take into account. Although he claims to rely largely on planetary positions, he does also make use of some conventional methods of forecasting. For example, there is a 27-day cycle for recurrent magnetic storms in the years approaching sunspot minima which can be used. To validate Nelson's work we should have to show that it produced better results than predictions based only on these conventional methods, and the only check we know of does not show this. Dean (1981) has assessed the accuracy of the daily forecasts made by the Central Radio Propagation Laboratory; for 1964 through 1969 it was consistently 97 or 98 per cent, which is even greater than that claimed by Nelson. (Similarly for 334 days in 1965 the correlation between actual and predicted radio conditions was 0·25 and for 335 days in 1964 it was 0·55, again much greater than that achieved by Nelson.) Admittedly the laboratory was working only between 1 and 7 days in advance, whereas Nelson's RCA predictions were made 10 to 40 days in advance, and the accuracy of these forecasts presumably depends very much on how far ahead they are made. Still, at the least one can say that if Nelson made even some use of conventional methods it could contribute towards the accuracy of his results, which in any case were not nearly so impressive as they seemed at first.

The last hope for a resurrection of Nelson's theory may come from a direct study of the association between planetary positions and radio conditions, but on the basis of our analysis of Nelson's predictions a positive outcome now seems very unlikely. From this unfortunate state of affairs we can at least point one clear moral. The whole value of a piece of work in the field of astrology and cosmobiology may turn on what to the layman seems an obscure and purely technical point. Nelson may well have been quite correct in claiming an accuracy of ninety per cent (which surely sounds impressive enough) on the strength of a method of evaluation backed (no less impressively) by the US Bureau of Standards. But if the method of evaluation is itself invalid, then only a proper statistical check will reveal the true state of affairs.

If only for that reason Nelson's work would be worth describing. But it is also relevant to the whole question of planetary influences and, as we have noted, the final verdict on the more general issue has not yet been reached. In any case, work which has attracted so much attention among followers of astrology deserves to be fully described and we hope that it has at least made an interesting story.

One last point is worth making. In our investigation of Nelson's work we came across a curious thing. It seems always to have been assumed that magnetic disturbance is associated with HF radio reception, and clearly this is a very important fact for anyone working in the field. But has it been checked and just what is the correlation? We were surprised to find that no such research seems to have been undertaken: at least we could not discover any. Organisations such as the Ionospheric Prediction Service (at Slough in England) and the British Broadcasting Corporation could offer us only subjective opinions, and these varied from claims of an almost one-to-one correspondence to a dismissal of the relationship as very slight. Provoked into making our own first assessment on the basis of data provided by Nelson we reached correlations of 0·36 for night-time and 0·39 for daytime waves. We offer this as at least a start, along with the observation that apparently scientists and technicians are not always careful to base their own judgements on facts and figures even when they are eager to blame astrologers for just that failing.

Earthquakes

The prediction of catastrophic events has always been popular with astrologers (the very word 'disaster' is derived from the Greek word for a star) and one form of catastrophe which they link with planetary forces is that of earthquakes.

There are many astrological studies of earthquakes but most of them are unconvincing. Rudolph Tomaschek, for example, a German physicist, plotted planetary positions at the time of 134 major earthquakes and claimed to find a connection (Tomaschek 1959). Certain of the planets, notably Uranus, Pluto and Jupiter, had hard angles at the times of the earthquakes to a significant degree, but then out of all the possible coincidences one would expect some to appear significant just by chance. Tomaschek seems also to have made serious mistakes of fact. He produced data showing that

Uranus was overhead in 15 out of 23 quakes during one three-year period, and within one hour of the meridian 39 times compared with an expectation of 22·3 times. However, Gauquelin (1975, personal communication) has pointed out that Tomaschek was ignoring the distortion due to the earth's inclination to the plane of the ecliptic and the effect of this on the apparent position of Uranus. When it is taken into account Uranus' position ceases to be significant.

One problem in gauging the value of any astrological theory of earthquakes is the sheer frequency with which they occur. Big, disastrous quakes are luckily not common but smaller ones most certainly are. On average there is one every half minute somewhere in the world! With such a number to choose from it should not be hard to find plenty of earthquakes to fit into any preconceived pattern.

All the same, there are a few studies that do seem rather more convincing, and the figure shows one of the clearer results in a study cited by Dewey and Mandino (1973). In this case the connection is with sunspots. It is worth having a look at some possible mechanisms that have been suggested to account for the influence of extraterrestrial events on earthquakes.

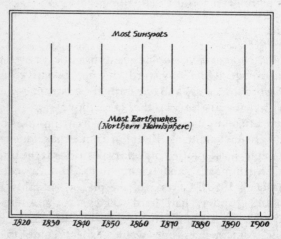

Earthquakes and sunspots, 1829-1896. Note that the first cycle is short for both sunspots and earthquakes, the next cycle is average for both, the third is long for both, and so on. (Based on Dewey and Mandino, 1973.)

One way to start is to look at moon quakes. Since the Apollo missions, which left seismic stations behind, the moon's surface has been continuously monitored and it seems to be established that moon quakes are more frequent when the earth is at its closest or farthest from the moon. These are the times when the earth's gravity would cause the strongest tidal strain on the moon's surface: is it possible that the moon also acts on the earth to influence, at least in some degree, the timing of earthquakes? Because of the relative sizes of the two bodies we should expect this effect to be much smaller and therefore much harder to detect, but many hundreds of studies seem only to have produced conflicting results. If there is a lunar effect all we can say is that it is not consistent and is less important than other variables.

What about the sun and the planets? Gribbin and Plagemann (1974) have prepared a case for believing in their influence, which rests on the idea that once stress has built up in a geological fault quite a minor force could trigger its release. The argument they present is complex, but essentially they suggest that a planetary alignment will cause a maximum tide on the sun, which will provoke an abundance of sunspots and hence a massive injection of particles into the earth's upper atmosphere. This will set up unusual movements of large air masses, which will affect the earth's rate of rotation, thus triggering regions of instability into earthquakes. They say that a major alignment of the planets occurs in 1982, and that tectonic movement along the San Andreas fault in California is long overdue, hence a major Californian earthquake is likely in 1982.

Their arguments have been widely and vigorously criticized by astronomers, such as Meeus (1979), on the grounds that each link in their chain of events is either not proven or is of such low probability that the overall probability is essentially nil. Fortunately it is not necessary to enter into the technicalities of the debate because two simple facts put everything into perspective.

First, the alleged alignment of 1982 does not exist. According to Meeus, the width of the sector which contains all nine planets reaches a minimum of 95 degrees on 10 March 1982, while the width of the sector containing the four largest planets is never less than 60 degrees throughout 1982. Planets spaced over 60 or 95 degrees hardly form an alignment!

Second, similar 'alignments' have occurred many times in the past at intervals of roughly 179 years. If they do in fact trigger earthquakes then an examination of earthquake records should settle the argument once and for all. Hughes (1977) cites an analysis of Chinese earthquake records dating continuously from 640 BC to the present, and it shows no evidence of such an effect. Such a simple test is conspicuously absent from Gribbin and Plagemann's book – obviously with good reason!

In any case, their prediction will be put to the test: before the end of 1982 it will be known whether a major earthquake has or has not occurred in California. If it has, it could, of course, just be a lucky shot by Gribbin and Plagemann, and if it has not their theory will appear to have received a severe blow.

Provisionally at least, we must conclude that planetary forces do not seem to have any clearly apparent effect either on the sun or directly on the surface of the earth. To believe otherwise would demand more convincing evidence than much of that which has so far been put forward. The only really promising studies concern the possible connection between planetary positions and the sunspot cycle. If such a connection does prove to be the case then of course we have evidence of an indirect link between the planets and any events on earth which are associated with sunspots.

9 The Moon

Galileo's opinion of the theory that tides are caused by the moon was terse and definite: 'Astrological nonsense.'

It is not known for sure how far back the theory goes. It is often ascribed to Kepler, but Copernicus, or even the ancient Greek philosopher Eratosthenes, may have anticipated him. What is interesting in the context of this book is that what seems to us such an obvious connection was missed for so many years, and even when it was proposed was hotly denied by men who ought to have been well qualified to judge. We must be cautious of too-easy scepticism as well as too-easy belief.

Many astrological doctrines centre around the moon and its supposed effect on men and women. We shall look at some of the more plausible ones and also at some cosmobiological ideas that do not necessarily tie in with traditional astrology. It is only fair to warn the reader in advance – since he or she must by now be getting used to our raising many fascinating theories only to dismiss most of them as false or at best unproved – that in this chapter again we shall not unearth much in the way of hidden gold. There are certainly some very interesting ideas that we cannot dismiss, but generally the closer they are to being established, the further they are from anything that would ordinarily be called astrology. However, no critique of astrology can ignore so obvious a subject as the moon, and we can promise at least that we have approached it open-mindedly and that some of the side turnings off the main road make the journey worthwhile.

Moon phases and tides

Newton's theory of universal gravitation made the explanation of how the moon draws up tides on earth obvious and simple. The part of the earth's surface closest to the moon is subject to

163

the strongest upward pull, so that the sea bulges up towards that point. On the opposite side of our globe the moon's pull is weakest, so that the sea there has a second bulge. As the earth rotates the bulges stay put relative to the moon, so that the earth moves round under the high tides – or, to look at it from our viewpoint, the tides surge round the earth.

The size of the tide depends on two things. The first is the moon's distance (when the moon is closest to earth its tidal force is 30 per cent higher than when it is furthest away) and the second is its position relative to the sun, whose tidal force (surprisingly) is nearly half that of the moon. Spring tides occur at new and full moon, when the sun and moon are aligned and so combine forces. Neap tides occur when they are at right angles, so that their forces partly cancel. If a spring tide coincides with the moon's closest distance, as it does about twice a year, the tide will be at maximum.

There are two major lunar cycles. The most obvious one to us is the progression from new moon to full moon and back, those being of course the times when the moon is between the earth and the sun (in conjunction) and therefore reflects little or no sunlight, and on the opposite side from the sun (in opposition) with its whole disc lit up to our view. This is known as the *synodic lunar cycle*.

The other – *sidereal* – lunar cycle is the time taken for the moon to make one complete revolution in its orbit round the earth, relative to the 'fixed' stars. This does not take quite the same time as the cycle from new moon to new moon because, while the moon passes round the earth, the earth itself is moving along its own orbit round the sun. To come between it and the sun, therefore, the moon must each month move into a slightly different position. The times occupied by the two cycles are 29·5 days for the synodic cycle (new moon to new moon) and about 27·3 days (it varies slightly) for the sidereal cycle.

There are a number of traditional beliefs about the effects of the lunar cycle, on the weather, on plants, on animals and on humans. We will deal with each of these in turn.

The weather

In the folklore of the countryside, the pattern of rain and shine is supposed to follow the rhythm of the moon. Bradley, Woodbury and Brier (1962) set out to find if there is any truth in this. They plotted the combined rainfall data from no less than 1544 weather stations in North America over a 50-year period starting in 1900, and they did indeed find a significant result. Rainfall was heaviest in the middle of the first and third weeks – that is, a few days after both full and new moon. It was lowest in the second and fourth quarters, before new and full moon.

To check their results they split the 50-year period in two and compared the data from the two 25-year periods with each other. The figures were very similar, with an excellent correlation between them (0·8).

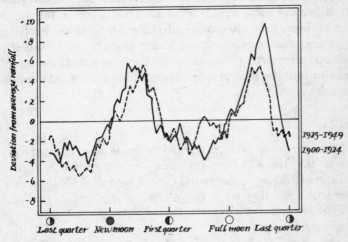

Between 1900 and 1950, widespread rainfalls recorded by all US weather stations occurred more frequently on days after the new and full moon. The solid line shows the data for the years 1900 to 1924, using 7,856 records, and the dotted line for the years 1925 to 1949, using 8,209 records. It can be seen how well the series match each other. (Based on Bradley, Woodbury and Brier, 1962.)

Brier and Bradley (1964) went on to make a further analysis of their rainfall data for the USA and found a 14·8-day cycle – half a lunar month. They also found a lunar 'tide' in barometric pressure, but the effect was very small.

165

Adderley and Bowen (1962) conducted a similar study in the southern hemisphere, but had delayed publication because 'to suggest a lunar effect on rainfall would simply not have met with the right response.' Their results from 50 weather stations in New Zealand over a 25-year period were very similar to those from North America.

These studies provide evidence that the moon can be used to predict an increased likelihood of rain a few days after it is new or full. The effect is very slight – it needed an enormous amount of data to demonstrate – but it is something that contemporary meteorologists should investigate. They have always assumed that the moon cannot be used to predict the weather, and in practical terms they are right; but that need not prevent them investigating theoretically interesting relationships.

A possible explanation of this effect is that the moon may act to deflect the 'solar wind', which causes changes in the upper atmosphere, and also to shield the earth from some of the meteoric dust around which water droplets may condense when rain is starting to form. An explanation of this kind would take us into the field of cosmobiology, but hardly into that of astrology.

Plants

In the past, when farmers wanted to decide when to plant their crops, they turned to the almanacs. There is a well established system of folklore connecting the moon with agriculture, and in particular dealing with the phases of the moon that are conducive to healthy growth. Modern researchers have tried to find evidence for this.

Over fifty years ago, a researcher in Stuttgart, Lili Kolisko, wrote a book called *The Moon and Plant Growth* describing how her experiments, conducted over a nine-year period, showed among other things that corn and other plants sowed two days before the full moon grew larger than if they were planted two days after it.

Apart from an astrological explanation, it is of course possible that the extra light from a full moon may help early growth: Paleg and Aspinall (1970) report that floodlights speed up barley growth by three to four weeks. But before seeking an explanation for Kolisko's result, we must ask how much confidence can be placed in it. Amazingly, there has been no systematic follow-up to this work. Researchers have instead been concerned with testing different theories, with the result that there are now a number of isolated findings associating the moon with plant growth, but with none of the findings directly replicated.

Best (1978) reviews these other studies and it is worth mentioning two of them here.

First, an astrological experiment concerned with moon *signs* and growth. In collaboration with a market gardener in Sussex, England, Kollerstrom planted twenty-four rows of potatoes, each row being sown at a different position of the moon over a two-month period. As a result of this and other experiments, in particular a series of studies by Maria Thun, he claimed that potatoes and other root crops are best sown when the moon is in earth rather than water signs, his earth-sign potatoes producing a 25 per cent better crop.

The second experiment concerned moon *phases*. Brown and Chow (1973) took daily measurements and found that the rate of absorption of water in bean seeds varied with the moon's phase. There was a maximum rate at new moon, at full moon and at the two quarters – four peaks in each month. However, when the experiment was controlled for temperature, only the peak at full moon remained significant. It is difficult to think of an explanation of this result, and anyway we must await replication.

One doubt which affects many experiments in this field arises from the fact that, as Ronald Fisher has demonstrated, a great deal of care has to be taken in the design and random allocation of plots in agricultural experiments if they are to have any validity. In some of the astrological work cited, there does not seem to be a full appreciation of the difficulties involved. Until the experiments are repeated with such factors as temperature and allocation carefully controlled, we must view their results with scepticism.

One quite different but very interesting effect is based on the voltage differences between different parts of trees. The pioneer in this work was Burr (1972) a professor emeritus of anatomy at Yale. He made painstaking measurements over a number of years, attaching electrodes to two different points on each tree, and found that a number of factors seemed to affect the difference in voltage between them. Among them, there appeared a cycle of 14·75 days, half the synodic lunar cycle. Burr also worked on voltage differences on the human body, as did a neurologist at Duke University, Leonard Ravitz (1962), and both of them claimed to find evidence of a lunar rhythm. But no replications have been published and until they are we can only regard these preliminary results as interesting curiosities.

Animals

There are numerous anecdotal reports of how some creatures are influenced by the moon, and many of them have been carefully documented. One example may suffice. According to Wing (1962), the breeding rhythm of the sooty tern on Ascension Island is unique. In other species, breeding usually takes place at the same time each year and is timed by various cues such as temperature. The sooty tern has a 9·7 month cycle, and its breeding rhythm, for some unknown reason, is adjusted to the tenth full moon. Pairing occurs at night under this full moon, and because of this night activity, the locals refer to the birds as the 'wide-awakes'. After breeding they fly away over the seas, only to return again at the time of the tenth full moon. Wing suggests that some physiological rhythm of near 9·7 months is triggered by the full moon. Anyway, this anecdote raises the question as to how many other species may be influenced in some aspect of their behaviour by the moon, and of course whether these species include man.

According to Lucilius, 'The moon feeds oysters, fills sea urchins, puts flesh on shellfish and on beasts.' Not surprisingly, the activity of certain forms of sea-life has often been observed to depend on the tides (and so on the phases of the moon). Oysters open their shells at high tide to feed, and close them at low tide to prevent being dried out. Biologists assume that oysters possess an internal clock that is somehow set in motion by the tides, but Frank Brown, professor of biology at Northwestern University, reasoned that it was equally possible that the oysters were sensitive to the direct action of the moon. He conducted what has become a classic study (Brown, 1954 and 1959).

Taking 12 oysters from the seashore of Long Island, Connecticut, he transported them a thousand miles inland to his laboratory in Evanston, Illinois. For the first ten days or so, the oysters continued opening and closing their shells as if they were back on Connecticut, consistent with the assumption that they possessed an internal clock. But their rhythm then changed to a new routine, according to what would have been high and low tide in Evanston – had it been furnished with a seashore! (It is possible to draw up theoretical tide times for anywhere on earth.) The oysters now opened their shells to feed when the moon was directly overhead in their new abode. Since light, temperature and pressure were being kept constant in the Evanston laboratory it seemed that they were responding directly to gravitational forces coming from the moon, and had reset their clocks by it. At any rate, there was no other apparent explanation for the result. Here then was evidence that distant celestial forces, although minute (the gravitation force from the moon is many times smaller than the tidal force exerted on you by this book), can affect living organisms.

Brown has extended his work to cover plants and animals as well as other forms of sea-life. He was the joint author of the study on beans cited in the last section and also of an interesting experiment on a rat kept in a cage under constant conditions of light and temperature (Brown and Terracini, 1959). When the moon was below the horizon, the rat was twice as active as when it was above the horizon. This was a single case study urgently in need of replication.

In another experiment (Brown and Park, 1967) four hamsters were studied over two years, using an activity wheel (a kind of treadmill which could be operated by the hamsters at will, with the number of revolutions being counted automatically). The animals were kept in a room that was illuminated according to a regular daily pattern, and they followed a clear 24-hour rhythm of activity – active in dark,

169

inactive in the light. The level of activity trailed off just *before* the light came on and then began again just before it went off; in other words, they appeared to be able to anticipate the light schedule.

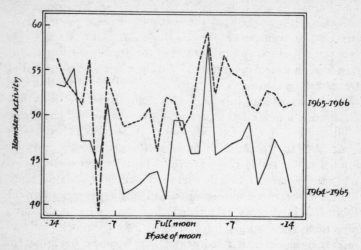

The activity of hamsters at different phases of the moon is shown for each of the two years of the study. It is measured in tenths of an hour per day. (Based on Brown and Park, 1967.)

The investigators also found evidence for a lunar rhythm. As shown in the figure, activity over the lunar month varied, with a peak four days after full moon and also high levels for a few days after the new moon. According to Brown and Park, these results are equivalent to most activity occurring just before moonrise and just after moonset, that is, during the dark times. As the figure shows, similar results were obtained over two years for the hamsters, the correlation being 0·52, which is highly significant. It seems therefore that biological rhythms may be under both solar and lunar direction. Lunar timing would have had a useful role in marine organisms, because of the tides, and remnants of this may still exist in species evolved from them. These results are interesting, but the sample is very small, as in all the previous work by Brown. Furthermore, in spite of the ingenuity of the work of Brown and his colleagues and the very positive results that they have reported, we should close this section with a warning that Klinowska (1972), who studied the activity of male hamsters for a whole year, found that individual variation was considerable but showed no peak after full moon. Here again we find contradictory results, and we can only hope that someone will at least replicate the oyster study, which is of quite fundamental importance in relation to the influence of the moon on sea life.

Mankind: birth and death

Does the moon influence man? Many beliefs have arisen, and we shall examine some of them in the next sections of this chapter. We will begin with beliefs about the moon's role in determining the time of birth and death, birth being supposed to occur more often at full moon and death when the moon is waning.

It is true that natural labour begins twice as often at midnight as at noon and that a midnight onset tends to lead to a faster and easier birth. But there is no need to bring in the moon: the effect could be simply explained in terms of the mother being more relaxed at night than during the day.

Is there nevertheless a relationship between birth and the phases of the moon? Menaker and Menaker (1959) analysed half a million births in New York hospitals over a nine-year period, plotting them against the 29·5 day lunar cycle. Slightly more births occurred during waning than waxing of the moon, with the maximum number around full moon and the minimum around new moon. However, the effect was only just detectable and other researchers have not confirmed it. McDonald (1966) found a different pattern in his study of negro deliveries in South Carolina, with more births occurring during full and new moon phases and least during the first quarter. He put this down to the effect of the moon's gravitational pull being combined with the sun's at full and new moon, but he also admitted that the result could have been influenced by the belief in the influence of the moon which is characteristic of Southern negro culture.

Phase of the moon	Number of births
First quarter	233
Full moon	276
Last quarter	254
New moon	282

In McDonald's study (restricted to full-term, spontaneous deliveries over a six-year period) most births were found to occur in the new and full moon periods. This analysis was based on 1,045 cases that fell clearly into one of these four categories, the remaining cases (out of the total of 1,907) being borderline. (Based on McDonald, 1966.)

Abell and Greenspan (1979) analysed nearly 12,000 births occurring in a US hospital over 51 lunar cycles from 1974 to 1978, and found no correlation with full moon or any other moon phase. The authors note that the results were a surprise to several of the hospital nurses, who had 'fully expected to find a strong correlation of birth rate with full moon'.

Another line of research has been to relate birth to the tides, which depend on geographical location as well as on the moon. (This, remember, was important in the case of the oysters.) Gauquelin (1973) cites a study by H. Kirchoff in Germany, who found an excess of births at or just after high tide, and another study in which a similar effect was found in Cologne. Without further replication we must be wary of accepting these results as indicating that the moon can influence the timing of births, but a slight effect, possibly due to gravitation, cannot be ruled out.

As to death and the moon, various claims have been made, but we know of no research results that confirm them in a clear-cut manner and that would be worth reporting in detail here.

Lunacy, crime and suicide

From very early times, people have believed that the moon influences the mentally ill. Hippocrates wrote: 'One who is seized with terror, fright, and madness during the night is being visited by the goddess of the moon.' And in Shakespeare, after Othello has murdered Desdemona, he exclaims:

It is the very error of the moon,
She comes more near the earth than she was wont
And makes men mad.

The word 'lunatic' comes from the Latin word for moon, and 'epilepsy' is associated with the Greek meaning 'to seize upon from the moon'. Other languages also bear testimony to the belief in an association between the moon and disturbed behaviour, and the same belief is incorporated in a number of legends, including that of the werewolf, which is of considerable antiquity. The transformation of a man into wolf, otherwise known as lycanthropy, is believed to be a form of madness caused by the moon, and a case of lycanthropy – a woman who at full moon believed that she was a wolf – has been reported recently in the *American Journal of Psychiatry*.

Other murders have also been thought to be influenced by the moon. In the 'Jekyll and Hyde' case, an English labourer named Charles Hyde was charged with murder and other criminal acts. His defence rested on the fact that his criminal acts were committed at new and full moon, and that he was suffering from a form of madness that was triggered by the moon.

Various researchers have set out to test the belief that the moon can influence murderers. In America, Lieber and Sherin (1972) analysed homicide records in Dade County from 1956 to 1970. In a total of 1,887 murders there was a significant tendency for them to occur at new or full moon, and this finding was strengthened by a similar result obtained for Cuyahoga County (Lieber, 1978), though in that one the figures were not statistically significant.

Other researchers have not found murder to be related to the moon, but Lieber points out that their analyses have only involved time of *death* and not the time of the *assault*, which in most places is not recorded. Dade County is a fortunate exception, since it also records the estimated time of attack. Lieber and Sherin suggest that if there is a very slight association between the moon and murder, then it may not become apparent if time of death is used instead, and they have demonstrated the force of this argument by taking the trouble to re-analyse their data using time of death. The slight moon effect obtained using time of attack disappeared.

Rather than moon phase a more appropriate measure might be the time of local high tide when the moon is directly overhead. An indication that an investigation along these lines might be worthwhile is given in the Cuyahoga County results where the peak incidence of homicide occurs three days after the full moon. Compared with the Dade County result, where homicide peaked at full moon, this may represent a lag in lunar effect due to geographical location.

Using this refinement, Lieber (1973) predicted that homicides would tend to cluster around the times of high tide (that is, the times of maximum daily gravitational attraction) with the least number of cases at moonrise and moonset (least gravitational attraction). Accordingly he plotted 424 homicides into these segments, and claims to have found the prediction to be supported.

As further support for a lunar effect that is related to local tide times rather than moon phase, Lieber points out that his Cuyahoga graph of homicide plotted against moon phase closely resembles a graph for metabolic activity in hamsters provided by Brown, and notes that Cuyahoga lies in the same latitude (41 degrees north) as Evanston, where the hamsters were studied. But this is hardly evidence; the similarity between the two sets of data was reported only because they were similar, and many other comparisons might have given different results.

If the moon does have a precipitating effect on the mentally unstable, then perhaps it will show up in forms of crime less extreme than murder. Tasso and Miller (1976) related phase of the moon to 34,318 criminal convictions, including rape, burglary and homicide. For most forms of crime they did find an increased rate at full moon, but not for homicide or car thefts. The size of the sample made their findings significant, but it has to be admitted that the effect was very slight. Other research has also shown a link between crime and moon phase – but not always the same phase, and obviously such studies only support each other if the same phase is involved each time.

Another form of action that might be influenced by the moon is suicide, that final and desperate solution to life's problems. The incidence of completed (that is, fatal) suicides at new and full moon has been compared with that at other times in five recent studies. One of them showed a slight, but not significant, tendency for suicide to be more frequent at new and full moon, as shown in the table (Garth and Lester, 1978). A similar study by Jones and Jones (1977) produced a significantly greater number of suicides during the period of new moon (129 compared with an expected 94) but the number at full moon was fractionally below chance expectation (93 instead of 94).

	Number of suicides	Expected number
New moon	60	49·7
Full moon	52	49·7
Other times	392	404·5

In this study, there was a slight, but not significant, tendency for suicides to occur at the times of new and full moon which were each taken as lasting three days. (Based on Garth and Lester, 1978.)

Combining all five studies, there is on balance a tendency for suicides to occur at new and at full moon, but the effect is very slight. It is also quite possible that any relationship with the moon is psychological rather than astrological. If someone is going to kill himself his timing of the act might be affected by knowing that astrology or superstition point to certain times as most appropriate.

Mental disorder

One way of assessing the effect of the moon on mental disturbance in general is to look at the admissions to psychiatric hospitals. The big problem here, as with murders but on a far greater scale, is that of delay. It has been estimated that some 85 per cent of homicide victims die within an hour of injury, but admission to hospital following a psychiatric crisis may be delayed for several days or even months. Because of this unknown degree of error, it is hardly surprising that studies have yielded conflicting results.

These studies have been well reviewed by Campbell and Beets (1978) and by Cooke and Coles (1978). In one of them, in which over a thousand admissions to a mental hospital in Ohio were analysed, time of disturbance was assumed to occur four days before admission to hospital for every patient (Osborn, 1968).

It would have been better if an estimate had been made in each individual case, but using this correction factor (and only then) mental breakdown was found to coincide with the full moon at a significant level. The effect was more apparent for psychotic than for neurotic disorders.

In another study with a similar outcome (psychiatric admissions being higher at the time of full moon) the authors checked to see whether the result still held when only cloudy nights were considered. It did. It is surprising that other researchers have not bothered to consider this variable, since if the moon is visible it could have a psychological effect – or even a practical one on a criminal weighing up his chances of getting caught on a dark or a moonlit night.

This sort of consideration is important when one thinks how small is the effect to be explained. Taken all together, there is a very slight tendency for a peak to occur at or around the time of full moon, both for hospital admissions and for emergency calls to a campus crisis centre (Weiskott, 1974, and De Voge and Mikawa, 1977). Just how slight we can illustrate by noting that in a study of 12,093 cases (Weiskott and Tipton, 1975) the result was statistically significant but the increase in admissions to hospital at the time of full moon was still only one per cent. In our opinion such a small variation could well have psychological causes, probably stemming from the patients' prior knowledge of the astrological doctrine. The self-fulfilling prophecy seems to us the most likely explanation.

Fertility

The moon has long been the female symbol of fertility. Aristotle wrote that menstruation begins when the moon is waning, and Darwin, noting that the lunar month coincides in length with a woman's month, wrote: 'Man is descended from fish . . . why should not the 28-day feminine cycle be a vestige of the past when life depended on the tides, and therefore the moon?'

Researchers have looked for a relationship between the lunar cycle and the onset of menstruation. Gauquelin (1973) cites the case of Svante Arrhenius who won a Nobel Prize for his research in chemistry at the turn of the century, and who also studied the influence of the moon on, for example, the female cycle. On the basis of 11,807 cases, he found that the onset of menstruation was higher during the waning than the waxing moon (supporting Aristotle) and reached a peak on the eve of new moon.

Other researchers, however, have obtained inconsistent results. Sometimes they have found no relationship; sometimes the new moon is implicated; at other times it is the full moon. One example may be given. Gunn and others (1937) designed the rigorous test of asking women to mail a postcard on the day that menstruation began, a more reliable method than trusting to memory. After ten thousand cards had been collected, the results were analysed. They revealed no relationship with the moon. Presumably Arrhenius' effect had been due to chance or to errors of memory. Even the results of Nobel Laureates cannot be accepted as gospel unless replicated!

Much has been made of the similarity between the length of the female cycle and that of the moon, and the fact that pregnancy lasts for exactly nine lunar months from the time of conception. Abell (1979) suggests that this is merely coincidence, and not a very good one at that, since the female cycle averages 28 days and the lunar cycle is 29·5. However, a large-scale survey by Gunn and Jenkins (1937) found the average female cycle to be 29·5 days, although we must remember that this is only an average, that many women diverge from it and that few have absolutely regular cycles.

If the moon does affect the female cycle, can we formulate any theories about how it does so? According to R.J. Reiter (1976), melatonin is produced during darkness – there is a five-fold increase at night – and melatonin inhibits hormone production. (Thus blind people tend to be less fertile than sighted people.) In an experiment by Dewan (1967 and 1969) women with menstrual irregularity who slept with the light on for the fourteenth and seventeenth nights of their cycle 'almost all' found the irregularity corrected. Dewan's sample was small (19 women) and no replications have been published, but there are other pointers, as for instance the fact that in Finland, where winter nights are very long, more twin conceptions occur in summer.

On this sort of basis it would be easy to speculate that the length of the female cycle is the evolutionary result of a long ancestry spent sleeping in the open under the moon; and indeed Gooch (1979) speculates that all Neanderthal women menstruated together at the time of the new moon. Unfortunately for this theory, the same long evolutionary exposure to the moon does not seem to have worked for other species. As Abell points out, the oestrous cycle varies in length for different mammals. For opossums it is 28 days, for sheep 11 days, for cows 21 days, for chimpanzees 37 days, and so on. To quote him: 'One could argue, I suppose, that the human female, being more intelligent and perhaps more aware of her environment, adapted to a cycle close to that of the moon, while lower animals did not. But then the 28-day period for the opossum must be a coincidence, and if it is a coincidence for opossums, why not for humans?' It is a valid point.

Such considerations, however, have not stopped some experimenters from formulating ways in which the lunar cycle could be used as a method of birth control. Eugen Jonas, a Czechoslovak psychiatrist, has developed a theory that predicts a woman's time of peak fertility and also the time most conducive to bearing a boy or girl. (His work is described by Ostrander and Schroeder, 1972.)

The first part of the theory is that ovulation is related to phases of the moon, with a peak time occurring when the sun and moon are in the same angular relationship as at the moment of birth. Jonas believed that intercourse at this time could trigger ovulation, which might or might not coincide with normal ovulation, and he claimed to have found that this astrologically determined time of peak fertility was responsible for around 80 per cent of pregnancies. Using both this and the conventional rhythm method of birth control for deciding when to abstain, he claimed 98 per cent effectiveness. Unfortunately it is not at all clear what this figure means. If we simply take the number of pregnancies per hundred acts of intercourse, then the average effectiveness of the ordinary rhythm method is at least 99·5 per cent (one pregnancy for each two hundred acts of intercourse). On that measure, Jonas's method seems to be a step in the wrong direction.

The second part of his theory is that the sex of the child can be predicted from the moon's position at the time of the mother's birth when this coincides with the time of conception. If it is in an odd-numbered or male sign, such as Aries, then the child will be a boy. Jonas claimed that in two surveys involving 200 women who followed this method, almost 90 per cent were successful in having what they wanted.

Not unnaturally, his claims were ridiculed and he was considered insane by his medical colleagues. Access to his original data (he claims to have based his research on 30,000 cases) is not possible since his work was stopped by the Communist government in 1970 for reasons unknown. However, several researchers have tried to replicate his findings, but without success. In one of these attempts, 100 Californian mothers with a known time of intercourse leading to conception were studied. The time was not related to moon phase in the women's birth charts. Nor in another 400 cases was the sex of the child related in any way to the phase of the moon.

As regards the question of sex (the second part of Jonas' theory), perhaps the most damning criticism is to ask why non-identical twins, who are conceived at exactly the same time, are of different sex as often as ordinary brothers and sisters, who are conceived at different times.

Playfair and Hill (1978) have assessed the research by Jonas, and in particular his claim of 98 per cent accuracy in birth control. They comment: 'We have yet to unearth a properly written report on any such test – and not without trying.' Since they went to extreme lengths to obtain details of many other research studies, such as travelling abroad to visit the scientists concerned, their failure to find documentation for a major part of Jonas' research speaks for itself. Needless to say, the Jonas methods are not accepted by conventional family planning clinics.

Surgery

Some early astrologers insisted that the moon influences blood flow. Surgeons in ancient India delayed operating until the wane of the moon in order to get less scarring, and even today some farmers avoid castrating animals during a full moon for fear that they will bleed to death; this is the kind of advice given in astrological almanacs.

Edson Andrews (1960), a Florida surgeon, recounts how his nurse noted the dates when excessive bleeding occurred after tonsillectomy operations, and found that they often coincided with the full moon. After this, relevant details were kept of all tonsil and adenoid cases from 1956 to 1958, by which time they numbered just over a thousand. Of these, 44 cases presented problems of operative or post-operative bleeding requiring unusual means of control, such as the patient being returned to the operating room, and when the dates of these cases were plotted against phases of the moon they supported the nurse's original observation. The problem cases were clustered around the full moon with a minimum number around the new moon: 82 per cent of the problem cases occurred in the second and third quarters, one week on either side of full moon.

Similar results were obtained from another hospital, involving 24 cases over a six-year period, and an analysis of 66 cases of bleeding peptic ulcers revealed a similar, but less marked, pattern. Although these results were not subjected to statistical analysis, the overall pattern might appear clear-cut enough not to be the result of chance. Andrews was sufficiently impressed to write: 'These data have been so conclusive and convincing to me, I threaten to become a witch doctor and operate on dark nights only, saving the moonlit nights for romance.'

Unfortunately, his study has yet to be independently replicated. This is a pity since it would be easy to do and a confirmation would have very important implications for the practice of surgery. Andrews also noted that he had fewer patients at the time of the full moon, and he suggests that laymen are reluctant to enter hospital at this time because they know more about these things than the doctors.

One last study of bleeding is worth mentioning. Rhyne (1966) analysed over a thousand cases of serious nosebleed from hospital records dating back to 1930. According to traditional astrology the signs of the zodiac are associated with different parts of the body and their specific illnesses. Rhyne found that more than 90 per cent of the cases of nosebleed were of patients whose moon signs were in Capricorn, Aquarius or Pisces. Compared with a chance expectation of 25 per cent this is highly significant, and the only trouble with it from the astrologer's point of view is that these are the wrong signs. They involve the body from the knee down to the foot! Rhyne attempts to rescue astrology by claiming that if a correction is made for the precession of the equinoxes the signs all move up one and this brings in the appropriate sign of Aries. Recalling a day when no less that five nosebleed cases came into his office, Rhyne mentions that on this day (24 January 1947) the moon was in Pisces, or in Aries if the correction is made for precession. Unfortunately Rhyne makes his correction in the wrong direction, a mistake which does not inspire confidence in his study as a whole. In any case it has not been replicated and we are not inclined to take it seriously.

Indeed we agree with George Abell (1979), the astronomer we have quoted earlier, when he writes: 'There may well be undiscovered lunar influences, and some of the alleged influences may possibly turn out to be real. But many of the incredible "facts" concerning the effect of the moon are simply not facts at all.'

It is sad to have to discard attractive theories, or at least retain one's scepticism and suspend judgement. Nevertheless we must be ruled by facts and be prepared to go in whatever direction they lead. But if one does this it is all the more exciting when one comes across theories which seem to fly in the face of conventional scientific preconceptions but which are backed by rigorous analysis and impeccable methods of research. To the reader who has followed us patiently through our largely negative findings so far we now offer an extraordinary story.

10 The Work of the Gauquelins

> Science is the knowledge of consequences
> and dependence of one fact upon another.
> *Thomas Hobbes*

Michel Gauquelin was born in Paris in 1928. He has been interested in astrology since childhood. No one in his family was an astrologer – they regarded it as a parlour game, nothing more – but his father had a friend who was interested, and it was his influence that sparked off the young Gauquelin's obsession with the subject. Outside the family he met many people who took astrology seriously and he was fascinated by what they told him. By the age of seven he was asking people their birthdays, and then telling them the zodiac sign under which they were born together with their supposed character. Soon he was nicknamed Nostradamus by his class-mates, and as a teenager he read all the astrology books he could lay his hands on. Up to this point he was very much a believer; he had never asked himself the question 'Is any of this true?'

He studied psychology and statistics at the Sorbonne, eventually obtaining a doctorate in psychology. It was during his student days that he discovered scepticism and Descartes' First Principle: 'Never accept anything as true unless you clearly and obviously know it to be true.' Accordingly it was only at this point in his career that he began to have doubts about astrology and to appreciate the need for proof. He then collected birthdates for the purpose of testing such astrological claims as 'Professional soldiers are often born under the sign of Aries or Scorpio, and rarely under Cancer.' His formal training in statistics provided the basis for testing such predictions against the laws of chance, and the results he obtained were consistently negative. Repeatedly, when astrological claims were put to the test, they failed.

Gauquelin extended his research to include planetary positions at the time of both birth and death. As regards death, he was forced early on to reject such claims as 'Death occurs more frequently under the influence of Saturn', put forward by previous researchers such as Krafft and Choisnard. Their research involved faulty methods and controls, or simply did not produce the same results when repeated.

It was when using time of birth that Gauquelin began to obtain positive results. (He was able to get the actual time of birth, as opposed to the mere birth-date, from registry offices, since it is recorded on birth documents in most European countries including Scotland, but unfortunately not in England, and more recently in the United States.) When he studied famous people from various occupations, such as acting and medicine, Gauquelin noticed that certain planets tended to be in particular positions at the time they were born. Could there really be a planetary influence on destiny? The idea is of course consistent with the general claims of astrologers but seems quite incompatible with modern scientific knowledge. So Gauquelin began the long task on which he has since spent many years and in which he has been joined by his wife Françoise who is also a psychologist, checking his results, trying out the same analysis on new sets of data, and exploring the ways in which a plausible pattern could have arisen by accident. For all his work he has not been able to disprove his basic finding: the planets really *do* seem to bear some inexplicable relationship with how a famous person develops.

Gauquelin represents a rare combination, possessing both a detailed knowledge of astrology and a genuine scientific outlook based on a formal academic training. He certainly does not see himself as an astrologer, and indeed he is very critical of astrology as a whole, having learned from his own research that much of it is untrue.

From the beginning he has had to provide his own funds for research, although he now does receive the occasional grant for his privately run laboratory. As we shall see, his work has involved getting data from birth certificates in registry offices all over the continent, and for financial reasons he has had to rely on public transport for much of this work. Since registry offices are typically open to the public on only a few days a week, it can be seen that there were many difficulties to overcome. Also his research had to be fitted in with part-time work to earn money. In this respect he provides the complete answer to astrologers who point to the lack of funds to explain astrology's lack of scientific progress; clearly what astrologers need is not so much funds as initiative and determination!

The results of Gauquelin's researches are summarised in his recent book *The Spheres of Destiny*. Full details are provided in a series of research documents which he has published privately, and which are listed in another recent book (Gauquelin, 1978). What follows in this chapter is a description and evaluation of his main findings.

Occupation

Gauquelin's first positive result was obtained for 576 members of the French Academy of Medicine. Doctors who had achieved academic distinction by virtue of their research were selected from medical directories, using objective criteria so as to avoid bias. Relative to theoretical expectation, the eminent doctors tended to have been born when Mars or Saturn had just risen, or had just passed the midheaven.

Before we discuss this result, it may help to spell out exactly what is involved. Since the earth is rotating, each planet appears to rise and set, like the sun and moon. It rises on the eastern horizon at the rising point and passes to its highest point at the midheaven or point of upper culmination, where it is exactly halfway in time between rising and setting. It then sinks to the setting point, and the same process (but of course inverted) is repeated below the horizon.

The path of the planet is divided by Gauquelin into 12 sectors which are similar to, but not identical with, the astrological houses. The divisions are arranged so that, unless there is a distorting astronomical influence, a planet will spend one-twelfth (8·33 per cent) of the time in each sector. This, of course, means that if the birth-times of any group of people are evenly spread, 16·7 per cent of them will fall when a planet is in a given pair of sectors. What Gauquelin found with his sample of eminent doctors was that appreciably more than 16·7 per cent of them were born with Mars or Saturn in the sectors following rising and upper culmination.

Unlike many previous results favouring astrology, this one

could not be explained in terms of any known effect of astronomy or demography. To make sure of this, Gauquelin collected the birth-times of a control group of people from the general population drawn at random from the electoral register and covering the same period of births as the doctors. This group confirmed theoretical expectation. How then could his result be explained? Since Gauquelin had tested so many astrological claims, one of them sooner or later was going to appear statistically significant by chance alone. Perhaps that was what had happened with the doctors. To test for this possibility it was necessary to repeat the study and, unlike so many other researchers, Gauquelin took the trouble to do this.

The replication was carried out on another group of French doctors who had undertaken important research. The same pattern emerged as before: this group of 508 doctors, too, showed an above-chance tendency to be born when Mars or Saturn had just risen or had just passed the midheaven. As a result of this confirmation of the original result, a much greater degree of confidence can be placed in the finding.

Intrigued by this, Gauquelin extended his research to include other professions and other countries. He travelled through Germany, Italy, Belgium and Holland until he had collected a total of over 25,000 birth dates from official registers. With few exceptions, positive results continued to emerge.

Two examples may suffice. First, Gauquelin looked at the distinction between arts and science that has long been recognised in education. He contrasted 5,100 successful artists with 3,647 successful scientists, and found that Saturn was the planet that best differentiated these two groups. As shown in the figure the scientists tended to have been born when this planet had just risen or had just passed the midheaven. In contrast, the artists were significantly less likely to have been born at these times; they showed a distinct tendency to avoid being born 'under' Saturn. Similarly contrasting results were obtained when certain other groups were compared, such as soldiers and musicians. In the case of musicians specialising in military music, their results tended to fall mid-way between the soldiers and other musicians!

The second example concerns Mars, which has long been

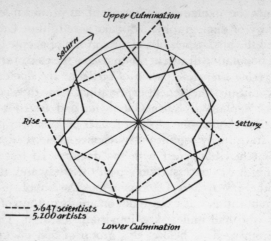

The dotted line shows how scientists tend to be born just after the rise or upper culmination of Saturn, while the births of artists (solid line) are least frequent at those times. It is interesting to see how closely the two curves run counter to each other. The circle shows the number of births to be expected at each time by chance alone. (Based on Gauquelin, 1978.)

recognized as the symbol of the god of war. Gauquelin looked to see if this planet occupied the critical zones (just past the rising point and just past the midheaven) in the charts of 3,438 military leaders. It did, with 680 cases in these zones instead of an expected 590. Moreover, Jupiter was even more apparent, with 703 cases instead of an expected 572.

Throughout this research it was found that the critical planetary positions tended to occur *only for the births of the famous or distinguished.* Just as control groups selected at random from the general population yielded results in accord with the laws of chance, so too did control groups formed from people in positions subordinate to those in the distinguished groups. In other words, there was no apparent planetary effect for ordinary or unsuccessful professionals. For example, Saturn did not occupy the critical zones more frequently than chance for a group of 1,458 ordinary scientists. Neither Mars nor Jupiter was predominant in the charts of 2,840 ordinary soldiers.

This seems to show that the planets are related to destiny, success and good fortune. To check this, Gauquelin decided to look at the charts of a group of young soldiers who had been shattered by death or crippling injuries before they had had a chance of becoming successful. Each was a war hero who had been decorated for bravery. This tragic group yielded results similar to those of the generals and other famous leaders, with Mars and Jupiter again predominant. This was a crucial finding, because it suggested that the relationship was not with destiny but with the character or personality that makes for success. It was to this variable, therefore, that the Gauquelins turned.

Character

Sport provides a good example of how the right temperament can help in reaching the top. Coaches have always recognised that physical attributes are only one component, and that psychological factors are often of far greater consequence. With two people of equal physical prowess, it is the one with the greater determination and confidence who is likely to win, and the same is true in many other areas of life – for example, the thrusting businessman or the dedicated scientist.

In looking through biographical descriptions of famous sportsmen, Gauquelin noticed that most possessed what might be called an 'iron-willed' temperament or character. They were characterised by their determination, bravery, energy, persistence, and so on. Having previously found that Mars tends to predominate in the charts of successful sportsmen, Gauquelin now repeated the analysis but this time in terms of personality. Two sub-groups of famous sportsmen were formed on the basis of their biographical descriptions. One group was composed of the typical 'iron-willed' sportsmen, and the other was made up of 'weak-willed' sportsmen characterised by descriptions such as 'inconsistent', 'dilettante', 'lacking in vigour', 'unambitious', 'gentlemanly' and so on. The former group included many famous names who had succeeded in spite of various physical limitations, and the latter group included many 'natural athletes' who had succeeded with the minimum of effort; presumably their physical attributes were more than enough to compensate for their lack of determination. How then were these two groups of famous sportsmen associated with Mars? As shown in the figure, the 'Mars effect' was found to apply only to the 'iron-willed' group; it was not associated with successful sportsmen who possessed an atypical personality. The planetary effect was again shown to be a matter of personality rather than of destiny.

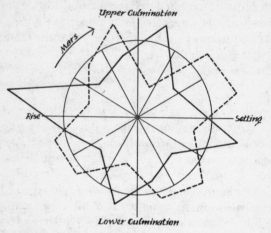

Mars and 'iron-willed' versus 'weak-willed' champions. The solid line represents the births of 'iron-willed' and the dotted line 'weak-willed' champions. (Based on Gauquelin, 1978.)

In another attempt to link planetary positions directly with personality rather than occupation, famous people wre classified in terms of their personalities as reflected in their biographies (Gauquelin and others, 1979). The subjects – 2,089 sportsmen, 1,409 actors, and 3,647 scientists – were classified by such descriptions as 'extravert', introvert', 'unstable', and 'toughminded'. These personality descriptions were then related to planetary positions at birth. This latter information had been independently charted and it was kept secret from the psychologist (Sybil Eysenck) who had rated each subject on the personality dimensions. This procedure (otherwise known as blind assessment), by which the two variables to be correlated are independently assessed, was in accord with the requirements of modern psychology.

What then did the results show? Regardless of occupation, it was found that *personality was associated with the planets being in one of the critical zones*. For example, extraverts and tough-minded people tended to be born 'under' Mars and Jupiter, while introverts and the tender-minded were born 'under' Saturn. It was personality rather than occupation that was related to the planets; and it was only because a particular personality tends to characterise success in given occupations that Gauquelin had obtained his original results.

Is it possible to arrive at a list of character traits representative of each planet? The Gauquelins have attempted to do exactly this. By comparing trait words with the owners' birth charts, they have constructed a list of traits associated with each of the planets studied. A summary of the key words for each planet is given in the table. What it means is that a person whose personality is described by these key words is more likely to have been born when the relevant planet, rather than any other, was just past the rising point or midheaven.

MARS	JUPITER	SATURN	MOON
active	at ease	formal	amiable
eager	ambitious	reserved	many friends
quarrelsome	opportunistic	conscientious	simple
reckless	authoritarian	cold	good company
combative	talkative	methodical	good-hearted
courageous	likes to assert himself	meticulous	accommodating
dynamic	sense of the comical	modest	disorderly
energetic	communicative	observant	absent-minded
fiery	debonair	organized	generous
untiring	spendthrift	not talkative	imaginative
fighting	gay	precise	easily influenced
aggressive	gesticulating often	reflective	fashionable
afraid of nothing	good-humoured	retiring	worldly
straightforward	independent	reserved	nonchalant
strong	happy	wise	poetic
daring	worldly	melancholy	dreaming
valiant	prodigal	timid	obliging
full of vitality	bantering	industrious	rather snobbish
lively	likeable	silent	superficial
self-willed	vain	sad	tolerant

What is important to note about these results is that the traits associated with each planet appear to form a meaningful pattern; each list does not consist of a lot of random unrelated traits.

Recent research has also uncovered a set of traits associated with tender-mindedness for Venus, but attempts to detect a personality relationship with the other planets have so far been unsuccessful. There is little or no such link apparent for the sun or Mercury, or for the distant planets, Uranus, Neptune and Pluto.

Before we go on to consider possible explanations of Gauquelin's results, we should mention one interesting study which he made on people who had achieved distinction in the fields he had found to be related to Mars, Jupiter, Saturn or the moon. He combined all these types as a single sample, which reached the very large size of 46,485, and the results as shown in the figure speak for themselves.

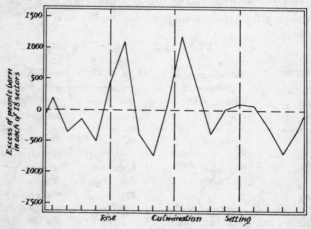

Gauquelin's combined sample of 46,485 people eminent in fields 'governed' by Mars, Jupiter, Saturn and the moon. The position of each person's planet depends on the birth time, and taken all together they show highly significant peaks after rise and upper culmination.

The search for an explanation

Having apparently established that there is a correlation between the positions of the planets at birth and subsequent personality, Gauquelin was left with the job of explaining how this could happen. It is important to distinguish between establishing that there is something to explain and then providing the explanation. The example has already been given of how some three hundred years ago, Newton established the case for gravity by providing laws that accurately described its effects, although he had no explanation as to how it worked (a state of affairs that still exists). A similar situation arose with electricity; scientists were making use of it long before they had any understanding as to how it worked, or even whether it was a unitary force.

With a few exceptions, Gauquelin's results tend to be consistent with the astrological characteristics of the planets, but to say that the planets influence us astrologically is of course no explanation; it is necessary to state how they could have this effect. In an attempt to throw light on the issue, Gauquelin next turned to an investigation of planetary associations with genetics – a scientifically established mechanism in personality development.

Planetary heredity

According to Kepler, 'There is one perfectly clear argument beyond all exception in favour of the authenticity of astrology. This is the common horoscopic connection between parents and children.'

In an earlier study, Gauquelin had found this assertion to be untrue with regard to signs of the zodiac; parents and their children showed little or no tendency to be born at the same time of year. It was now necessary to re-analyse the data to see if any correspondence could be obtained not for signs of the zodiac but for planetary positions. Accordingly, the positions of the major planets at the time of birth of 15,000 couples and their children were noted. Kepler was now found to be right! If one or both parents had been born when a planet was just past the rising point or midheaven, then there was a significant tendency for their children also to be born 'under' this particular planet. This is shown in the figure. The effect was most marked for the moon, Venus and Mars, followed by Jupiter and Saturn; it was not apparent for the sun, or for

Mercury or the outer planets. It may be noted that, as with the previously discovered relationships, this is consistent with the 'distance-mass' law of physics; the effect applied only to the large or near planets. It may also be noted that this study demonstrates a planetary effect for ordinary people, whereas the previous studies found an effect only for eminent people.

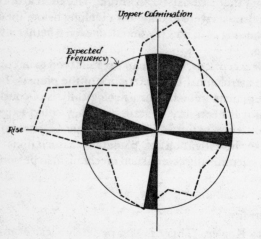

When the parents were born with the moon, Venus, Mars, Jupiter or Saturn in one of the solid areas, the chances of the child being born 'under' the same planet are much higher. The dotted line shows the number of such children born at the time of each position of their parents' planet, and it can be seen that their births tend to concentrate just after its rise and upper culmination. (Based on Gauquelin, 1978.)

Replication was of course necessary in order to establish this effect as real, but before doing this Gauquelin was distracted by the realisation that a perfect test of astrology presented itself. If the planets really do influence our destiny at birth, as is popularly supposed, then it should not matter whether the birth is natural or induced. Accordingly, in order to test this hypothesis, Gauquelin divided the group into those two categories. (Induced births were taken to include those that involved drugs as well as delivery by forceps and caesarian section.) And he found that the planetary effect applied *only* to the natural births. This suggests that the planets, rather than affecting development, are instead influencing the natural timing of birth, making it more likely that a person of a certain type will be born at one time rather than another.

In conventional medicine, it is not yet known what initiates the birth process; there is believed to be a complex interaction of hormonal influences acting between mother and child, but the timing mechanism is unknown. Gauquelin's work introduces a new possibility, namely that the planets are somehow acting as celestial midwives. Some kind of signal emanating from the planets may somehow interact with the foetus in the womb, stimulating it to struggle into birth at a certain time. This is consistent with what Hippocrates wrote some 2,500 years ago: 'When the time comes, the baby stirs and breaks the membranes containing it and emerges from its mother's abdomen.'

The destiny of a child is known to depend to some extent on genetic predisposition. Perhaps it is this predisposition that makes a child 'choose' to be born when a particular planet has just risen or culminated. In other words, the unborn child tends to initiate its own birth process in response to a particular planetary configuration. Which planet acts as a trigger will depend on the genetic characteristics of the child, and these same genetic characteristics can also play a part in determining later character and career success.

However, this solution is by no means as straightforward as it might appear. If the planet sends some kind of signal that initiates the birth process, there will obviously be a lag between the signal and the resulting birth that is equal to the duration of labour. That duration varies considerably, from a single hour to many hours: first births average 9 hours, second births 5 hours, and night labours average 25 per cent less than day labours. This compares with the average time between rise and culmination of about six hours. In other words, even if the births of all future sports champions began the moment that Mars was in one of certain specified positions, the resulting spread in the durations of labour should be enough to degrade the effect virtually beyond detection. This objection would be lessened if the planetary signal came after the onset of labour and closer to birth, but in that case the signal would be unnecessary!

On the other hand, if the planetary signal coincides with the birth moment, what initiates the birth process? And of course there remains the problem of what the signal is. Gravity or magnetism seem unlikely since the sun has no effect. Direct electromagnetic radiation seems unlikely because it would already have been detected; in any case either terrestrial walls would block it or terrestrial sources would drown it. Furthermore, whatever the signal may be, how can the various planets have such qualitatively and quantitatively different effects? Extra-sensory or psi effects are unlikely, due to the known absence of planetary inhabitants! If it is argued that some extra-sensory power of the unborn child senses the planet's position directly, this involves the further problem of explaining why they would choose one planet rather than another, and indeed why they would want to do this anyway. After all, on evolutionary grounds it is very hard to see what advantage one birth time would have over another.

Gauquelin's interpretation, therefore, involves us in real difficulties, but it is consistent with his results. Further evidence is provided by the fact that the correspondence between child and parent is apparent for both mother and father, their relative contribution being roughly equal. A child tends to be born under a particular planet if one of the parents, either mother or father, was also born at that time. The finding that the father has such a role can only mean that it is the child, and not the mother who initiates the birth process. Moreover, Gauquelin found that if both parents were born when a given planet was in a critical position, then the chances of their child being born 'under' this planet were doubled. This is in accord with the laws of genetics.

In yet another analysis, Gauquelin looked at the effect of magnetically disturbed days. The figure shows that children were more likely to be born 'under' the same planet as their parents if the magnetic field of the earth was disturbed on that day. It is not known how magnetic storms or the associated sunspots could affect the issue, unless it is that when the planets are strongly affecting a birth they are also strongly affecting the sun.

According to the French mathematician Laplace, 'the weight

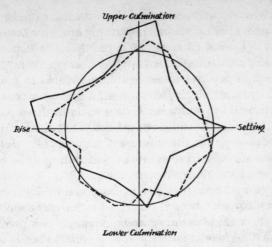

A child born of a parent who was born when the planet had just passed the horizon or the meridian is twice as likely to be born under a similar planetary configuration if he is born on a magnetically disturbed day (unbroken line) than if he is born on a quiet day (dotted line). The results from the five planets have been combined. (Based on Gauquelin, 1978.)

of the proofs must be suited to the oddness of facts.' Prompted by this principle, the Gauquelins recognized that it was necessary to replicate their results on heredity. This they did with two new samples each involving over 15,000 couples and their children. (Note that, unlike most replication attempts, the sample size was increased rather than decreased.) Again it was demonstrated that the effect is independent of the sex of the parent; that its intensity increases if both parents have the same planetary heredity; that the effect vanishes if the delivery of the child is induced; and that the effect is increased if the geomagnetic activity is disturbed.

Gauquelin points out some of the implications of his findings. For example, the planets may influence the timing of a birth and so may help to indicate the type of personality that the baby is born with, but they do not otherwise influence its destiny. This of course goes against the view of astrologers that the planetary positions at a child's birth correlate with its fortunes from that time on. To an astrologer, therefore, it does not matter whether a birth is natural or induced: if a person is destined to be born at a certain time then that destiny will be

195

fulfilled, by whatever means, and the birth chart will be valid.

Gauquelin's findings do not necessarily prove the astrologers wrong on this point. Although an induced birth will mean that Gauquelin's indicators will not apply, it does not follow that the child's personality and future will be unrelated to the chart prepared by an astrologer, who will use a number of factors not yet investigated by Gauquelin. If these other factors work, they may not be affected by induction of birth. The point is naturally very important for the whole future of astrology at a time when most births are induced so as to take place during 'office hours'; but only empirical research can settle it.

Gauquelin admits that his findings are of little use for predicting anyone's future. Since, with the exception of the heredity effect, the planetary correlations apply only to eminent people we need to wait until someone is eminent before we can know whether they apply to him. By that time it is a little late to be predicting his career.

Evaluations and replications

From an early stage, Gauquelin sent his results to other scientists for evaluation. Few were prepared to comment, and only now are researchers beginning to conduct their own studies. In Belgium, however, there is a team of thirty astronomers, demographers, statisticians, and other scientists known as the Committee for the Scientific Investigation of Alleged Paranormal Phenomena (the Committee Para for short). Their express purpose is to examine evidence that is claimed to support the existence of paranormal phenomena. Their motto is 'Nothing rejected a priori. Nothing affirmed without proof.' In practice, they have usually been able to demolish rather than verify the claims they have investigated.

After fifteen years' perusal, having found no serious errors in Gauquelin's methods and calculations, they decided to supervise a replication, choosing famous sportsmen for this purpose. Earlier, as we have seen, Gauquelin had found that relative to both a control group of ordinary sportsmen and theoretical expectation, Mars tended to be in one of the critical zones at the birth of 1,553 sports champions. This study was repeated for a new group of 535 sports champions from France and Belgium. The same result as before was obtained, as shown in the figure. In the original study, 21·4 per cent of the champions were born in one of the two critical sectors, while in the replication the proportion was 22·2 per cent. (Chance expectation in both cases is 16·7 per cent.) The odds against this result occurring by chance were now several millions to one.

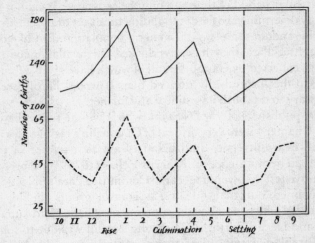

The two curves show the frequency of births of sports champions at different positions of Mars. The upper curve is Gauquelin's sample of 1,553; the lower curve is the independent sample of 535 studied by the Committee Para. (Based on Gauquelin, 1978.)

In spite of this apparently very successful replication, the Committee Para was not convinced. In a short statement published in 1976, they suggested that the results could be due to an artefact, saying: 'The Committee Para cannot accept the conclusions of the research of M. Gauquelin based on hypotheses in which the committee has found inexactitudes.'

Their doubts concerned the theoretically expected value of 16·7 per cent. Only if birth frequency was stable over the course of every 24 hours, and only if the frequency of births was stable over the period under investigation which ranged from 1872 to 1945, would this theoretical value always be true. But this may be seen as a very weak objection since any departure from such 'ideal' conditions would make very little difference. Moreover, in advancing their objection they overlooked the fact that control group data for 717 ordinary sportsmen and for various other groups were available; this information has each time provided results very close to the theoretically expected value of 16·7 per cent.

Various other critics have noted that the actual distribution of births when a planet is in one of the two critical positions over a particular period of time can only be estimated; it cannot be exactly determined without tabulating the exact time of birth of a truly random sample of the general population. But like the Committee Para they have overlooked the available control groups collected by Gauquelin, all of which have given a figure close to the theoretically derived one. It would hardly seem necessary to establish its validity any further.

The publishers of *The Humanist*, who it will be remembered from Chapter 1 were very critical of Gauquelin's claims, agreed to call in a university statistician to act as a referee in the debate. The man chosen, Marvin Zelen (1976), proposed a definitive test that would meet the Committee Para's objection. He pointed out that, ideally, a control group should be assembled which matched the sportsmen as to the approximate date and place of birth. If Gauquelin's result was due to some demographic artefact, then such a control group should also display the Mars effect. In response to *The Humanist*'s offer to publish the results of such a test, no matter what the outcome (previously they had only published criticisms of astrology), the Gauquelins went back to their birth data and constructed charts for 16,756 people born around the same date and in the same areas as 303 of the champions (matching control data were not readily available for the others). Upon analysing this newly assembled data it was found that the Mars effect was apparent for the sub-group of 303 champions with 66 of them (22 per cent) being born in the critical zones. It was not apparent for the control group. Even for 474 controls who had been matched with the 66 champions born under Mars, only 82 had also been born under Mars (again close to the chance expectation of 16·7 per cent). This result effectively answers the Committee's objection about theoretical expectancies.

In spite of this apparent confirmation, *The Humanist*, like the

Committee Para, decided to conduct yet another study. They wanted to see if the Mars effect could be replicated with US sports champions. The study, which was conducted by the US Committee for the Scientific Investigation of Claims of the Paranormal, ran into difficulties when most states refused to provide the required information on account of the 1974 US Privacy Act. It had been intended to obtain a sample of 605 US champions, but it was possible to obtain birth times for only 128. For what it is worth, 20·3 per cent of this group displayed the Mars effect. Although just significant, this sample was considered too small, so it was enlarged by adding more cases. Unfortunately these extra cases included many sportsmen who were well below international class. For the total group (now 408) there was no significant Mars effect and the Committee reached a negative conclusion.

The Gauquelins have pointed out that this test of their work was unfair because the required standards of sporting achievement were lowered too much in order to increase the sample size (Gauquelin and Gauquelin, 1979). For the extra 280 cases, the Mars effect applied to only 11 per cent, which is significantly below chance level. (Why this group of ordinary sportsmen should have yielded such a small number of births under Mars is a mystery. As already discussed, it is entirely counter to expectation in terms of the link between Mars and Personality.)

The Gauquelins have also pointed out that no real attempt was made to select natural births; it will be remembered that only in such cases is there a planetary effect. Since it is only in the last quarter century that inducement of birth has become a routine practice, the researchers could have avoided this problem by selecting earlier births. Consistent with this it was noted in the first stage of the Committee's research, that the Mars effect was stronger for pre-1930 births (27 per cent) than it was for the whole group (20·3 per cent).

By using objective criteria of success, such as being an Olympic champion, the Gauquelins divided the total sample into highly successful and less successful sportsmen, and found once again that the Mars effect was limited to the highly successful. It was significantly higher for 88 outstanding sportsmen than it was for the remaining 320, who while good had never quite reached the top. Moreover, for 20 Olympic champions in the sample, the Mars effect was 35 per cent.

Being aware of the difficulties in obtaining a suitable sample of outstanding sportsmen in the USA, the Gauquelins decided to conduct yet another replication attempt of their own. They located the birth times of 432 new international sportsmen in Europe, together with a control group of 423 new sportsmen below international level. The renowned group yielded a proportion of 24·5 per cent born with Mars in one of the two critical zones, and the control group a proportion of 16 per cent. This result for the renowned group was significant beyond the 1 per cent level.

In general it has to be said that, while the Gauquelins' own replications have been well devised and carried out, the same cannot be said for independent replications by others. The main fault lies in the sizes of the samples. If we are replicating, say, a study that found 21 per cent of sports champions born when Mars was in one of the critical positions, then we can calculate the *minimum* sample size needed to give a significant result. In this example, at least 300 people would be needed to give a result significant at the 1 per cent level, and of course if we want a level of significance comparable with that obtained by the Gauquelins, we would need a sample of similar size to theirs. What sample sizes have in fact been used in the replication attempts? In the studies we have managed to locate they have mostly been below 100! It is unfair to judge Gauquelin's findings on the basis of such obviously inadequate studies, though for what it is worth the results have tended to be consistent with the original studies: a slight excess of sports champions, extraverts, etc. has been found with the predicted planet in one of the critical positions.

Gauquelin's critics

Before coming to our general evaluation of the work reported by the Gauquelins, we wish to say a few words about their critics, particularly those with a scientific background. We have found that far from showing the impartiality popularly associated with science, critics have gone out of their way to demonstrate bias, prejudice and hostility. Much of the conduct of the critics has been less than ethical. Thus, to take but one example, the Belgian Committee Para, which set out to disprove Gauquelin's findings, decided against publishing its full report when its findings in fact supported them. This is a very unusual thing to do in science. It means that our knowledge of the Committee's findings derives mainly from Gauquelin's quotations and discussions of them; and while we have little doubt that these are accurate (because otherwise the Committee would certainly have issued a disclaimer) it would still have been preferable to have the Committee's own report available for consultation.

Again, the American Committee, as we have stated before, raised certain statistical objections and agreed with the Gauquelins that if these could be met then their findings would have to be accepted. The Gauquelins collected a large body of data which fulfilled the conditions laid down, with results entirely supporting their case. Nevertheless, the Committee refused to agree that the Gauquelins had now proved their case! This again is an unusual kind of procedure in science, and one which does not do credit to the Committee. A full account of what went on 'behind the scenes' in this intriguing but unfortunate episode has been provided by Rawlins (1981) and by Curry (1982). If these accounts are true the Committee has a lot to answer for.

Other critics like Culver and Ianna (1979) tend to play down the Gauquelins' results by giving so little space to a description of their work that the innocent reader would be quite unable to see the immense labour that has gone into it and the resounding success of much of it, including the numerous replications. Undue weight is given to small and badly executed replications that fail to reach the required level of significance, usually because of the inclusion of less eminent groups which in any fair test ought to have been excluded. This is, however, not generally explained by the critics.

When statistical criticisms are mentioned, this is often done in a way that does not enable the reader to understand what the issue is, or to evaluate the criticism. Thus Culver and Ianna have this to say:

Basically, the Gauquelins' analysis has been criticised on a number of counts, the bulk of which centre on the counting scheme and the computation of the number of degrees of freedom in the data. The claim is made that if these factors are properly introduced, the Gauquelins' odds against the random distribution drop considerably from the value of roughly 10^{-6} quoted in their early work on the subject.

Note that in this rather vague statement Culver and Ianna do not even say that they agree with these criticisms; they simply quote them as claims but do not attempt to evaluate their accuracy. Nor do they mention that when the conditions laid down by a noted statistician to set aside all doubts about the theoretical expectation were in fact followed by the Gauquelins, the results still held up. This is not proper scientific criticism, but merely an attempt to mislead readers into thinking that errors were committed when in fact there were no errors.

We have looked carefully at the arguments concerning statistical evaluation and experimental design, and we have inspected with great interest the debates between the Gauquelins and their critics on various points. We have come to the definite conclusion that the critics have often behaved in an irrational and scientifically unusual manner, violating principles they themselves have laid down, failing to adhere to their own rules, failing to consult the Gauquelins on details of tests to be carried out, or failing to inform them on vital points of the results. We have not found any similar misdemeanour on the part of the Gauquelins, who seem to have behaved throughout in a calm, rational and scientifically acceptable manner, meeting criticism by appropriate re-analysis of the data, by the collection of new data, however laborious the process might have been, and by rational argument. We do not feel that the 'scientific' community emerges with any great credit from these encounters.

Alternative explanations

Even if the Gauquelins' work stands up well to further replication, we also need to ask whether there may not be some

interpretation other than planetary influences that would account for the facts. Is it, for instance, conceivable that famous athletes or soldiers had been prompted to take up such a career because they had discovered that Mars, the god of war, was in a prominent position at the time of their birth? This 'prior knowledge' argument was discussed in Chapter 4. Throughout the centuries, Mars has been the planet of energy, aggression and combat, and it is this planet rather than any other that tends to be in a particular position in the birth charts of outstanding sportsmen, in whom these qualities play an obvious part. A similar parallel can be drawn for most of the other findings; for example, it is Saturn which is traditionally associated with the saturnine or reflective temperament that is prominent in the charts of scientists. The extent to which tradition accords with Gauquelin's findings, while consistent with astrological teachings, is also consistent with a 'normal' explanation in terms of knowledge of astrology influencing a person's development and choice of career or life style. Remember that, as we noted before, it would need only a small proportion of such cases to yield a statistically significant result.

However, while this interpretation explained the 'Mayo effect', it does not appear to fit the present case. In the first place, not all the results are consistent with traditional astrology. In particular, Venus and Mercury do not figure in the charts of musicians and artists as would have been predicted by most astrologers; and the sun has no effect at all, which is in complete conflict with traditional claims for its over-riding importance. Still, on balance the associations with astrology seem rather impressive, and individual variation among astrologers, plus research error, might be enough to explain the few instances of lack of agreement, if it were not for one important way in which the results depart from traditional astrology.

Gauquelin's two critical positions are just *past* the rising point and just *past* the midheaven, and in traditional astrology these two zones in the sky coincide approximately with the cadent or weak houses (they are the twelfth and ninth houses respectively). Presumably, if some of the famous sportsmen born 'under' Mars had consulted an astrologer in their youth

203

they would not have been told that they had a 'Martian' temperament or that they were suited to a 'Martian' type of career. To have been told this they would have had to be born an hour or so earlier, when Mars would have fallen in the preceding house, since in traditional astrology, it is the first house, just *before* the ascendant, that is concerned with personality and character, and the tenth house, just *before* the midheaven, that is concerned with profession, vocation, awards and honours. The 'prior knowledge' explanation would thus apply only to people born with planets in these houses, and Gauquelin's results do not show an excess in either of them.

It is of course interesting to note that, according to traditional astrology, Gauquelin's results are just one house out of phase in each case. This may be just coincidence, or it may mean that the 'significant' time of birth should instead refer to a stage two hours or so earlier in the birth process, though it cannot be the start of birth, since this generally begins five to ten hours earlier. The displacement cannot be put down to inaccuracy in recording birth-times unless it can be shown that such errors are systematically an hour or so out. The Gauquelins checked this and found no evidence of a systematic error.

One other point works against any explanation in terms of 'prior knowledge', and that is Gauquelin's finding on 'planetary heredity'. For this to be caused by prior knowledge both mother and father would have to be deliberately trying to ensure that their children were born under the same planets as themselves. Moreover, they would only do this if they had been born when a planet was in one of Gauquelin's two critical sectors. This type of explanation is unlikely enough to dismiss; but it does mean that the finding on heredity assumes a new importance. Because of its obvious independence from prior knowledge it is the most convincing of Gauquelin's results. Accordingly, it is the one result that the Committee Para and the American Committee should have attempted to replicate. For the time being we shall have to be content with the replications that the Gauquelins carried out themselves.

Various critics have put forward other interpretations of Gauquelin's results. Since none of them appear to stand up to scientific scrutiny, they may be briefly dealt with. For example,

Jerome (1977) states that 'Gauquelin has confused cause and effect . . . people with differing temperaments just happen to be born at differing times of the day.' He gives as an example soldiers who might be born at 'off' times of the day which might just happen to correspond with Jupiter being in one of the two critical zones of the sky. Rather than merely stating such an objection as if it had an element of truth, Jerome should have checked it against astronomical and birth information, or at least have studied Gauquelin's research documents which provide the necessary information complete with references which would enable anyone to check it. Had he done so, he would have found that military men are born throughout the day with the same frequency as other people. Even if their births did tend to cluster at some particular time, the effect could only arise if Jupiter spent an excessive length of time in the two critical positions at that time, and that could only have happened if the period of the study had been restricted to a few weeks or even days. In fact it extended over several decades.

Another explanation frequently put forward concerns the use of probability testing. The most extreme statement of this view was made in the *New Scientist* by David Cohen who, after considering Gauquelin's work, concluded that his results 'could reflect the fact that probability theory (at least as used in the life sciences) makes rather primitive assumptions about how the world should work. Gauquelin may have learned not so much anything about the planets as something important about probability.' All that this rather vague statement could mean is that apparently significant results have been obtained only because of the very large number of factors that exist in astrology, so that 'significant' results can and do arise every so often by chance alone. But the likelihood of this can be calculated, and the effect can be obviated by replication since of course such an explanation becomes increasingly unlikely each time a similar result is obtained. In this case the replications show that Cohen's objection is invalid.

Objections

None of the alternative explanations that have been offered, then, seem to us convincing. There are, nevertheless, some subtantial objections to Gauquelin's theories that need to be stated.

Potentially the most serious of them concerns the tendency for significant results to apply only to the elite in a given profession. Gauquelin has shown that the connection is really with personality and not with occupation, so the planetary effect should apply to the whole of a profession that is characterised by a particular personality, not just to its elite.

To take one example, sportsmen are characterised by an extravert personality, regardless of their level of success (Eysenck and others, 1982). In our own research, athletes and physical education students have obtained higher extraversion scores from questionnaires than most other occupational groups tested. Moreover, their level of extraversion appears to be unrelated to success, with the average athlete tending to be just as extraverted as the star. On the basis of research so far, it appears that extraverts are attracted to sport but that this personality trait is not related to success – indeed, the unsuccessful athlete may need a high level of extraversion if he is to continue. If this finding is also true of the athletes in Gauquelin's sample (and due to differences in conditions and customs it may not be – most of them were born quite a time ago between 1860 and 1930) the non-elite should tend to display at least as strong a planetary effect as the elite. Why then does the Mars effect apply only to sportsmen at the very top?

It is not good enough to postulate that the Mars effect is related to a very specific aspect of personality, since this would be counter to the finding that Mars is related to extraversion (which is a major dimension of personality shared by everybody). Rather we must just note that a marked discrepancy is apparent in the results, and that further research is needed on the characteristics of sportsmen who show the Mars effect and those who do not. The same argument probably applies to soldiers, actors, scientists, and indeed all Gauquelin's groups. In other words the question is what is so special about eminence? The fact that eminence is also a potent factor in season of birth effects (Chapter 6) may provide a clue to the answer.

A second objection comes from a fact that has often been pointed out, namely that if a 'true' correlation has been discovered by research, then an even better correlation should be produced by further research as more information is uncovered. Has this happened in the case of Gauquelin's results? The original finding that a planetary effect applies to just over 20 per cent of cases, instead of the 16·7 per cent expected by chance, has not been significantly improved in the replication attempts. The effect has in fact remained at much the same level. But clearer results have been obtained by changing from an analysis of occupation to one of personality, and a further improvement should also be possible if cases of induced birth were to be left out of the analysis. This is based on the family studies finding that the planetary effect disappears altogether with induced births. This extension of the research has not been carried out, and it is difficult anyway to discover whether a birth was induced or not. There is no central source of information and, short of searching through confidential hospital records, all that can be done is to ask the parents and hope that they knew in the first place and have remembered correctly.

Against these objections is the fact that Gauquelin did encounter failures which were as inexplicable as his successes, and which may serve to reassure us that the statistical methods he adopted for analysis, and the experimental design, are capable of generating null results as well as positive ones!

For example we have already mentioned his failure to demonstrate sign effects. Another arose from the attempts of the Gauquelins to analyse the births of more than 6,000 mental patients diagnosed as functional psychotics. Gauquelin (1980) summarised the results of this study as follows:

The results were never positive; there was no correlation between births under any one planet and mental illness in general or any particular kind of mental illness. Saturn does not rule schizophrenia, and where one might have expected Jupiter to be present at the birth of paranoid patients – whose illusions are often very grand indeed – our results again revealed nothing positive. As far as we know, no planetary temperament seems connected with mental illness.

207

Thus, even with such a clearly marked out group as functional psychotics, there is no connection with planetary influences. The fact that the method can result in failure is a reassuring indication that the successes are not merely statistical artefacts.

Conclusion

In spite of the very convincing case that Gauquelin has made for a planetary effect, most orthodox scientists remain sceptical. The astronomer Abell (1979) who is one of the few to have familiarised himself with the research, points out that 'Gauquelin's findings represent an anomalous result that remains unconfirmed to the degree necessary to be accepted as scientific fact.' If the results were in accord with some already established theory, then there would be no problem. The case is already stronger than that for almost any area of research in psychology. It is only because of the nature of the findings, which seem to invoke planetary influences unrecognized by science, that a higher level of proof is called for.

Regardless of the scepticism expressed over Gauquelin's findings, most critics recognize the potential importance of the work. Such a sentiment is well expressed by Abell (1979) who wrote: 'I strongly suspect that in the end Gauquelin's results will turn out to be spurious. But if by any (to me) miraculous chance they should be even partly correct, it would be a tremendous milestone in establishing cosmic influence on man.' British astrologer, John Addey has compared Gauquelin's life-long endeavour with that of Darwin. Like Darwin's monumental collection of data, Gauquelin's too may lead to a scientific revolution.

For ourselves, faced by Gauquelin's research at its present stage of development, we feel obliged to admit that there is something here that requires explanation. However much it may go against the grain, other scientists who take the trouble to examine the evidence may eventually be forced to a similar conclusion. The findings are inexplicable but they are also factual, and as such can no longer be ignored; they cannot just be wished away because they are unpalatable or not in accord with the laws of present-day science.

208

Because Gauquelin has, all along, published full details of his research in a series of documents, it is possible to evaluate independently the design and methods used in the research. This we have done, and we have been unable to find anything seriously wrong. On the contrary we have been impressed by the meticulous care with which the data have been set out and analysed. As we see it, the only way in which these results will be invalidated will be by failure to replicate. Because of the number of successful replications already conducted, this appears to be a very remote possibility. Rather the task is to explain how the planets could possibly be related to character, and perhaps to extend the area of study to hitherto unexplored factors such as aspects.

The evidence summarised in this chapter represents what must be the most convincing case that can be made for the basic astrological premise, that there is a connection between the affairs of man and the position of the planets at the time of birth. In the words of Mather (1979): 'It is probably not putting it too strongly to say that everything hangs on it.' If Gauquelin's results are ever shown to be spurious then, relatively speaking, the positive evidence that remains for astrology is weak. But while this possibility must be granted, it does not seem to us that it is at all likely that what has been established on so many cases, and replicated so many times, will be found to be due to chance or error. Perhaps the time has come to state quite unequivocally that a new science is in process of being born. Amid all the dross, there does seem to have been a nugget of gold.

11 Verdict and Prospect

Do not judge, and you will never be mistaken.
Jean-Jacques Rousseau

We have reviewed a large body of evidence in this book, and we have additionally read an even larger amount of material in the form of books, articles, letters, unpublished manuscripts and submissions – our library shelves are spilling over into boxes which threaten to engulf the offices in which we work, and yet there seems to be no end to the flood of printed and written material on our topic. Can we come to any sort of final evaluation which might be accepted by readers as coming near the truth? In this final chapter we shall try to indicate how we interpret the evidence, and why we think that our labours may have been worth while. We do not flatter ourselves that we shall move those readers who start out with strong preconceived ideas; the Law of Certainty which we invoked at the beginning makes this unlikely. But the majority of readers may be more likely to pay attention to the evidence, and it is to them that we address ourselves.

We started out by making a distinction between traditional astrology as taught to aspiring students and incorporated in numerous textbooks, and cosmobiology, as we like to call it, which concerns the factual study of relations between planetary movements and other cosmic forces, and events on this earth. We could perhaps have added a third category, popular or newspaper astrology, which does not concern itself with individual interpretation or prediction, and which does little but generalise about the likely fate of all those born under one or other of the sun signs. We have not done so because this sort of thing is despised by serious astrologers. Those who churn it out for a credulous public usually know perfectly well that what they are doing has no meaning and no relation to real astrology. Needless to say, they have made no effort to provide any kind of evidence for the truth of what they write, and the studies which have been made by others give it no support whatsoever.

210

Popular astrology is frankly an exercise in money-making, it has no interest or value, and it is disowned precisely by those who place value in the possible contributions to society which traditional astrology may be able to make. Insofar as the anti-astrology manifesto we quoted in the first chapter is directed against this variety, we fully agree with it; popular astrology is nonsense, and the newspapers and magazines which print it should be thoroughly ashamed.

It may be true that it does no great harm. The occasional neurotic may become addicted to these columns, even dependent on them, but this is not likely to occur on any large scale, and if this source of superstition were to be withdrawn, no doubt some other would take its place. People often seem to have an insatiable appetite for being cheated. On the other hand what is published is published under false pretences. It is not labelled as entertainment only, and as we have shown, many people do believe that these columns are something more than fun.

Traditional astrology

When we turn to traditional astrology, we find a very different picture from the obvious charlatanism of the popular columns. In general, serious astrologers are genuine and sincere, are convinced of the truth and value of their efforts, and are intent on improving and perfecting what they conceive of as a valid technique. Does the evidence that we have surveyed in this book support their belief that 'astrology works'? To answer this question we have to rephrase it more precisely, because everything depends on what we mean by 'astrology' and 'works'.

If the question is 'Does astrology provide an individual with apparently meaningful insight into his existence?' the answer may be yes. The key word is 'apparently'. What astrology does in effect is to provide a dazzling symbolic superstructure that could hardly be better suited to provide 'meaning', even though the descriptions and predictions may be unrelated to the objective world. In this respect it is no worse than some psychological techniques such as inkblots, which are widely

211

used although no one pretends that inkblots contain real meaning. In fact astrology may be superior because its concepts have undeniable beauty and appeal, and because taken one at a time they are attractively simple. Thus unlike ids and superegos, the aggressive energy of Mars and the loving harmony of Venus are open to understanding by all. Moreover, in combination they can approach every complexity of human experience; such all-embracing application is certainly beyond any existing psychological technique, and indeed may deserve to be ranked as a religion! In itself this ability to provide 'meaning' is not necessarily without merit, and in fact a small but increasing number of therapists are finding that astrological concepts can provide a useful framework for exploring and describing persons and situations in understandable and very human terms. Such benefits would of course apply whether astrology was objectively true or not.

If the question is 'Are astrological assertions true?' the answer is yes and no, but mostly no. We have seen that the assertions about signs have no basis in fact, and that those about houses seem equally invalid. On the other hand some planetary attributes have been confirmed by the work of the Gauquelins, leading to the finding that their effect varies according to the position of the planets with respect to the horizon. (This is the concept of angularity, which has nothing necessarily to do with houses.) No verdict is possible for aspects and certain other factors such as midpoints because they have yet to be properly investigated. To the extent that many of the more scientific astrologers consider aspects to be the most important single factors in a birth chart, this leaves a major unknown in our assessment of astrology.

If the question is 'Do descriptions based on the whole birth chart accurately describe the individual?' no reliable answer is possible because definitive tests have yet to be made. We have shown that matching tests such as the experiments of Vernon Clark appear to support astrology but have weaknesses which rule them out as decisive evidence. On the other hand they have been addressed not to personality, which is the one area that astrology pre-eminently claims to describe, but to things like cerebral palsy and suicide, which few astrologers would have

212

confidence of finding in a birth chart.

Overall, then, in response to the question 'Does astrology work?', we would agree with the summing up of Dean and others (1977), that 'the picture emerging suggests that astrology works, but seldom in the way or to the extent that it is said to work.' In terms of the question posed by the title of this book, we therefore conclude that astrology is largely (but not entirely) superstition. However, because of the important areas which remain to be investigated, this conclusion may need future qualification. We should not be dogmatic.

Science and astrology

In this book we have been critical of scientists and their refusal to look seriously at the experimental work done by astrologers; yet we can quite see why this should be so. Science follows certain rules of procedure which have become sanctified over the centuries because they have been found to work. Most astrologers fail to follow these rules, and commit all sorts of solecisms which infuriate the orthodox. They make claims which lack substance, or at least substantiation; and the very facts which many of them adduce as being in their favour, such as the claim that astrology has a long ancestry – and most astrologers do hark back to the teachings of those early days – count against them in scientific circles. If astrology is a science, then we would expect it to have outgrown the primitive rules and injunctions laid down some two thousand years ago. Why has there been so little progress? Why are we no nearer any proper proof of astrological assertions now than we were then?

With whatever regret, we have to admit that these criticisms carry weight. In this book we have tried to examine the best research done by supporters of astrology and all too often we have been forced to admit that it was amateurish in its conception, faulty in its execution and less than rigorous in its statistical analysis of the data. Even the most often quoted studies have weaknesses which rule them out as decisive evidence.

Perhaps we should not be too surprised. Science is a

demanding discipline which requires training and experience. There are many rules of experimentation and statistical analysis which may seem pedantic to an outsider but are in reality vital for success. We have given examples in this book of seemingly trivial technical points that completely switched the results of an experiment.

The major failure to which we have returned time after time is the lack of replication. It is not enough for a second researcher to set off on a similar trail of his own. If he is to validate the original research he must replicate it *in the same form*. Only if he then reaches the same results does his work serve as confirmation. Of course it is more exciting to initiate new ideas than to check someone else's, and of course a believer does not feel much pleasure at the idea of disproving a result that supports his belief. But that it the only way in which any true science can advance. A hypothesis must survive repeated attempts to break it down. Only then can we place reliance on it.

Replication becomes particularly important if the outcome of an experiment is unexpected and has implications that would revolutionise its field of study. Quite reasonably, other scientists will be unwilling to accept that theories built up over many years of painstaking and rigorous research should be thrown out of the window because one experiment disagrees with them. They will demand really convincing evidence, and a scrupulous researcher will set out to give it to them.

A situation of this kind arose with the classic Michelson and Morley experiments. In 1887, these physicists attempted to measure the absolute speed of the earth in space through the hypothetical ether by comparing the speed of light in different directions. To their complete surprise the speed seemed to be the same in all directions – as if the earth was not moving at all! They did not accept their own results; instead they repeated the experiment but with better apparatus. The results were the same as before. It was not until they had performed many subsequent replications that their finding was accepted as fact. Note that they did not reject their first result as obviously wrong, nor did they accept it uncritically. A scientist does not have to believe a result to be true or false, but can defer judgement until he is in a position to offer an informed opinion. The Michelson and Morley finding could not be explained in terms of existing theories; it was incompatible with the theories of Galileo and Newton. A new theory was required to deal with the results, and this was later provided in Einstein's relativity theory.

There can be no doubt that, if the tenets of traditional astrology were proved to be true, it would revolutionise our study of the physical world. This would be so even if the deviation from the expected run of events was quite small. If the sun signs really did correlate with personal destiny, for example, it would be enough to show that this influence occurred at all, however slight in comparison with other factors, and we would be forced to adjust our existing ideas quite radically.

This of course has been the fascination of looking at many of the studies we have described. For it has to be admitted that very few of them, even if they were convincingly replicated time after time, would offer us anything much in the way of practical guidance. If a man born under a particular planetary configuration has a very slight extra chance of marrying unhappily – say one per cent above the normal expectation – how much help are you really giving him by telling him so? It would be sensible for him to act on this knowledge – for instance by staying unmarried – only if the influence were many times greater. In none of the more convincing studies we have surveyed is there any indication that we are dealing with an effect that is decisive enough to be of practical importance. It would be roughly true to say that, the more persuasive the experiment, the more it tends to deal with tiny deviations from chance expectations that could certainly have revolutionary implications for science, but equally certainly would give no help to anyone in his personal decisions.

The roots of belief

All these criticisms, then, can be levelled against traditional astrology, as well as the damning fact that its practitioners are divided against each other. There is not one astrology but several – European, Indian, Chinese – and different astrologers would therefore make different predictions from the same facts. In contrast, the laws of physics and astronomy are the same all over the world, and one would expect the same to be true of astrology if it did indeed have any factual basis. Science is international in its theories and findings, and astrology's failure to arrive at a set of universally agreed rules must speak heavily against it. Why, then, do so many people – both astrologers and their clients – believe in astrology and regard it as an important source of understanding?

We have mentioned its quasi-religious function in providing a 'meaning' to life. Less exaltedly, let us remember an experiment carried out many years ago by B.F. Skinner. A number of hungry pigeons were allowed a free run in a laboratory in which, every few minutes at regular intervals, some grains of corn were automatically dispensed by a machine. The next morning it was observed that the pigeons showed very strange behaviour; some ran around with their heads held high up in the air, others trailed one wing on the floor while holding up the other, and others made different obsessional movements of one kind or another. What happened was this. The hungry pigeon, in running around the laboratory, makes all sorts of movements; when, quite by accident, some grain is thrown on the floor while it is making one particular movement, it gets the message that because the corn was thrown *after* it made a certain movement, therefore it was thrown *because* it made that movement! The bird is now more likely to make the movement again, in the hope of encouraging more manna from heaven. By pure chance, on each occasion, food will again be thrown on the floor, and the bird will be confirmed in its (entirely erroneous) hypothesis. Thus the probability of its making the movement will increase, until by the morning it will be running around making it all the time! In this fashion are superstitions born.

In the same way, an astrologer or his client will remember the occasions when the grain of corn, in the shape of a prophecy fulfilled, came their way. They will forget the occasions it did not. No one has to consciously deceive himself or anyone else: we have already noted that serious astrologers are on the whole honourable, intelligent and discerning. It is the nature of the subject that makes belief so easy and, for many people, disbelief so hard.

Aside from its capacity to offer a 'meaning' to life, and the reluctance this produces to be sceptical about it, there are difficulties in the very nature of the material involved, human behaviour. This presents many problems for the experimentalist, as demonstrated in the present uncertain state of psychology – in William James' words a hope of a science, rather than a developed science as yet. It is usually possible to be fairly certain about statements regarding physical substances, but it is much less easy to arrive at certainty regarding psychological states. If we say, as an astrologer might, 'This person has a good sense of humour,' precisely what do we mean? That he laughs frequently; or that he laughs at the jokes we make; or that he makes witty remarks; or that he doesn't take himself too seriously; or what? The astrologer who says that his client has a good sense of humour can hardly go wrong; everybody has (or thinks he has) a good sense of humour in one of the many senses of that phrase, and will interpret the astrologer's statement in that sense. This acceptance by the client will, in turn, convince the astrologer of the accuracy of his statement and of his 'science', and his beliefs will once more be reinforced.

Then there is the fact that astrology can be a self-fulfilling prophecy. We explored this problem in connection with the hypothesis that introverts are born under the even-numbered signs of the zodiac, extraverts under the odd-numbered ones. Once this sort of prophecy is known widely enough, many people will be influenced by it in making self-judgments, and when the self-judgments form the criterion of the astrologer's art, then apparently positive results will be produced, though they will have no value as evidence. This ever-present danger has not on the whole been guarded against in the experiments we have come across, nor in the views of astrologers about their ability to diagnose personality from astrology. If it plays as important a part as we believe the evidence demonstrates, it would be another weighty factor in making astrologers and their clients believe in the value of astrology.

If astrologers are to persuade us that there are better reasons

217

than these for believing in the truth of their doctrines – or even if they are to decide among themselves which of the contradictory schools of astrology is the true one – then those who genuinely believe that they are practising and teaching a valid set of principles must get down to the hard job of finding proper proofs for their hypotheses and theories, using the well-developed methods of the social sciences, particularly psychology. There is no real problem in mounting a series of decisive experiments in this field; the need is to make them sophisticated enough to take into account the many traps we have pointed out in the course of our discussion of previous experiments. We hope, therefore, that astrologers will take seriously the task of building up a science, and provide doubters with the proof that has so far escaped them of the validity of astrological assertions.

Is this likely to happen? On past performance it seems more likely that most astrologers will continue to eschew the laborious task of scientific enquiry, and to reject the very criteria of science as being out of place or irrelevant to their art. We have often heard complaints about interfering, hard-nosed scientists who really have no role to play in astrology; astrologers convinced of the great truth of their discipline feel only too often that no proof is needed beyond that given by their experience. Desirable as it would be for them to accept the burden of objective proof, we see little probability that they will. The most likely outcome is a continuation of present policies, with claims and counter-claims being bandied about in the absence of proper factual support.

Cosmobiology

If, in judging classical or traditional astrology, we have had to side with those scientists who find little good to say about it, the position is rather different when we turn to cosmobiology. Here we find that those astronomers and physicists who have shown any interest in the matter have overdone the cautious, critical attitude which quite properly characterizes 'hard' scientists, and have treated the Gauquelins, Frank Brown, and other prominent exponents rather badly, often criticizing them in terms of what they might have done rather than judging them on what they actually did. If astrologers of the traditional school are often non-factual in their claims and arguments, so have many scientists been in dealing with the claims of cosmobiology.

We have tried to demonstrate how this happens by reference to the Gauquelins' great contribution. Our conclusion with respect to their results has already been stated; we can find no valid major criticism of their conclusions, methods, or statistics. If there is any value in the scientific method as usually employed in studies of this kind, and if the laws of statistics apply here as they do elsewhere, then these discoveries must stand as clear indications that our conceptions of the universe we live in are not as final and complete as we might like to think, and that there are certain facts urgently in need of a good hypothesis to explain them.

One point may be important in this discussion, and needs to be clarified. We have spoken of traditional astrology and cosmobiology as if these were quite distinct entities, without overlap, but this is clearly not quite correct. It is just possible that early astrologers may have noted intuitively some of the regularities, cycles or phenomena associated with cosmobiological forces, and based their astrological rules on these observations. If this were so, and if there is any scientific validity in cosmobiological factors, then to that extent there might be some scientific truth in the pronouncements of astrologers. The curious relationships between Gauquelin's findings of planetary association with prominence in different occupations, and the astrological symbolism of the planets concerned, suggest such a link, and other possible associations could be mentioned.

It is only fair to add that, although the Gauquelins' work is often quoted in support of traditional astrology, they themselves do not agree. Michel Gauquelin has written: 'It is now quite certain that the signs in the sky which presided over our births have no power whatever to decide our fate, to affect our hereditary characteristics, or to play any part, however humble, in the totality of the effects, random or otherwise, which form the larger part of our lives and mould our impulses to actions.' And in another place he had this to say: 'Every effort made by astrologers to defend their basic postulate, that the movement of the stars can predict destiny, has failed . . . . Statistics have disposed of old arguments once and for all: the numbers speak without bias, and they leave no room for doubt. Whoever claims to predict the future by consulting the stars is fooling either himself or someone else.' The Gauquelins' work must be regarded as support for cosmobiology; they themselves regard it as quite irrelevant to traditional astrology. We believe that they carry this distinction a little too far, in view of the obvious symbolic relationship between astrology and their findings, and they have yet to investigate aspects adequately; but on the whole they are probably right in declining to see their work as supporting the bulk of traditional astrology.

Orthodox scientists have for the most part made little distinction between astrology and cosmobiology: their attitude to the latter, as to the former, has been hostile in the extreme. John Gribbin, who with Steven Plagemann wrote *The Jupiter Effect*, a book we have already referred to, mentions a telling episode. Plagemann, then working for NASA, was approached by a colleague working in the same building. 'You know,' he said, 'I'm really glad to see that stuff in print. I've been working on predicting solar flares for years, and I've got a file of evidence which shows a definite relationship with Jupiter-Saturn alignments. But I daren't put that in my report – it's more than my job is worth.' John Gribbin continues his account: 'Steve, of course, is now farming in Ireland, while his anonymous colleague still has a desk job in NASA.' This is the climate of the inquisition, not of factual, unbiased enquiry; many of the people in the scientific establishment would have fitted well into the panel which condemned Galileo! We have become aware of this climate of censorship and intolerance, both through reports from individuals directly affected and from remarks warning us that even criticizing astrology in detail, and showing familiarity with its pronouncements, would undermine our scientific standing and reputation. So much for the religion of the open mind.

The work of the Gauquelins, to go no further, stands up to a careful degree of scrutiny, and compares favourably with the best that has been done in psychology, psychiatry, sociology or any of the social sciences. But there are other discoveries, recounted in previous chapters, which are of great interest and possible importance, and which appear to have been investigated with considerable scientific integrity and competence. The only fault we have to find with them is simply that they have not been replicated; we have made replication the corner-stone of what is and what is not properly acceptable to science, and hence have to assign most of these studies to the category of 'not proven'. Nevertheless, the evidence for them looks much more secure than that for any of the traditional astrological beliefs.

There are, however, other criticisms or rather objections which orthodox scientists have to make of much of this work, and these cannot be rejected so easily. Science abhors the 'one-off' type of phenomenon, particularly one which cannot be fitted into its customary framework. Science proceeds by building up a coherent structure of theories, and naturally scientists prefer to get on with that job rather than let themselves become entangled with what at the time is impossible to explain. This has inevitably been the fate of cosmobiological discoveries, and in terms of their own preconceptions one can but sympathize with traditional scientists in their reluctance to be embroiled with these threatening new complications.

One-off phenomena have another drawback, apart from being far removed from orthodox theories; they do not seem to hang together in any meaningful manner. Cosmobiology is not a logically consistent body of knowledge. It is rather a string of 'one-off' phenomena, equally mysterious, equally lacking in proper physical explanation, and only linked together because of the (probably correct) belief that they are all caused or affected by planetary or other cosmic influences. This is a can of worms particularly designed to frighten off cautious scientists, and when to the claims of cosmobiologists is added the taint of 'astrology' the scientific reaction of disdainful withdrawal becomes intelligible. One may even begin to understand why sensible and apparently open-minded physicists and astronomers will go to any lengths to deny the claims of the

221

Gauquelins and of the many other researchers we have quoted as providing evidence for some sorts of cosmobiological phenomena.

But the fact that these reactions are psychologically understandable does not mean that they are scientifically excusable. Scientists are supposed to be open-minded, impartial, unbiased, dispassionate and objective; we know of course that this picture distorts reality to the point of caricature, but the values embodied in the ideal are still very real, and may serve to shame some scientists at least into taking a closer look at the evidence before condemning the whole enterprise. It may be that, were they to do that, they might find, as we have done, that a number of phenomena, apparently isolated and disjointed, begin to come together and suggest theories which, while at the moment obviously vague and nebulous, nevertheless promise at least the possibility of a proper physical explanation of many of these odd and contentious phenomena.

As an example of such a theory, consider a number of phenomena apparently quite disparate and disjointed. Why did certain species of bacteria suddenly become extinguished at certain remote periods? Why do potatoes, crabs, snails and bean seeds obey similar cyclic fluctuations? How do homing pigeons and honey bees find their way in the absence of ordinary landmarks? Why do certain types of bacteria swim northwards, and how do they manage to do this? Why does bone regeneration work better at certain times than at others? How do sting rays learn that food is available in the east (or west) basket when two alternatives are offered them?

All these phenomena are in fact explicable in terms of the earth's magnetic field, and are thus truly cosmobiological. Many animals respond to magnetism, carrying ferromagnetic pieces of metal which enable them to 'feel' the direction of the field. This makes the bacteria swim towards the magnetic pole which, except at the equator, also means downwards along the angle of dip, thus taking them to a more favourable habitat. When the magnetic field reverses, as it has done occasionally in the past, it leads to the extinction of certain species of bacteria. Variations in the strength of the field produce all sorts of cyclic phenomena, and the field is affected by the solar wind, and by solar flares. It is possible to link together a large number of apparently odd and unrelated phenomena once the general hypothetical connection has been unearthed. If only scientists could be interested in the other phenomena discussed in this book, replicating the findings and looking for links and explanations, we feel certain that many important new truths could be discovered. Scientific advance is often most impressive at the border of the unknown; it is here that the greatest rewards may often be reaped, and the phenomena of cosmobiology are crying out for a more concerted scientific attack than the desultory skirmishes to which they have been exposed to date.

What are the most likely candidates for the role of 'link' between extra-terrestrial events and biological and other phenomena here on earth? The most promising of course are sunspots and other solar disturbances and the various wave and particle emissions caused by them; the possibility that these in turn are affected by the planets involves the whole planetary system in this attempted explanation. Many cyclical events could be explained along these lines, although the details have not as yet been worked out in any testable manner. The interaction between solar events, the earth's magnetic field, and many other terrestrial and extra-terrestrial phenomena produces many well-established effects, and it does not take too large a jump of the imagination to think of factors of this kind as being responsible for many of the better authenticated phenomena described on previous pages. The task of turning such a vague and obviously unspecific hypothesis into a testable prediction is not an easy one, but it seems to us an important one in our unending efforts to understand and control the physical and biological universe. Science should not abdicate its mandate because it fears ridicule by being associated with 'astrology'.

Do we believe in astrology?

'If you wish to strive for peace of soul and pleasure, then believe,' said Nietzsche; 'if you wish to be a devotee of truth, then enquire.' Unfortunately both astrologers and scientists have sought rather for peace of soul than for truth, and proper factual enquiry has languished – apart from the work of a few intrepid souls, like the Gauquelins and Geoffrey Dean. We find this regrettable, and can only voice our hope that the future will see a reversal of this trend – with astrologers conceding the need for impartial enquiry, and scientists conceding the occurrence of phenomena that may be odd but that are well enough authenticated to call for investigation and explanation.

The shape of the theories that will finally account for all the bits and pieces of evidence we have looked at is something we can only guess at; but that they will bring about a better understanding of nature we have no doubt.

In the end, the reader who is looking for simple certainties is bound to ask, as many people have asked us: 'But do you believe in astrology?' If we have achieved anything in this book it is surely to have shown that, although this sounds like a simple question, there is no simple answer. And of course the question of our belief is finally irrelevant. What matters – all that matters – is fact. We have done our best to present the major relevant facts to the reader in as unbiased a form as possible; the ultimate decision must be left to him. We have indicated the sort of conclusion we would draw from the material surveyed. It may be the right conclusion or it may not. Only time will tell.

Bibliography

Abell, G.O. (1976) One astronomer's views. *The Humanist*, January.

Abell, G.O. (1979) Review of Dean's *Recent Advances*. *Zetetic Scholar*, April.

Abell, G.O. (1979) Review of Lieber's *The Lunar Effect*. *Skeptical Inquirer*, Spring.

Abell, G.O. and Greenspan, B. (1979) Human births and the phase of the moon. *New England Journal of Medicine*, 300, 96.

Abetti, G. (1963) *The Sun*. London: Faber & Faber.

Adderley, E.E. and Bowen, E.G. (1962) Lunar component in precipitation data. *Science*, 137, 749–750.

Addey, J.M. (1961) The scientific starting point in astrology: A new discovery. *Astrological Journal* (UK), 3, 4-13.

Addey, J.M. (1968) Astrology and genetics: Red hair. *Astrological Journal* (UK), 10, 5-18.

Addey, J.M. (1974) *The Discrimination of Birthtypes in Relation to Disease*. Wisconsin: Cambridge Circle.

Allan, T.M. (1964) Lung cancer and month of birth. *Lancet*, i, 439-440.

Andrews, E.J. (1960) Moon talk: The cyclic periodicity of postoperative haemorrhage. *Journal of the Florida Medical Association*, 46, 1362-1366.

Bailar, J.C. and Gurian, J.M. (1964) Month of birth and cancer mortality. *Journal of the National Cancer Institute*, 33, 237-242.

Barry, H. and Barry, H. (1961) Season of birth. *Archives of General Psychiatry*, 5, 292-300.

Barry, H. and Barry, H. (1964) Season of birth in schizophrenics. *Archives of General Psychiatry*, 11, 385-391.

Best, S. (1978) Lunar influence in plant growth: A review of the evidence. *Phenomena*, May.

Best, S. and Kollerstrom, N. (1980) *Planting by the Moon*. London: Foulsham.

Bok, B.J. (1975) A critical look at astrology. *The Humanist*, September.

Bok, B.J., Jerome, L.E. and Kurtz, P. (1975) Objections to astrology: A statement by 186 leading scientists. *The Humanist*, September.

Bortels, H. (1951) Beziehungen zwischen Witterungsablauf, physikalisch-chemischen Reaktionen, biologischem Geschehen und Sonnenaktivität. *Naturwissenschaften*, 38, 165-176.

Bradley, D.A., Woodbury, M.A. and Brier, G.W. (1962) Lunar synodical period and widespread precipitation. *Science*, 137, 748-749.

Brier, G.W. and Bradley, D.A. (1964) The lunar synodical period and precipitation in the United States. *Journal of the Atmospheric Sciences*, 21, 386-395.

Brown, F.A. (1954) Persistent activity rhythms in the oyster. *American Journal of Physiology*, 178, 510-514.

Brown, F.A. (1959) Living clocks. *Science*, 130, 1534-1544.

Brown, F.A. and Chow, C.S. (1973) Lunar-correlated variations in water uptake by bean seeds. *Biological Bulletin*, 145, 265-278.

Brown, F.A. and Park, Y.H. (1967) Synodic monthly modulation of the diurnal rhythm of hamsters. *Proceedings of the Society of Experimental Biology and Medicine*, 125, 712-715.

Brown, F.A. and Terracini, E.D. (1959) Exogenous timing of rat spontaneous activity patterns. *Proceedings of the Society for Experimental Biology and Medicine*, 101, 457-460.

Buck, C. and Simpson, H. (1978) Season of birth among the sibs of schizophrenics. *British Journal of Psychiatry*, 132, 358-360.

Burr, H.S. (1972) *Blueprint for Immortality*. London: Neville Spearman.

Buttery, T.J. and White, W.F. (1978) Student teachers' affective behavior and selected biorhythm patterns. *Perceptual and Motor Skills*, 46, 1033-1034.

Campbell, D.E. and Beets, J.L. (1978) Lunacy and the moon. *Psychological Bulletin*, 85, 1123-1129.

Caroli, G. and Pichotka, T. (1954) Weitere Untersuchungen zur Beziehung zwischen Blutgerinnung und Wetter. *Archiv Met. Geophys. Bioklimat.*, 5, 403-412.

Clark, V. (1961) Experimental astrology. In *Search*, Winter/Spring. (Reprinted in *Aquarian Agent*, 1970.)

Clark, V. (1970) An investigation of the validity and reliability of the astrological technique. *Aquarian Agent*, Autumn.

Cohen, D. (1975) Gauquelin hits back. *New Scientist*, October.

Cole, L.C. (1957) Biological clock in the unicorn. *Science*, 125, 874-876.

Committee Para (1976) The Committee Para replies to Gauquelin. *The Humanist*, January.

Cook, E.R. and Jacoby, G.C. (1977) Tree-ring–drought relationships in the Hudson Valley, New York. *Science*, 198, 399-401.

Cooke, D.J. and Coles, E.M. (1978) The concept of lunacy: A review. *Psychological Reports*, 42, 891-897.

Cooper, H.J. (1973) Occupation and season of birth. *Journal of Social Psychology*, 89, 109-114.

Cooper, H.J. and Smithers, A.G. (1973) Do the seasons govern your career? *New Society*, 5 April.

Cooper, H.J. and Smithers, A.G. (1975) Birth patterns among American army officers. *Journal of Social Psychology*, 97, 61-66.

Cowling, T.G. (1977) *Isaac Newton and Astrology*. Leeds: University Press.

Culver, R.B. and Ianna, P.A. (1979) *The Gemini Syndrome*. Arizona: Pachart.

Cunningham, M.R. (1979) Weather, mood, and helping behavior. *Journal of Personality and Social Psychology*, 37, 1947-1956.

Curry, P. (1982) Research on the Mars effect. *Zetetic Scholar*, Spring.

Dalén, P. (1968) Month of birth and schizophrenia. *Acta Psychiatrica Scandinavica*, 203, 55-60.

Dalén, P. (1975) *Season of Birth: A Study of Schizophrenia and other Mental Disorders*. New York: Elsevier.

Daneel, R. (1970) Ehescheidung und Geburtssternbild. *Kosmobiologie*, November.

Daneel, R. (1972) Ehescheidung und Geburtsdatum. *Zeitschrift für Parapsychologie, und Grenzgebiete der Psychologie*, 14, 37-43.

Davies, J.M. (1963) Lung cancer and month of birth. *Lancet*, ii, 1283.

Dean, G.A. (1981) 'Shortwave radio propagation: Non-correlation with planetary positions'. Unpublished manuscript.

Dean, G.A., Mather, A.C.M. and fifty-two others (1977) *Recent Advances in Natal Astrology: A Critical Review 1900–1976*. Perth: Analogic. (Distributed by Recent Advances, 36 Tweedy Road, Bromley, Kent, England; and by Para Research, Whistlestop Mall, Rockport, Massachusetts 01966, USA.)

Delaney, J.G. and Woodyard, H.D. (1974) Effects of reading an astrological description on responding to a personality inventory. *Psychological Reports*, 34, 1214.

De Voge, S.D. and Mikawa, J.K. (1977) Moon phases and crisis calls: A spurious relationship. *Psychological Reports*, 40, 387-390.

Dewan, E.M. (1967) On the possibility of a perfect rhythm method of birth control by periodic light stimulation. *American Journal of Obstetrics and Gynecology*, 99, 1016-1019.

Dewan, E.M. (1969) Rhythms. *Science and Technology*, January, 20-28.

Dewey, E.R. and Mandino, O. (1973) *Cycles: The mysterious forces that trigger events*. New York: Manor.

Dobyns, Z.P. (1970) Personality assessment through astrology. *Aquarian Agent*, Summer.

Dobyns, Z.P. (1975) The Vernon Clark experiment. *Astrology Now*, November.

Dobyns, Z.P. (1976) Results of the Vernon Clark experiment. *Astrology Now*, April.

Dobyns, Z.P. and Roof, N. (1973) *The Astrologer's Casebook*. Los Angeles: TIA.

Düll, B. and Düll, T. (1939) Neuer Beitrag zur Erforschung des Bioklimas. *Die Umschau*, 31, 715-745.

Düll, T. and Düll, B. (1934) Über die Abhängigkeit des Gesundheitszustandes von plötzhichen Eruptionen auf der Sonne und die Existenz einer 27-tägigen Periode in den Sterbefällen. *Virschow Archiv*, 292, 272-319.

Düll, T. and Düll, B. (1935) Zusammenhänge zwischen Stärungen des Erdmagnetismus und Häufungen von Todesfällen. *Deutsche Medizinische Wochenschrift*, 61, 21-43.

Eddy, J.A. (1976) The Maunder Minimum. *Science*, 192, 1189-1202.

Emerson, A.C., Lichtblau, N.S. and Sansbury, R. (1975) The era of continuous or 'field' astrology: A preliminary study of hemophilia. *Journal of Geocosmic Research*, 1, 50-54.

Eriksen, W.K. (1976). The inaccuracy of astrological research. *The Humanist*, November.

227

Eysenck, H.J. (1945) Graphological analysis and psychiatry: An experimental study. *British Journal of Psychology*, 35, 70-81.

Eysenck, H.J. and Eysenck, S.B.G. (1976) *Pychoticism as a Dimension of Personality*. London: Hodder & Stoughton.

Eysenck, H.J., Nias, D.K.B. and Cox, D.N. (1982) Sport and personality. *Advances in Behaviour Research and Therapy* (Monograph).

Farley, F.H. (1968) Season of birth, intelligence and personality. *British Journal of Psychology*, 59, 281-283.

Feyerabend, P. (1978) *Science in a Free Society*. New York: Schocken.

Findeisen, E. (1943) Experimentelle Untersuchungen über den Einfluss des Witterungsablaufes auf die Beständigkeit eines Kolloids. *Bioklimatische Beiblätter* 10, 23-34.

Forer, B.R. (1949) The fallacy of personal validation: A classroom demonstration of gullibility. *Journal of Abnormal and Social Psychology*, 44, 118-123.

Forlano, G. and Ehrlich, V.Z. (1941) Month and season of birth in relation to intelligence, introversion-extraversion, and inferiority feelings. *Journal of Educational Psychology*, 32, 1-12.

Friedman, H., Becker, R.O. and Bachman, C.H. (1963) Geomagnetic parameters and psychiatric hospital admissions. *Nature*, 200, 626-628.

Furze-Morrish, L. (1959) Correlation test of human affinities and celestial patterns. In *Search*, Autumn. (Reprinted in *Aquarian Agent*, 1970.)

Furze-Morrish, L. (1971) Mutual planetary aspects in relationships. *Astrological Journal* (UK), 13, 33-34.

Gallant, R.A. (1974) *Astrology: Sense or Nonsense?* New York: Doubleday.

Garcia-Mata, C. and Schaffner, F.I. (1934) Solar and economic relationships. *Quarterly Journal of Economics*, 49, 1-51.

Garth, J.M. and Lester, D. (1978) The moon and suicide. *Psychological Reports*, 43, 678.

Gauquelin, M. (1970) *Astrology and Science*. London: Peter Davies. (Original French edition, 1966.)

Gauquelin, M. (1971) *How Atmospheric Conditions Affect Your Health*. New York: Stein & Day.

Gauquelin, M. (1973) *The Cosmic Clocks*. London: Paladin.

Gauquelin, M. (1978) *Cosmic Influences on Human Behavior*. New York: ASI.

Gauquelin, M. (1979) *Dreams and Illusions of Astrology*. Buffalo: Prometheus.

Gauquelin, M. (1980) *The Spheres of Destiny*. London: Dent.

Gauquelin, M. and Gauquelin, F. (1979) Star US sportsmen display the Mars effects. *Skeptical Inquirer*, Winter.

Gauquelin, M., Gauquelin, F. and Eysenck, S.B.G. (1979) Personality and position of the planets at birth: An empirical study. *British Journal of Social and Clinical Psychology*, 18, 71-75.

Geddes, S. (1976) *Astrology*. London: Macdonald.

Gooch, S. (1979) *Guardians of the Ancient Wisdom*. London: Wildwood House.

Goodavage, J. (1966) *Astrology the Space Age Science*. New Jersey: New American Library.

Goodavage, J. (1976) Attacks on Astrology: They come in threes. *Horoscope*, July.

Goodavage, J. (1979) *Write Your Own Horoscope*. New York: New American Library.

Goodstein, L.D. and Brazis, K.L. (1970) Credibility of psychologists: An empirical study. *Psychological Reports*, 27, 835-838.

Gribbin, J.R. (1979) Wizard idea. *New Scientist*, 28 June.

Gribbin, J.R. and Plagemann, S.H. (1974) *The Jupiter Effect*. London: Macmillan.

Gunn, D.L. and Jenkins, P.M. (1937) Lunar periodicity in homo sapiens. *Nature*, 139, 84.

Gunn, D.L., Jenkins, P.M. and Gunn, A.L. (1937) Menstrual periodicity: Statistical observations on a large sample of normal cases. *Journal of Obstetrics and Gynaecology*, 44, 839.

Hare, E.H. (1975) Manic-depressive psychosis and season of birth. *Acta Psychiatrica Scandinavica*, 52, 69-79.

Hare, E.H. (1976) The season of birth of siblings of psychiatric patients. *British Journal of Psychiatry*, 129, 49-54.

Hare, E.H. (1978) Variations in the seasonal distribution of births of psychotic patients in England and Wales. *British Journal of Psychiatry*, 132, 155-158.

Hare, E.H., Price, J.S. and Slater, E. (1974) Mental disorder and season of birth. *British Journal of Psychiatry*, 124, 81-86.

Hartmann, F. (1973) *Paracelsus: Life and Prophecies*. New York: Steiner.

Harvey, C. (1965) Zodiacal physiognomy. *Astrological Journal* (UK), 8, 17-25.

Hawkins, L.H. and Barker, T. (1978) Air ions and human performance. *Ergonomics*, 21, 273-278.

Heuts, B.A. and Kop, P.P.A.M. (1974) Human aggression in relation to month of birth and partner choice in marriage. *Journal of Interdisciplinary Cycle Research*, 5, 331-339.

Houghton, A., Munster, E.W. and Viola, M.V. (1978) Increased incidence of malignant melanoma after peaks of sunspot activity. *Lancet*, i, 759-760.

Hudson, L. (1972) *The Cult of the Fact*. London: Cape.

Hughes, D.W. (1977) Planetary alignments don't cause earthquakes. *Nature*, 265, 13.

Hughes, D.W. (1977) The Inconstant Sun. *Nature*, 266, 405-406.

Hume, N. and Goldstein, G. (1977) Is there an association between astrological data and personality? *Journal of Clinical Psychology*, 33, 711-713.

Huntington, E. (1938). *Season of Birth: Its Relation to Human Abilities*. New York: Wiley.

Hyman, R. (1977) 'Cold reading': How to convince strangers that you know all about them. *Skeptical Inquirer*, 1, 18-37.

Illingworth, D.J. and Syme, G.J. (1977) Birthdate and femininity. *Journal of Social Psychology*, 103, 153-154.

Jerome, L. (1977) *Astrology Disproved*. Buffalo: Prometheus.

Jones, P.K. and Jones, S.L. (1977) Lunar association with suicide. *Suicide and Life-Threatening Behavior*, 7, 31-39.

Joseph, R.A. (1975) A Vernon Clark-model experiment distinguishing exceptionally gifted high performance from profoundly retarded low performance children. *Journal of Geocosmic Research*, 1, 55-72

Jourard, S. (1978) Astrological sun signs and self-disclosure. *Journal of Humanistic Psychology*, 18, 53-56.

Jung, C.G. (1960) *The Structure and Dynamics of the Psyche*. London: Routledge & Kegan Paul.

Kamimura, K. (1976) Epidemiology of twin births from a climatic point of view. *British Journal of Preventive and Social Medicine*, 30, 175-179.

Kanekar, S. and Mukerjee, S. (1972) Intelligence, extraversion, and neuroticism in relation to season of birth. *Journal of Social Psychology*, 86, 309-310.

Kaulins, A. (1979) Cycles in the birth of eminent humans. *Cycles*, 30, 9-15.

Kelly, I.W. (1979) Astrology and Science: A critical examination. *Psychological Reports*, 44, 1231-1240.

King, J.W. (1973) Solar radiation changes and the weather. *Nature*, 245, 443-446.

Klinowska, M. (1972) A comparison of the lunar and solar activity rhythms of the Golden Hamster. *Journal of Interdisciplinary Cycle Research*, 3, 145-150.

Knobloch, H. and Pasamanick, B. (1958) Seasonal variation in the births of the mentally deficient. *American Journal of Public Health*, 48, 1201-1208.

Knox, E.G. and 5 others (1979) Heart attacks and geomagnetic activity. *Nature*, 281, 564-565.

Kolisko, L. (1936) *The Moon and Plant Growth*. London: Anthroposophical Foundation.

Kollerstrom, N. (1981). A lunar sidereal rhythm in crop yield and its phasing in the zodiacal circle. *Correlation*, I, 44-53.

Kop, P.P.A.M. and Heuts, B.A. (1974) Month of birth and partner choice in marriage. *Journal of Interdisciplinary Cycle Research*, 5, 19-39.

Krips, H. (1979) Review of Gauquelin's *Cosmic Clocks* and *Cosmic Influences*. *Erkenntnis*, 14, 373-392.

Kuhn, T.S. (1970) *The Structure of Scientific Revolutions*. Chicago: University of Chicago Press.

Lewis, M.S. and Griffin, P.A. (1981) An explanation for the season of birth effect in schizophrenia and certain other diseases. *Psychological Bulletin* 89, 589-596.

Lieber, A.L. (1973) Lunar effect on homicides: A confirmation. *International Journal of Chronobiology*, 1, 338-339.

Lieber, A.L. (1978) *The Lunar Effect: Biological Tides and Human Emotions*. New York: Doubleday.

Lieber, A.L. and Sherin, C.R. (1972) Homicides and the lunar cycle: Toward a theory of lunar influence on human emotional disturbance. *American Journal of Psychiatry*, 129, 69-74.

Lipa, B.J., Sturrock, P.A. and Rogot, E. (1976) Search for correlation between geomagnetic disturbances and mortality. *Nature*, 259, 302-304.

Luce, G.G. (1971) *Body Time*. London: Temple Smith.

Lynn, R. (1971) *Personality and National Character*. Oxford: Pergamon.

McDonald, R.L. (1966) Lunar and seasonal variations in obstetric factors. *Journal of Genetic Psychology*, 108, 81-87.

McNeil, T., Kaij, L. and Dzierzykray-Rogalska, M. (1976) Season of birth among siblings of schizophrenics. *Acta Psychiatrica Scandinavica*, 54, 267-274.

Malin, S.R.C. and Srivastava, B.J. (1979) Correlation between heart attacks and magnetic activity. *Nature*, 277, 646-648.

Mann, T. (1979) *The Round Art: The Astrology of Time and Space*. London: Dragon's World.

Martini, R. (1952) Der Einfluss der Sonnentätigkeit auf die Häufung von Unfällen. *Zentralblatt für Arbeitsmedizin*, 2, 98-104.

Mather, A.C.M. (1979) Response to Abell's review of *Recent Advances. Zetetic Scholar*, April.

Mayes, B. and Klugh, H.E. (1978) Birthdate psychology: A look at some new data. *Journal of Psychology*, 99, 27-30.

Mayo, J., White, O. and Eysenck, H.J. (1978) An empirical study of the relation between astrological factors and personality. *Journal of Social Psychology*, 105, 229-236.

Meeus, J. (1979) Planets, sunspots and earthquakes. *Mercury*, 72-74.

Menaker, W. and Menaker, A. (1959) Lunar periodicity in human reproduction: A likely unit of biological time. *American Journal of Obstetrics and Gynecology*, 77, 905-914.

Metzner, R. (1979) An empirical study of the astrological elements and physical appearance. *Cosmecology Bulletin*, March.

Metzner, R., Holcomb, R. and Holcomb, J. (1980) Astrological elements and personality types: An empirical study. *Journal of Geocosmic Research*, 1, 16-29.

Michelson, L., Wood, R., Wilson, J., Silverstein, L. and Piland, J. (1977). The astrophysical diagnosis of respiratory distress syndrome. *CAO Times*, 3 (1), 21-23 and 3 (2), 9-13.

Moos, W.S. (1964) The effects of 'föhn' weather on accident rates in the city of Zurich (Switzerland). *Aerospace Medicine*, 35, 643-645.

Mörth, H.T. and Schlamminger, L. (1979) Planetary motion, sunspots and climate. In B.M. McCormac and T.A. Seliga (eds), *Solar-Terrestrial Influences on Weather and Climate*. Holland: Reidel.

Nelson, J.H. (1974) *Cosmic Patterns: Their influence on man and his communication*. Washington, D.C.: American Federation of Astrologers.

Nelson, J.H. (1978) *The Propagation Wizard's Handbook*. New Hampshire: '73' Magazine.

Newmeyer, J.A. and Anderson, S. (1973) Astrology and addiction: An empirical probe. *Drug Forum*, 2, 271-278.

Nolting, W.J.J. de Sauvage (1968) Seasonal variations in birth-rates of cancer patients. *International Journal of Biometeorology*, 12, 293-295.

Omwake, L. (1937) A study of sense of humor. *Journal of Applied Psychology*, 21, 608-704.

Osborn, R.D. (1968) The moon and the mental hospital: An investigation of one area of folk-lore. *Journal of Psychiatric Nursing*, 6, 88-93.

Ostrander, S. and Schroeder, L. (1972) *Astrological Birth Control*. Englewood

231

Cliffs: Prentice-Hall.

Paleg, L.G. and Aspinall, D. (1970) Field control of plant growth and development through the laser activation of phytochrome. *Nature*, 228, 970-973.

Parker, D. and Parker, J. (1975) *The Compleat Astrologer*. London: Mitchell Beazley.

Parker, G. and Neilson, M. (1976) Mental disorder and season of birth: A southern hemisphere study. *British Journal of Psychiatry*, 129, 355-361.

Pawlik, K. and Buse, L. (1979) Selbst-Attribvierung als differentiell-psychologische Moderatorvariable. *Zeitschrift für Sozialpsychologie*, 10, 54-69.

Pellegrini, R.J. (1973) The astrological 'theory' of personality: An unbiased test by a biased observer. *Journal of Psychology*, 85, 21-28.

Persinger, M.A., Cooke, W.J. and Janes, J.T. (1978) No evidence for relationship between biorhythms and industrial accidents. *Perceptual and Motor Skills*, 46, 423-426.

Phillips, D.P. (1978) Airplane accident fatalities increase just after newspaper stories about murder and suicide. *Science*, 201, 748-750.

Piccardi, G. (1962) *The Chemical Basis of Medical Climatology*. Springfield: Thomas.

Pintner, R. and Forlano, G. (1934) The birth month of eminent men. *Journal of Applied Psychology*, 18, 178-188.

Pintner, R. and Forlano, G. (1943) Season of birth and mental differences. *Psychological Bulletin*, 40, 25-35.

Pittock, A.B. (1978) A critical look at long-term sun–weather relationships. *Reviews of Geophysics and Space Physics*, 16, 400-420.

Playfair, G.L. and Hill, S. (1978) *The Cycles of Heaven*. London: Souvenir.

Pokorny, A.D. and Mefferd, R.B. (1966) Geomagnetic fluctuations and disturbed behavior. *Journal of Nervous and Mental Disease*, 143, 140-151.

Popper, K.R. (1972) *Conjectures and Refutations*. London: Routledge & Kegan Paul.

Press, N., Michelsen, N.F., Russell, L., Shannon, J. and Stark, M. (1978) The New York suicide study. *Journal of Geocosmic Research*, 2, 23-47.

Ravitz, L.J. (1962) History, measurement, and applicability of periodic changes in the electromagnetic field in health and disease. *Annals of the New York Academy of Sciences*, 98, 1144-1201.

Rawlins, D. (1981) Starbaby. *Fate*, October.

Reiter, R. (1952) Verkehrsunfallziffer und Reaktionzeit unter dem Einfluss verschiedener meteorologischer, komischer und luftelektrischer Faktoren. *Meteorologische Runschau*, 5, 14-17.

Reiter, R. (1956) Einfluss des Wetters auf die Häufigkeit von Unfällen im Untertagebetrieb. *Arbeitsschutz*, 133-134.

Reiter, R.J. (1976) Pineal and associated neuroendocrine rhythms. *Psychoneuroendocrinology*, 1, 255-263.

Rhyne, W.P. (1966) Spontaneous hemorrhage. *Journal of Medical Association of Georgia*, 55, 505-506.

Rim, Y. (1975) Psychological test performance during climatic heat stress from desert winds. *International Journal of Biometeorology*, 19, 37-40.

Rim, Y. (1977) Psychological test performance of different personality types on Sharav days in artifical air ionisation. *International Journal of Biometeorology*, 21, 337-340.

Rockwell, T., Rockwell, R. and Rockwell, W.T. (1978) Irrational rationalists: A critique of *The Humanist*'s crusade against parapsychology. *Journal of the American Society for Psychical Research*, 72, 23-34.

Rosen, G.M. (1975) Effects of source prestige on subjects' acceptance of the Barnum effect: Psychologist versus astrologer. *Journal of Consulting and Clinical Psychology*, 53, 95.

Rosenberg, H.M. (1966) *Seasonal Variation of Births, United States 1933-1963*. Washington, D.C.: National Center for Health Statistics.

Rosenstock, H.A. and Vincent, K.R. (1977) A case of lycanthropy. *American Journal of Psychiatry*, 134, 1147-1149.

Rosenthal, R. (1964) The effect of the experimenter on the results of psychological research. In B.A. Maher (ed.), *Progress in Experimental Personality Research* (Vol. 1). New York: Academic Press.

Rosenthal, R. (1978) How often are our numbers wrong? *American Psychologist*, 33, 1005-1008.

Rothen, A. (1976) A 24-hour periodicity in the course of immunologic reactions carried out at a liquid–solid interface due to possible extra-terrestrial influences. *Journal of Interdisciplinary Cycle Research*, 7, 173-182.

Salter, C.A. and Routledge, L.M. (1974) Intelligence and belief in the supernatural. *Psychological Reports*, 34, 299-302.

Schultz, N. (1960) Les globules blancs des sujets bien portants et les taches solaires. *Toulouse Médical*, 10, 741-757.

Sechrest, L. and Bryan, J.H. (1968) Astrologers as useful marriage counselors. *Trans-Action*, 6, 34-36.

Selvin, S. and Janerich, D.T. (1972) Seasonal variation in twin births. *Nature*, 237, 289-290.

Shaffer, J.W., Nurco, D.N. and Bonito, A.J. (1977). Is there a relationship between astrology and addiction? A re-examination. *Drug Forum*, 6, 137-141.

Shanks, T.G. (1978) *Research on astrological factors between married couples*. Wisconsin: Cambridge Circle.

Silverman, B.I. (1971) Studies of astrology. *Journal of Psychology*, 77, 141-149.

Smit, R.H. (1977) Astrology in Holland. *Phenomena*, October.

Smith, H.C. (1966) *Sensitivity to People*. New York: McGraw-Hill.

Smithers, A.G. and Cooper, H.J. (1978) Personality and season of birth. *Journal of Social Psychology*, 105, 237-241.

Snyder, C.R. (1974) Why horoscopes are true: The effects of specificity on acceptance of astrological interpretations. *Journal of Clinical Psychology*, 30, 577-580.

Snyder, C.R., Larsen, D.L. and Bloom, L.J. (1976) Acceptance of general personality interpretations. *Journal of Clinical Psychology*, 32, 258-265.

Standen, A. (1975) Is there an astrological effect on personality? *Journal of Psychology*, 89, 259-260.

Stur, D. (1953) Karzinomexitus und Geburtsmonat. *Wien Klinical*

Wochenschrft, 65, 898-901.

Sundberg, N.D. (1955) The acceptability of 'fake' versus 'bona fide' personality test interpretations. *Journal of Abnormal and Social Psychology*, 50, 145-147.

Suppe, F. (ed.) (1974) *The Structure of Scientific Theories*. Illinois: University of Illinois Press.

Takata, M. (1951) Über eine neue biologisch wirksome Komponente der sonnenstrahlung. *Archiv Met. Geophys. Bioklimat*, 2, 482-507.

Tasso, J. and Miller, E. (1976) The effects of the full moon on human behavior. *Journal of Psychology*, 93, 81-83.

Thun, M. (1976) *Work on the Land and the Constellations*. Sussex: Lanthorn Press.

Thouless, R.H. (1935) The tendency to certainty in religious beliefs. *British Journal of Psychology*, 26, 16-31.

Tobey, C.P. (1936) Research. *American Astrology*, October.

Tobey, C.P. (1937) Research. *American Astrology*, June.

Tocquet, R. (1951) *Cycles et rythmes*. Paris: Dunod.

Tomaschek, R. (1959) Great earthquakes and the astronomical position of Uranus. *Nature*, 184, 177-178.

Toulmin, S. and Goodfield, J. (1965). *The Fabric of the Heavens: The development of astronomy and dynamics*. New York: Harper and Row.

Tramer, M. (1929) Über die biologische Bedeutung des Geburtsmonates, insbesondere für die Psychoseerkrankung. *Schweizerisches Archiv für Neurologie und Psychiatrie*, 24, 17-24.

Tromp, S.W. (1963) *Medical Biometeorology*. New York: Elsevier.

Tromp, S.W. (ed.) (1977) *Progress in Biometeorology*. Amsterdam: Swets & Zeitlinger.

Truzzi, M. (1979) Astrology: A Review Symposium. *Zetetic Scholar*, April.

Tyson, G.A. (1977) Astrology or season of birth: A 'split-sphere' test. *Journal of Psychology*, 95, 285-287.

Van Deusen, E. (1976) *Astrogenetics*. New York: Doubleday.

Vidmar, J.E. (1979) Astrological discrimination between authentic and spurious birthdates. *Cosmecology Bulletin*, March.

Weiskott, G.N. (1974) Moon phases and telephone counseling calls. *Psychological Reports*, 35, 752-754.

Weiskott, G.N. and Tipton, G.B. (1975) Moon phases and state hospital admissions. *Psychological Reports*, 37, 486.

West, J.A. and Toonder, J.G. (1970) *The Case for Astrology*. London: Macdonald.

Wing, L.W. (1962) The effect of latitude on cycles. *Annals of the New York Academy of Sciences*, 98, 1202-1205.

Woody, E. and Claridge, G. (1977) Psychoticism and thinking. *British Journal of Social and Clinical Psychology*, 16, 241-248.

Zelen, M. (1976) Astrology and statistics: A challenge. *The Humanist*, January.

INDEX